C000054251

The People's Liberation Army's Search for Overseas Basing and Access

A Framework to Assess Potential Host Nations

CRISTINA L. GARAFOLA, TIMOTHY R. HEATH, CHRISTIAN CURRIDEN, MEAGAN L. SMITH, DEREK GROSSMAN, NATHAN CHANDLER, STEPHEN WATTS

Prepared for the United States Army
Approved for public release; distribution unlimited

For more information on this publication, visit **www.rand.org/t/RRA1496-2**.

About RAND

The RAND Corporation is a research organization that develops solutions to public policy challenges to help make communities throughout the world safer and more secure, healthier and more prosperous. RAND is nonprofit, nonpartisan, and committed to the public interest. To learn more about RAND, visit www.rand.org.

Research Integrity

Our mission to help improve policy and decisionmaking through research and analysis is enabled through our core values of quality and objectivity and our unwavering commitment to the highest level of integrity and ethical behavior. To help ensure our research and analysis are rigorous, objective, and nonpartisan, we subject our research publications to a robust and exacting quality-assurance process; avoid both the appearance and reality of financial and other conflicts of interest through staff training, project screening, and a policy of mandatory disclosure; and pursue transparency in our research engagements through our commitment to the open publication of our research findings and recommendations, disclosure of the source of funding of published research, and policies to ensure intellectual independence. For more information, visit www.rand.org/about/research-integrity.

RAND's publications do not necessarily reflect the opinions of its research clients and sponsors.

Published by the RAND Corporation, Santa Monica, Calif.
© 2022 RAND Corporation
RAND® is a registered trademark.

Library of Congress Cataloging-in-Publication Data is available for this publication.
ISBN: 978-1-9774-1037-5

Cover: Xinhua / Alamy Stock Photo.

Limited Print and Electronic Distribution Rights

This publication and trademark(s) contained herein are protected by law. This representation of RAND intellectual property is provided for noncommercial use only. Unauthorized posting of this publication online is prohibited; linking directly to its webpage on rand.org is encouraged. Permission is required from RAND to reproduce, or reuse in another form, any of its research products for commercial purposes. For information on reprint and reuse permissions, please visit www.rand.org/pubs/permissions.

About This Report

This report documents research and analysis conducted as part of a project entitled *Alternative Futures for Competition with China: The PLA Goes Global*, sponsored by U.S. Army Pacific. The purpose of the project was to assess China's development of basing, access, and military capabilities that will allow it to project power beyond the Indo-Pacific region and examine the implications for the U.S. Army as it prepares to compete with China in a global context over the next ten to 20 years.

This research was conducted within RAND Arroyo Center's Strategy, Doctrine, and Resources Program. RAND Arroyo Center, part of the RAND Corporation, is a federally funded research and development center (FFRDC) sponsored by the United States Army.

RAND operates under a "Federal-Wide Assurance" (FWA00003425) and complies with the *Code of Federal Regulations for the Protection of Human Subjects Under United States Law* (45 CFR 46), also known as "the Common Rule," as well as with the implementation guidance set forth in DoD Instruction 3216.02. As applicable, this compliance includes reviews and approvals by RAND's Institutional Review Board (the Human Subjects Protection Committee) and by the U.S. Army. The views of sources utilized in this report are solely their own and do not represent the official policy or position of DoD or the U.S. government.

Acknowledgments

This report would not have been possible without significant assistance, contributions, and insights from many individuals. We would first like to thank the sponsor of this research, BG Andrew D. Preston, Chief of Staff, U.S. Army Pacific, for his support, as well as Rod Laszlo, LTC Steven Lewentowicz, LTC Jonathan Warr, LTC William Duncan, LTC Tim Doyle, and MAJ Douglas Yoon for their direction and feedback throughout the course of the project. We would also like to thank Jennifer Kavanagh, director of RAND Arroyo Center's Strategy, Doctrine, and Resources Program, for her advice and guidance during the course of this work. We additionally thank RAND Arroyo Center Fellow LTC Andrew Canfield and RAND colleagues Caroline Baxter, Nathan Beauchamp-Mustafaga, Scott Boston, Michael Chase, Brandon Corbin, Abby Doll, Bradley Martin, David Ochmanek, and J.D. Williams for their many helpful insights raised throughout the research process. Katherine Wu brought our data to life with creative visualizations, and Kristin Leuschner helped draw out key points from the text. We benefited greatly from proofreading and editing by Jordan Bresnahan. We are also grateful to the reviewers of this report, Isaac Kardon (U.S. Naval War College) and Lyle Morris (Asia Society Policy Institute), for their thoughtful comments.

Summary

While China's growing economic power began reshaping the global economy in the 2000s and Beijing's foreign policy approach has increasingly sought to reshape the international order since the 2010s, the future role of China's rapidly improving military, the People's Liberation Army (PLA), on the global stage remains unclear. However, General Secretary Xi Jinping's 2017 assertion that the PLA will transform into "world-class forces" by 2049 implies that China will seek to develop at least some level of global military power over the next three decades.[1]

How expansive might China's future overseas basing and access become? In this study, we sought to understand where China might seek to gain basing and access for PLA forces abroad and what types of operations it might carry out there. We focus on three primary questions:

- How are China's national interests evolving, and how do these changes drive China to seek overseas military access and basing?
- Which countries or regions is China most likely to pursue for overseas basing and access, and what types of operations may Chinese forces carry out at these overseas locations?
- What are the implications for the U.S. government, the U.S. Department of Defense (DoD), and the U.S. Army?

This research builds on the existing literature on China's evolving overseas interests, including Chinese sources. We developed a framework to systematically assess valuable attributes from Beijing's perspective, focusing not only on the utility of potential host nations but also on China's ability to secure access. We augmented existing country-level or regional assessments by evaluating 108 countries across three regions, with the goal of understanding which countries and regions may be viewed by Beijing as especially promising host nations for PLA basing or access. This report harnesses unclassified sources, and our research should not be viewed as a substitute for classified reporting. Rather, we leverage unclassified sources to develop a framework to assess what the world may look like in the 2030–2040 time frame.

How Are China's National Interests Evolving?

Several Trends Shape Demand for PLA Overseas Activities

Our analysis of official Chinese documents and Western and Chinese scholarly literature identified several key trends that we assess will significantly shape demand for PLA activities abroad.

- **Shifting balance of international power.** China's economic might provides an incentive for China's military to prioritize the building of bilateral and multilateral security partnerships with other developing countries to help shape an international order that better suits Beijing's needs.
- **Evolution of the Chinese economy and the global economy.** China's expanding overseas interests provide compelling incentives for Chinese leaders to expand the PLA's operational presence abroad,

---

[1] Xi Jinping, "Secure a Decisive Victory in Building a Moderately Prosperous Society in All Respects and Strive for the Great Success of Socialism with Chinese Characteristics for a New Era," remarks delivered at the 19th National Congress of the Communist Party of China, Xinhua, October 18, 2017.

especially in developing countries located along Belt and Road Initiative (BRI) routes through Eurasia, the Middle East, Africa, Latin America, and perhaps even the Arctic.

- **Reality of an intensifying great-power competition.** Intensifying competition with the United States and other rival Asian powers could motivate the PLA to consider a broader range of operations abroad than the military conducts today, including some form of combat operations.

China's Expanding Interests Drive Requirements for Overseas Military Power

Chinese leaders' responses to these trends are also informed by the priorities and policies Chinese leaders have set for the nation. These include fulfillment of the "China Dream," achieving a high living standard for all Chinese citizens and the country's revival as a prosperous, great power under Chinese Communist Party (CCP) rule. Given Beijing's assessment that continued economic growth is the foundation of CCP legitimacy and an important source of that growth will rely on China's activities abroad, China's overseas interests provide compelling incentives for Chinese leaders to expand the PLA's operational presence abroad, especially in developing countries located along BRI routes. In other words, the key drivers to send the PLA abroad are domestically oriented, especially those related to proliferating China's overseas economic interests and to shore up perceived threats to the homeland, rather than to impose costs on other countries, such as the United States. Our review of China's overseas economic activity, energy imports, and related security concerns indicates that China is likely to prioritize three regions for basing and access: the Middle East, Africa, and the broader Indian Ocean region, including the Indo-Pacific beyond the first island chain.

The pursuit of a China Dream gives rise to three areas of emphasis in foreign policy that could affect U.S. interests: building new China-led networks of partnerships, supporting multilateral security fora (as opposed to others' unilateral or Western-led initiatives), and seeking to erode established security alliances. Although in the post–Cold War period China has maintained that it is opposed in principle to military intervention, officials and analysts now argue that Chinese military involvement in other countries does not violate the "non-interference" principle if it occurs with the consent or at the request of host nations and under certain multilateral conditions. One PLA mission requires the PLA to improve its ability to protect overseas Chinese personnel, resources, shipping lanes, and interests.[2]

Which Countries or Regions Is China Most Likely to Pursue for Overseas Basing and Access?

Although we do not attempt to definitively predict what China will do with its growing capabilities, our research seeks to understand China's long-term priorities for stationing forces abroad. A growing body of literature by Chinese military analysts and academic researchers explores potential criteria for overseas PLA locations, as well as options for prioritizing locations for future PLA basing or access. Building on the discussion in Chinese sources of desirable political, economic, military, and other attributes for potential host nations—along with recognition in those sources that PLA presence and operations would require significant buy-in from a host nation's political leadership—we developed a framework comprising 17 indicators. We then matched the indicators to available quantitative and qualitative data to assess and rank potential host nations, with a focus on the 2030–2040 time frame. The indicators capture two dimensions for prioritiz-

---

[2] Yan Wenhu [闫文虎], "Correctly Understand the Military's Missions in the New Era" ["正确理解新时代军队使命任务"], *China Military Online* [中国军网], July 26, 2019.

ing potential host nations: (1) *desirability*, or a country's utility for overseas Chinese military operations; and (2) *feasibility*, or China's ability to obtain basing or access in a given country.

Key themes in the desirability dimension of our framework include the military utility of a potential host nation, its utility for protecting China's economic interests, and low or acceptable political or other risks to China of stationing forces in the country. The feasibility dimension of our framework highlights the potential host nation regime's alignment with the People's Republic of China (PRC), China's influence in the country, and potential obstacles in China's relationship with the country. Table S.1 lists the specific indicators that we used to assess each potential host nation.

TABLE S.1

Indicators for Assessing Potential Host Nations, by Dimension

Theme	Indicator
Desirability	
Military utility	D1. Known Chinese interest in basing and access
	D2. Within rapid steaming distance of China
	D3. Within military airlift range of China
	D4. Coastal country
	D5. Close proximity penalty
	D6. Level of human development
Utility for protecting China's economic interests	D7. Level of Chinese investment
	D8. BRI member or participant
Low or acceptable political or other risks	D9. Political stability and absence of violence
	D10. Risk of climate change
Feasibility	
Regime alignment with the PRC	F1. Authoritarian regime
	F2. Aligned voting with China
	F3. Perceptions of corruption
	F4. Partner engagement
China's influence in the country	F5. Arms sales or transfers
	F6. Tensions in relations
Potential obstacles in China's relationship with the country	F7. Official recognition of the PRC over the Republic of China (Taiwan)

SOURCE: Authors' analysis of sources cited in Chapter 3 and Appendix A.

Potential Host Nations for Future Chinese Basing and Access Locations

Our framework identified 24 countries that may be especially well suited to Beijing's pursuit of basing and access over the next one to two decades. Figure S.1 depicts these 24 countries, which scored in the top 50th percentile for both desirability and feasibility, with flag icons in three colors:

- China's inaugural host nation of overseas forces, Djibouti, is depicted with a black flag icon. Although Djibouti already hosts PLA forces, we opted to evaluate all 108 countries in the three priority regions to see how Djibouti would score based on our framework.
- Red flag icons indicate countries that scored highly across both the desirability and feasibility dimensions. These four countries (Pakistan, Bangladesh, Cambodia, and Myanmar) have attracted significant attention in both PLA and Western analyses as future basing or access locations for China. Pakistan and Myanmar have been listed in PLA studies as promising potential host nations.[3]
- Orange flag icons indicate countries that scored either high or medium in both desirability and feasibility, but not high for both dimensions. These 20 countries (19 in orange, plus Djibouti, which also scored in this range) include various Middle East countries that could become strategic partners, particularly on counterterrorism issues for countries on China's periphery; coastal African countries in three regions; and a variety of countries in the Indo-Pacific beyond the second island chain.

Among the top 24 overall scorers, countries in the U.S. Central Command's area of responsibility appear to present especially compelling options and variety for PLA basing and access given their proximity to key sea lines of communication and counterterrorism concerns, their source of energy exports to China, and their willingness to increase investment and, potentially, security ties with Beijing.

Linkages to Desired Overseas Power Projection Capabilities

Although Chinese sources are not explicit about the types of future roles, missions, and forces that the PLA may be called on to conduct overseas, we find some key elements relevant for overseas power projection noted in PLA sources, including the need for maritime replenishment and strategic airlift. PLA analysts also recognize that sending troops overseas will also impose greater requirements on networking the force, building overseas logistics capability, coordinating across civilian and military bureaucracies, increasing the level of personnel training and skills, and determining how best to leverage overseas commercial assets.

What Are the Implications for the U.S. Government, the U.S. Department of Defense, and the U.S. Army?

As this research indicates, growing overseas PLA presence is not a matter of if, but when. In the immediate future, for example, there are strong indications that Djibouti will not remain China's sole overseas naval facility; Cambodia could be the most likely to next join these ranks based on ongoing Chinese activities at Ream Naval Base. In the long term, China's growing overseas interests are driving China to examine a range of locations abroad, but key questions remain regarding the extent of China's future global presence and the

---

[3] Li Shougeng [李守耕], Chen Tieqi [陈铁祺], and Wang Feng [王丰], "Research on Pre-Positioned Reserves Methods for Combat Readiness Materiel" ["战备物资预置储备模式研究"], *Journal of Military Transportation University* [军事交通学院学报], July 2019; Wang Tianze [王天泽], Qi Wenzhe [齐文哲], and Hai Jun [海军], "An Exploration of Transportation and Projection Support for Overseas Military Bases" ["海外军事基地运输投送保障探讨"], *Traffic Engineering and Technology for National Defence* [国防交通工程与技术], Vol. 16, No. 1, 2018.

FIGURE S.1

Top Potential PLA Basing and Access Locations Based on Framework Dimension Scores

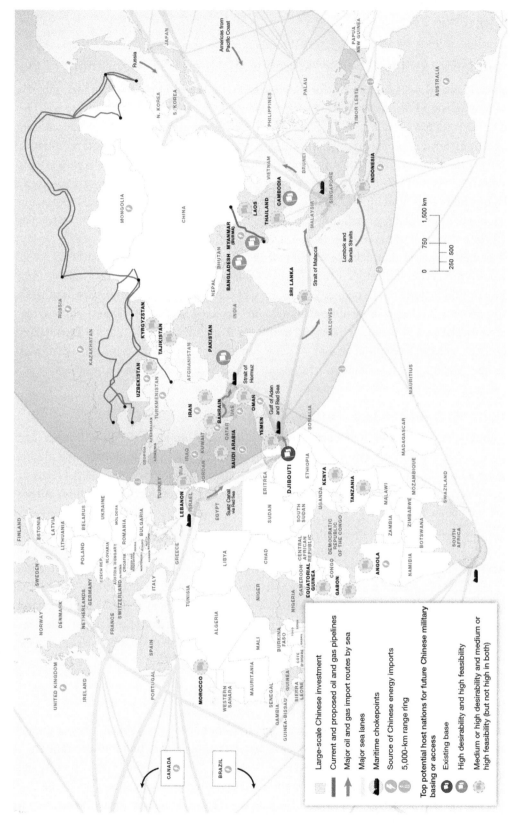

NOTE: Flag icons represent Tier 1 and Tier 2 countries. Tier 1 consists of countries that scored in the top quartile (high) of all 108 countries' scores across both dimensions. Tier 2 consists of countries that scored in the top 50 percent (high or medium) across both dimensions but lower than the Tier 1 countries. Icon placement is approximate and does not reflect specific potential basing or access locations within these countries.

types of power-projection activities it will undertake to leverage overseas basing and access. The following recommendations focus on further understanding China's plans for additional overseas basing and access and prioritizing risks to U.S. forces.

Recommendation for the U.S. Government and the U.S. Department of Defense

Develop indications and warning (I&W) for new overseas PLA locations. The primary purpose of our analysis was to understand Beijing's likely long-term aspirations for overseas basing and access. Our framework might be adapted, however, to help develop a set of I&W for China's future pursuit of access and basing in specific locations. Such a framework might be used to inform U.S. diplomatic and other initiatives.

In thinking through a potential I&W framework, nine of our 17 indicators are relatively slow to change given that countries' economies and domestic and foreign policies evolve over many years or even decades. However, eight of our indicators might change more rapidly (such as within one year) depending on the behavior of China or potential host nations, or both. Assessing these eight indicators more frequently may identify shifts in potential host nations' scores for desirability and feasibility.

An I&W framework could also include indicators with even shorter time frames, such as weeks or months, and could benefit from other indicators that we were not able to assess given currently available information. Such indicators could include the frequency and recency of China's or a host nation's request, the scale and scope of BRI partnership, the presence of key Chinese military-civil fusion equipment, Chinese reactions to ongoing geopolitical shifts, PLA engagement with multilateral organizations, PLA activities not leveraged for propaganda effect, splits in a potential host nation's foreign policy approach, risk of revolution in a potential host nation's government, and new acute security needs unmet by the United States or others.

Recommendation for the U.S. Army

Prioritize countries of concern for Army organizations and forces. Building on the countries identified in the framework as priority host nations that China might pursue, the Army could assess the implications of China securing a base or long-term access by performing country-level or facility-level risk assessments for specific mission sets that it currently conducts or may be called on to conduct in the future, during periods of both crisis and competition.

Two additional lenses may be beneficial: (1) the Army's ability to conduct Army-specific missions and roles and (2) the Army's ability to conduct missions and roles that support broader joint force missions and activities. Areas of emphases in assessments should include the risk to U.S. forces if China were to establish significant presence and conduct various military activities, as well as general threats to force protection or other challenges posed by Chinese forces present in close proximity to U.S. forces, such as counterintelligence issues and operations' security considerations. These reviews would identify options to mitigate near-term or less-severe risks, as well as gaps to address such risks, which would increase mission success in a more complex operating environment.

Areas for Future Research

As more information becomes available, additional research would prove valuable in further understanding the role that China's military forces will play overseas. First, it is important to better understand the risks that China may incur in expanding its operations overseas. Potential risks range from the difficulty of conducting force protection missions in insecure regions and potential counterintelligence risks to the challenge of conducting expeditionary warfare operations far from home. A second topic for future research concerns the role of private security contractors in supporting overseas PLA basing and access.

Contents

About This Report... iii

Summary v

Figures and Tables xiii

CHAPTER 1

Introduction 1

    What Is at Stake?.. 2

    Prior Research on China's Pursuit of Overseas Basing and Access 3

    Research Approach 6

    Definitions... 7

    Structure of This Report 8

    Limitations of the Scope of This Research.. 8

CHAPTER 2

China's Overseas Interests and Requirements for Global Military Power..................... 9

    Strategic Trends Shaping a More Global PLA... 9

    Chinese National Strategy, Foreign Policy, and Military Strategy 14

    Core Interests, Threats, and Strategic Response Options 17

    Implications for China's Pursuit of Overseas Basing and Access............................... 23

    Conclusion 23

CHAPTER 3

A Framework for Assessing China's Pursuit of Overseas Basing and Access Locations 25

    China's Growing Interest in Overseas Military Basing and Access............................ 26

    Assessing Potential Future PLA Basing and Access Locations 30

    Desirability... 31

    Feasibility 38

    Limitations of Our Approach 44

    Linkages to Desired Overseas Power Projection Capabilities 46

    Conclusion 55

CHAPTER 4

Evaluating Potential Host Nations as Future Chinese Basing and Access Locations......... 57

    Results of Framework Analysis 57

    Key Themes in Country Scoring... 60

    Examining Rankings Independently of Demonstrated Chinese Interest 65

    Conclusion 66

CHAPTER 5

Synthesis of Findings and Recommendations 69

    China's Expanding Interests Drive Requirements for Overseas Military Power 69

    A Mix of Factors Shapes China's Pursuit of Overseas Locations 69

    Potential Host Nations for Future Chinese Basing and Access Locations 70

Policy Recommendations 70

Areas for Future Research 76

APPENDIXES

A. Methodology for Basing and Access Framework 79

B. Country Scores 95

Abbreviations 107

Bibliography 109

Figures and Tables

Figures

S.1. Top Potential PLA Basing and Access Locations Based on Framework Dimension Scores ix
2.1. Overseas Chinese Investment, Resources, and Security Interests 24
4.1. Assessed Desirability and Feasibility of Potential PLA Basing and Access Locations 58
4.2. Top Potential PLA Basing and Access Locations Visualized 59
4.3. Top-Scoring 24 Potential Host Nations, by U.S. Combatant Command............................. 61
4.4. Top Potential PLA Basing and Access Locations Visualized with Improved Feasibility 64
4.5. Alternative Assessment of Potential PLA Basing and Access Locations (Without
Demonstrated Chinese Interest Indicator Scores) 66

Tables

S.1. Indicators for Assessing Potential Host Nations, by Dimension..vii
1.1. Key Term Definitions 7
2.1. Key Strategic Trends and Implications for PLA Presence Abroad 10
2.2. National Strategy, Foreign Policy, and Military Strategy: Implications for PLA Activities
Abroad 14
2.3. Chinese Interests, Potential Threats, and Potential PLA Response Options 17
3.1. Framework Indicators for Assessing China's Pursuit of Overseas Basing and Access
Locations, by Dimension 43
5.1. Speed at Which Framework Indicators May Change, by Dimension.................................. 71
5.2. Additional Potential Indicators of China's Pursuit of Basing and Access Locations................. 73
A.1. Desirability Indicator Values... 81
A.2. Feasibility Indicator Values 88
B.1. Country-Level Composite Scores and Tiers, by Dimension... 95
B.2. Country-Level Scores, by Desirability Indicator 98
B.3. Country-Level Scores, by Feasibility Indicator 102

CHAPTER 1

Introduction

While China's growing economic power began to reshape the global economy in the 2000s and Beijing's foreign policy approach has increasingly sought to reshape the international order since the 2010s, a key unknown remains the future role of China's rapidly improving military, the People's Liberation Army (PLA), on the global stage. The U.S. Department of Defense (DoD) assesses that China "has marshalled the resources, technology, and political will over the past two decades to strengthen and modernize the PLA in nearly every respect"; increasingly, this includes sending military forces to conduct operations beyond Chinese shores in order to advance Beijing's overseas interests.[1]

Two developments in 2017 led to intense speculation regarding the future trajectory of the PLA's overseas presence and operations. First, China established its first overseas military base in Djibouti. Second, at a key Chinese Communist Party (CCP) leadership meeting, General Secretary Xi Jinping set forth two milestones for the PLA to improve its capabilities that are relevant for overseas operations. He stated, "We will make it our mission to see that by 2035, the modernization of our national defense and our forces is basically completed; and that by the mid-21st century our people's armed forces have been fully transformed into world-class forces."[2] Although Chinese political and military leaders have not defined specific requirements for a future "world-class" military, the concept implies that the PLA will seek to develop at least some level of global military power over the next three decades—a transformation likely to have significant implications for the United States and its allies and partners.

Despite the keen interest of many observers, however, much about China's objectives for overseas basing and access remains unclear because Chinese officials have not publicly laid out in great detail their objectives for a more global PLA, priority locations for basing and access, or desired types of future overseas operations. Thus, in this report, we assess the potential for China to develop overseas military basing, access, and power-projection capabilities over roughly the next ten to 20 years—in other words, relevant to the 2030–2040 time frame. We focus in particular on potential basing and access in the Middle East, Africa, and the broader Indo-Pacific. We seek to provide insights into Chinese policy and its implications for U.S. defense policy generally and for the U.S. Army specifically. We do not attempt to definitively predict what China will do with its growing capabilities. Instead, we seek to understand China's long-term priorities for stationing forces abroad, as well as the potential security implications if China does pursue an array of overseas access and basing locations. Specifically, we address three primary research questions:

- How are China's national interests evolving, and how are these changes driving China to seek overseas military access and basing?

---

[1] Office of the Secretary of Defense (OSD), *Military and Security Developments Involving the People's Republic of China: 2020 Annual Report to Congress*, Washington, D.C.: U.S. Department of Defense, August 2020, p. i.

[2] Xi Jinping, "Secure a Decisive Victory in Building a Moderately Prosperous Society in All Respects and Strive for the Great Success of Socialism with Chinese Characteristics for a New Era," remarks delivered at the 19th National Congress of the Communist Party of China, Xinhua, October 18, 2017.

- Despite the lack of information regarding Beijing's intentions, which countries or regions is China most likely to pursue for overseas basing and access, and what types of operations may Chinese forces carry out at these overseas locations?
- What are the implications for the U.S. government, DoD, and the U.S. Army?

This report and its companion report document research conducted by the RAND Arroyo Center for U.S. Army Pacific as part of an overarching analysis of the implications of future Chinese overseas basing and access.[3]

What Is at Stake?

Expanding the PLA's overseas basing and access appears to be one component of China's global military ambitions based on information available at the date of this writing in fall 2021. A leading Chinese military publication indicated China must

> Build overseas strategic strongpoints [海外战略支点] that rely on the homeland, radiate into the periphery, and venture toward the [Pacific and Indian] Oceans. These sites are to provide support for overseas military operations or act as forward bases for deploying military forces overseas, exerting political and military influence in relevant regions.[4]

There are increasing signs that overseas PLA activities are being integrated into China's broader foreign and economic policy efforts as well. Calls by senior Chinese leaders for the military to support and align its activities under the Belt and Road Initiative (BRI), Xi Jinping's signature foreign policy initiative announced in 2013, have led to concerns that BRI projects and partnerships may act as stepping-stones for future global Chinese military access. China's 2019 defense white paper also increased its emphasis on the PLA's role in protecting China's overseas interests compared with its 2015 predecessor.[5]

Accordingly, some Western observers have warned of the strategic implications of China's pursuit of overseas access and basing, as well as links to initiatives, such as BRI. As part of his written testimony during a Senate nomination hearing, the current Assistant Secretary of Defense for Indo-Pacific Affairs, Ely Ratner, asserted that China views BRI as a means to expand China's global military presence:

> China's overseas infrastructure projects are a mechanism for increased influence overseas and a potential inroad for establishing overseas logistics and basing infrastructure. The PLA's growing access to foreign ports and airfields allows the preposition of logistic support necessary to sustain military operations abroad. This includes naval deployments in the Indian Ocean, the Mediterranean Sea, and the Atlantic Ocean. A global network of PLA logistical support facilities and installations could enable China to project and sustain military power at greater distances, reinforce its overseas interests, interfere with U.S. military operations, and potentially support offensive operations against the United States and U.S. interests.[6]

---

[3] Stephen Watts, Scott Boston, Pauline Moore, and Cristina L. Garafola, *Implications of a Global People's Liberation Army: Historical Lessons for Responding to China's Long-Term Global Basing Ambitions*, Santa Monica, Calif.: RAND Corporation, RR-A1496-3, 2022.

[4] Shou Xiaosong [寿晓松], ed., *Science of Military Strategy* [战略学], Beijing: Academy of Military Science Press [军事科学院], 2013, p. 254.

[5] State Council Information Office of the People's Republic of China, *China's Military Strategy*, trans., Beijing, May 2015b.

[6] Ely Ratner, "Advance Policy Questions for Mr. Ely Ratner, Nominee to be Assistant Secretary of Defense for Indo-Pacific Security Affairs," responses, Washington, D.C.: Senate Armed Services Committee, undated, p. 18.

More broadly, senior U.S. government officials see competition with China as a key long-term challenge for the United States and view China's military as the main pacing threat for DoD strategy, planning, partnerships, posture, modernization, and acquisition priorities. The Biden administration's *Interim National Security Strategic Guidance* released in March 2021 states that China "is the only competitor potentially capable of combining its economic, diplomatic, military, and technological power to mount a sustained challenge to a stable and open international system."[7] Deputy Secretary of Defense Kathleen Hicks echoed this language in her first public remarks in that role, concluding that "Secretary Austin and I believe that the PRC [People's Republic of China] is the pacing challenge for the United States military."[8]

That said, the extent to which a more global Chinese military creates additional strategic and operational challenges for DoD depends on how many locations China pursues for basing and access, what types of locations China pursues, and the types of operations it plans to conduct at those locations. How expansive might China's future overseas basing and access become in future decades? As the companion report explores in greater detail, the Soviet Union's experience suggests what China might be able to accomplish if Beijing decided that overseas basing was a sufficient priority to invest sizeable resources, both diplomatic and financial.[9] In the span of only 20 years, from 1955 to 1975, the Soviet Union developed a truly global reach, with significant bases on every continent.[10] Although China currently operates only one modest overseas base in Djibouti and the international system and geopolitical context of today are very different than those of 1955, China could conceivably develop a global network similar in scope to that of the Soviet Union's. Chinese basing decisions in the next ten to 20 years could thus significantly change the scope and degree of threat that the PLA could pose to the United States and its allies and partners.

Prior Research on China's Pursuit of Overseas Basing and Access

Growing PLA presence abroad has led to increasing scrutiny by policymakers and researchers, as well as broader speculation regarding future overseas PLA basing and access. In this section, we briefly highlight research and debates about the locations that China is most likely to pursue for overseas basing and access.

Following the Chinese government's announcement in late 2015 that China planned to construct a military facility in Djibouti, the base officially opened in August 2017.[11] Although China's base in Djibouti represents a new milestone in the access, scale, and types of Chinese military units stationed on foreign soil, it is not the only overseas location where China has secured access for PLA forces. The PLA Strategic Support Force (SSF) operates at least three tracking, telemetry, and command (TT&C) stations in Namibia, Pakistan, and Argentina, and it is involved in additional overseas space partnerships and access agreements in Chile

---

[7] Joseph R. Biden, Jr., *Interim National Security Strategic Guidance*, Washington, D.C.: White House, March 2021, p. 8.

[8] As cited in Paul McLeary, "New Pentagon No. 2 Hits China in First Speech as Tensions Rise," *Breaking Defense*, March 19, 2021.

[9] Watts et al., 2022.

[10] See Harkavy, 2007, for a list and description of Soviet bases. Note that bases and other military facilities can range from austere operating locations with minimal infrastructure to facilities the size of small cities (Robert E. Harkavy, *Strategic Basing and the Great Powers, 1200–2000*, New York: Routledge, 2007).

[11] Ministry of National Defense of the People's Republic of China, "Defense Ministry's Regular Press Conference on Nov. 26," November 26, 2015a, Google cached version; Ministry of National Defense of the People's Republic of China, "Defense Ministry's Regular Press Conference on Dec. 31," December 31, 2015b, Google cached version. A bilateral defense and security partnership agreement facilitating the PLA base in Djibouti was reportedly signed in February 2014. See "Djibouti and China Sign a Security and Defense Agreement," AllAfrica, February 27, 2014; and Andrew S. Erickson, "U.S. Wary of Its New Neighbor in Djibouti: A Chinese Naval Base, *Andrew S. Erickson Blog*, February 25, 2017.

and other locations.[12] China and Malaysia signed an agreement for PLA Navy (PLAN) access to the port of Kota Kinabalu in 2015, and China has also reportedly obtained access to overseas signals intelligence sites in at least one country via an agreement with Cuba.[13] China is additionally constructing guard outposts and a training facility in the tri-border region with Tajikistan and Afghanistan, and Chinese paramilitary forces are reportedly patrolling in Tajikistan as well.[14]

However, many external observers think that China is likely to pursue more locations overseas, including formal bases. In 2020, DoD named countries in the Middle East, Africa, and the Indo-Pacific that China "has likely considered . . . for PLA military logistics facilities," listed others where China has "probably already made overtures," and noted that China and Cambodia had both publicly denied finalizing an agreement for PLAN access to a Cambodian naval base.[15] DoD updated its assessment the next year, stating that China is "pursuing additional military facilities to support naval, air, ground, cyber, and space power projection."[16] Since 2019, media reports have detailed an alleged 30-year lease for the PLA's use of Ream Naval Base in Cambodia and increasing PLA activities in UAE.[17] Rumors of Chinese interest in dozens of locations in Africa, Europe, the Indo-Pacific, Latin America, the Middle East, and Oceania have additionally emerged, though none have been confirmed by Chinese officials.[18] Although PLA sources rarely list specific countries

---

[12] OSD, 2020, pp. 63, 129. For more information on overseas ground stations in China's space program, including dual-use applications and ties to the SSF, see Peter Wood, Alex Stone, and Taylor A. Lee, *China's Ground Segment: Building the Pillars of a Great Space Power*, Montgomery, Ala.: China Aerospace Studies Institute, March 2021, especially pp. 22–25, 34–35, 61–75.

[13] On the Malaysia agreement, see Isaac B. Kardon, "China's Overseas Base, Places, and Far Seas Logistics," in Joel Wuthnow, Arthur S. Ding, Phillip C. Saunders, Andrew Scobell, and Andrew N.D. Yang, eds., *The PLA Beyond Borders: Chinese Military Operations in Regional and Global Context*, Washington, D.C.: National Defense University Press, 2021, pp. 83, 102, fn. 62; and Prashanth Parameswaran, "Why Did China's Navy Gain Use of a Malaysia Port Near the South China Sea?" *The Diplomat*, November 24, 2015. On Cuba, see Kimberly Underwood, "China Advances Signals Intelligence," *Signal*, August 13, 2018.

[14] OSD, 2020, pp. 127–128. Media reports have investigated uniformed Chinese troops operating from facilities in Tajikistan (Gerry Shih, "In Central Asia's Forbidding Highlands, a Quiet Newcomer: Chinese Troops," *Washington Post*, February 18, 2019).

[15] The 12 countries "likely considered" are Myanmar, Thailand, Singapore, Indonesia, Pakistan, Sri Lanka, United Arab Emirates (UAE), Kenya, Seychelles, Tanzania, Angola, and Tajikistan. The three countries that China may have reached out to are Namibia, Vanuatu, and the Solomon Islands (OSD, 2020, pp. 128–130). An unclassified 2021 U.S. Intelligence Community assessment echoed DoD's finding in broad terms: "We expect the PLA to continue pursuing overseas military installations and access agreements to enhance its ability to project power and protect Chinese interests abroad" (Office of the Director of National Intelligence, *Annual Threat Assessment of the U.S. Intelligence Community*, Washington, D.C., April 9, 2021, p. 7). See also Defense Intelligence Agency, *China Military Power: Modernizing a Force to Fight and Win*, Bethesda, Md., January 2019, p. 29. In comparing the 2021 and 2020 reports, we found that DoD removed two countries from the list for which China has likely made overtures: Vanuatu and the Solomon Islands. DoD also clarified that China is likely considering Cambodia (OSD, *Military and Security Developments Involving the People's Republic of China 2021: Annual Report to Congress*, Washington, D.C.: U.S. Department of Defense, November 2021, p. 132).

[16] OSD, 2021, p. 132.

[17] In June 2021, the Cambodian defense minister stated that China was building infrastructure at Ream Naval Base but that Chinese military personnel would not be allowed to remain at the base (Jeremy Page, Gordon Lubold, and Rob Taylor, "Deal for Naval Outpost in Cambodia Furthers China's Quest for Military Network," *Wall Street Journal*, July 22, 2019; Warren P. Strobel and Nancy A. Youssef, "F-35 Sale to U.A.E. Imperiled over U.S. Concerns About Ties to China," *Wall Street Journal*, May 25, 2021; Sun Narin, "Defense Minister Says Ream Being Made into a Geopolitical Issue by 'Them,'" Voice of America Khmer, June 9, 2021).

[18] See, for example, Craig Singleton, "Beijing Eyes New Military Bases Across the Indo-Pacific," *Foreign Policy*, July 7, 2021. The Chinese Foreign Ministry refused to comment on allegations of Chinese troops in Tajikistan, and on the potential Cambodia basing deal, it stated China hoped others would "not over-interpret the normal cooperation between China and Cambodia." The ministry again denied Chinese interest in hosting military assets at a different location in Cambodia in 2020 (Ministry of Foreign Affairs of the People's Republic of China, "Foreign Ministry Spokesperson Geng Shuang's Regular Press

of interest, two PLA studies have discussed ten countries as recommended or potential future hosts: Pakistan, Myanmar, Sri Lanka, Djibouti, the Seychelles, Tanzania, UAE, Singapore, Indonesia, and Kenya.[19]

Analyses by external observers have sought to understand likely locations and requirements for future PLA bases, facilities, and access agreements beyond China's borders.[20] However, there is little consensus regarding desired locations that the PLA will pursue. Many observers agree that the Indian Ocean is a key focus for growing PLA presence, and some see compelling reasons for China to pursue bases and access in the Indo-Pacific beyond China's immediate periphery.[21] Others note that the participation of countries in Latin America, Oceania, and Africa into BRI and growing digital, space, and polar BRI components could provide opportunities for security partnerships farther afield—and in new domains—that enhance the PLA's capa-

---

Conference on February 19, 2019," 2019; Ministry of Foreign Affairs of the People's Republic of China, "Foreign Ministry Spokesperson Geng Shuang's Regular Press Conference on July 22, 2019," July 23, 2019; Ministry of Foreign Affairs of the People's Republic of China, "Foreign Ministry Spokesperson Wang Wenbin's Regular Press Conference on July 16, 2020," July 17, 2020).

[19] In 2014, scholars from PLAN's Naval Research Institute listed potential locations of "overseas replenishment and support points" [海外补给点和保障点] for PLAN operations, recommending Myanmar, Pakistan, Djibouti, the Seychelles, Sri Lanka, and Tanzania (Li Jian [李剑], Chen Wenwen [陈文文], and Jin Jing [金晶], "The Structure of Indian Ocean Maritime Rights and the Indian Ocean Expansion of China's Maritime Rights" ["印度洋海权格局与中国海权的印度洋拓展"], *Pacific Journal* [太平洋学报], Vol. 22, May 2014, pp. 74–75). In 2018, scholars from the PLA's Transportation University stated that "on this foundation . . . of building the first overseas base in Djibouti, in order to better safeguard our growing overseas development interests, our country will step by step plan to build overseas military bases (or overseas strongpoints) [海外军事基地 (或海外保障支撑点)] in Pakistan, the United Arab Emirates, Sri Lanka, Myanmar, Singapore, Indonesia, Kenya, and other countries through various methods such as purchase, leasing, and cooperation, and gradually build and form a networked system for China's overseas logistics support" (Wang Tianze [王天泽], Qi Wenzhe [齐文哲], and Hai Jun [海军], "An Exploration of Transportation and Projection Support for Overseas Military Bases" ["海外军事基地运输投送保障探讨"], *Traffic Engineering and Technology for National Defence* [国防交通工程与技术], Vol. 16, No. 1, 2018, p. 32). All ten countries listed in these two Chinese studies are located in the three regions assessed in our study.

[20] Key studies and conference volumes include Daniel J. Kostecka, "Places and Bases: The Chinese Navy's Emerging Support Network in the Indian Ocean," *Naval War College Review*, Vol. 64, No. 1, Winter 2011; Christopher D. Yung, Ross Rustici, Scott Devary, and Jenny Lin, *"Not an Idea We Have to Shun": Chinese Overseas Basing Requirements in the 21st Century*, Washington, D.C.: Center for the Study of Chinese Military Affairs, Institute for National Strategic Studies, National Defense University Press, China Strategic Perspectives No. 7, October 2014; Roy Kamphausen and David Lai, eds., *The Chinese People's Liberation Army in 2025*, Carlisle, Pa.: Strategic Studies Institute, U.S. Army War College Press, July 2015; Erica Downs, Jeffrey Becker, and Patrick deGategno, *China's Military Support Facility in Djibouti: The Economic and Security Dimensions of China's First Overseas Base*, Arlington, Va.: CNA, July 2017; Devin Thorne and Ben Spevack, *Harbored Ambitions: How China's Port Investments Are Strategically Reshaping the Indo-Pacific*, Washington, D.C.: C4ADS, 2017; Andrew Scobell and Nathan Beauchamp-Mustafaga, "The Flag Lags but Follows: The PLA and China's Great Leap Outward," in Phillip C. Saunders, Arthur S. Ding, Andrew Scobell, Andrew N.D. Yang, and Joel Wuthnow, eds., *Chairman Xi Remakes the PLA: Assessing Chinese Military Reforms*, Washington D.C.: National Defense University Press, 2019; Nadège Rolland, ed., *Securing the Belt and Road Initiative: China's Evolving Military Engagement Along the Silk Road*, Seattle, Wash.: National Bureau of Asian Research, NBR Special Report 80, September 2019; Roy Kamphausen, David Lai, and Tiffany Ma, eds., *Securing the China Dream: The PLA's Role in a Time of Reform and Change*, Washington, D.C.: National Bureau of Asian Research, 2020; Peter A. Dutton, Isaac B. Kardon, and Conor M. Kennedy, *Djibouti: China's First Overseas Strategic Strongpoint*, Newport, R.I.: U.S. Naval War College, China Maritime Studies Institute, China Maritime Report No. 6, April 2020; Chad Peltier, Tate Nurkin, and Sean O'Connor, *China's Logistics Capabilities for Expeditionary Operations*, Jane's, 2020; Isaac B. Kardon, Conor M. Kennedy, and Peter A. Dutton, *Gwadar: China's Potential Strategic Strongpoint in Pakistan*, Newport, R.I.: U.S. Naval War College, China Maritime Studies Institute, China Maritime Report No. 7, August 2020; Jeffrey Becker, *Securing China's Lifeline Across the Indian Ocean*, Newport, R.I.: U.S. Naval War College, China Maritime Studies Institute, China Maritime Report No. 11, December 2020; Charlie Lyon Jones and Raphael Veit, *Leaping Across the Ocean: The Port Operators Behind China's Naval Expansion*, Barton ACT: Australian Strategic Policy Institute, February 2021; and Joel Wuthnow, Arthur S. Ding, Phillip C. Saunders, Andrew Scobell, and Andrew N.D. Yang, eds., *The PLA Beyond Borders: Chinese Military Operations in Regional and Global Context*, Washington, D.C.: National Defense University Press, 2021.

[21] Peltier, Nurkin, and O'Connor, 2020; Thorne and Spevack, 2018; Yung et al., 2014; Kostecka, 2011.

bilities abroad.[22] Some researchers also highlight the potential for PLA presence in Europe and the Atlantic Ocean, leveraging the western coasts of both Africa and Latin America.[23]

Many of these assessments have focused on specific sites; one report by Jane's identified 18 potential overseas base locations in 14 countries, of which Jane's assessed six locations were particularly likely candidates for Chinese basing.[24] Maritime researchers have honed in on Chinese analysts' use of the term "strategic strongpoints" to examine ports that China may pursue for basing and access, building on China's experience in Djibouti to analyze the potential for PLA presence at the port of Gwadar in Pakistan.[25] However, few studies have examined a large number of potential hosts across various factors to evaluate specific attributes that China seeks from host nations and which countries are most favorable from Beijing's perspective to host PLA forces in the future.

This research builds on the existing literature in three ways. First, we review China's evolving overseas interests to determine trends that will likely continue to shape PLA presence and activities in the 2030–2040 time frame. Second, we leverage Chinese sources to develop a framework to systemically assess valuable attributes from Beijing's perspective, focusing not only on the utility of potential host nations but also on China's ability to secure access. We also build upon the existing PLAN-centric discussion, which typically focuses on analysis at the port level, to incorporate criteria for air and ground forces and assess and rank locations at the country level. Finally, we augment existing country- or regional-level assessments by evaluating 108 countries across three regions, with the goal of understanding which countries and regions may be viewed by Beijing as especially promising host nations for PLA basing or access.

Research Approach

In this report, we use a framework to assess the potential for China to develop overseas military basing, access, and power-projection capabilities relevant to the 2030–2040 time frame, with a focus on the Middle East, Africa, and the broader Indo-Pacific. We examine these three regions based on an assessment of China's growing overseas interests, threats to those interests, and potential roles for the PLA in mitigating those threats overseas—particularly roles that would be enabled or bolstered by expanding the PLA's overseas basing and access posture. Although China has economic and security interests in Europe and the Americas, and the PLA conducts a variety of activities in both regions, Chinese interests and perceived threats in Europe can be advanced via a host of diplomatic and economic tools and fora. Compared with the three regions of focus in our analysis, we also found fewer drivers leading China to prioritize PLA basing and access in the Western Hemisphere in the 2030–2040 time frame.

To construct our framework for assessing countries as potential basing and access locations for the PLA, we leveraged authoritative and semi-authoritative Chinese sources, including policy documents, military texts, and Chinese research and analyses on desired attributes of overseas basing and access points and on the types of operations and forces that the PLA seeks to carry out abroad. We also augmented these sources with U.S. government assessments and other secondary sources. In assessing the 108 countries in the three priority regions, we leveraged established data sets from international institutions and academic researchers. Our quantitative data focus on Chinese overseas political, economic, and military activities, and country-

---

[22] Rolland, 2019.

[23] Jones and Veit, 2021; Peltier, Nurkin, and O'Connor, 2020.

[24] Peltier, Nurkin, and O'Connor, 2020, pp. 26–27. The top six sites from this assessment were in Cambodia, Pakistan, Myanmar, Oman, Vanuatu, and Namibia. Other reports focus on site assessment, including Thorne and Spevack, 2018.

[25] Dutton, Kardon, and Kennedy, 2020; Kardon, Kennedy, and Dutton, 2020.

level geographical data, scientific projections, domestic development and political indicators, and foreign policy preferences.

This report and its companion report document research conducted by the RAND Arroyo Center for U.S. Army Pacific as part of an overarching analysis of the implications of future Chinese overseas basing.[26] Across the two reports, we address three overarching questions:

- Where might China seek to gain basing and access for PLA forces abroad, and what types of operations might they carry out there?
- What are the long-term implications for the United States and DoD if China were to achieve some form of global presence and operations in the future?
- And how in turn might Beijing's future basing decisions have important implications for present-day U.S. defense planning?

In this report, we primarily focus on addressing the first question, while the companion report leverages historical case studies and other research to primarily address the second and third questions.

Definitions

Given our frequent use of three key terms—*base*, *access*, and *power projection*—we define them upfront, particularly because there is not a consensus in how these terms are defined across the literature that we reviewed. Table 1.1 summarizes our use of these terms in this report.

TABLE 1.1
Key Term Definitions

Term	Definition
Base	As Robert Harkavy notes, the term *base* often has sensitive political connotations, and thus many countries with overseas bases—including China—prefer to use the term *facility*.[a] In this report, we use these two terms interchangeably, although we typically adopt the more commonly used term, base. DoD defines a military base as "[a]n area or locality containing installations which provide logistics or other support."[b]
	The PLA's dictionary defines a military base as "an area where a certain number of military personnel are stationed, a considerable number of weapons, equipment, and military materials are stored, and corresponding organizations and facilities are established to carry out specific military activities."[c] Drawing on this definition, some PLA military transportation researchers have proposed the following definition for an overseas military base: "An area where a certain number of armed forces are stationed in overseas commons, territories, dependent territories, overseas trusteeships, and on the land of other countries, with corresponding organizations and facilities to achieve specific military functions."[d]
Access	We use the term *access* to refer to a sovereign state's granting of permission for foreign military forces to be positioned on, temporarily stop in, or pass across its territory, airspace, or territorial waters. Access arrangements may involve a formal signed agreement. Although access can include relatively minimal operations, such as port calls or the occasional overflight, our particular focus in this report is on long-term or repeated access that could involve significant use of a host nation's facilities.[e]

---

[26] Watts et al., 2022.

Table 1.1—Continued

Term	Definition
Power projection	*Power projection* refers to the ability of a state to exercise effective military power, in peace or in war, at a substantial distance from its own territory. Our focus is on operations that leverage access or basing on another country's territory.[f]

[a] Harkavy, 2007.

[b] Joint Chiefs of Staff, *DOD Dictionary of Military and Associated Terms*, Washington, D.C., November 2021, p. 23.

[c] Academy of Military Science, *People's Liberation Army Military Terminology* [中国人民解放军军语], 2nd ed., Beijing: Academy of Military Science Press, December 2011, p. 7.

[d] Wang, Qi, and Hai, 2018, p. 32. For a nearly identical definition in an earlier article, see Jiang Deliang [姜德良], Zhang Ren [张韧], and Ge Shanshan [葛珊珊], "Natural Risk Scenario Simulation Assessment of Overseas Support Bases Based on Uncertain Knowledge" ["知识不确定条件下的海外保障基地自然风险情景模拟评估"], *Marine Science Bulletin* [海洋通报], Vol. 36, No. 5, October 2017, p. 504.

[e] The PLA dictionary does not define *access*, nor did we find a definition for this concept in the other PLA literature that we reviewed.

[f] Although the PLA has a concept known as "strategic power projection" or "strategic delivery" [战略投送], the term is not analogous to Western concepts of power projection. For example, the PLA dictionary's definition focuses on leveraging "transportation strengths" to move groups of armed forces to the conflict or "crisis" area (Academy of Military Science, 2011, p. 58). In broader writings, the Y-20 transport aircraft is cited as a key system that facilitates strategic delivery. Our thanks to Isaac Kardon for suggesting that we include this term.

Structure of This Report

The analysis in this report proceeds in four steps. In Chapter 2, we analyze China's strategic objectives, the threats to those objectives that Beijing perceives, and high-level military options that China could undertake to secure those objectives. This preliminary discussion helps to provide context, showing the ways in which overseas basing and access might support Chinese objectives, as well as the many alternatives that Beijing has to protect its interests.

In Chapter 3, through a detailed review of Chinese authoritative and semi-authoritative or so-called gray literature, we assess Chinese strategic discourse and analysis to develop a framework for understanding what makes a potential location for basing and access desirable to China. We also examine factors that may make it feasible for Beijing to secure an agreement from a host nation. We then translate this framework into 17 quantitative and qualitative indicators to evaluate future basing and access locations from the perspective of Chinese policymakers and analysts. We also highlight key forces, systems, and enablers that experts see as likely to participate in power projection via overseas Chinese bases and access in the future.

In Chapter 4, we use the framework to evaluate 108 countries in the Middle East, Africa, and the broader Indo-Pacific. We analyze the results by key themes, focusing on the top-scoring countries, regional dynamics, and host nations' agency in shaping some elements of our framework by the 2030–2040 time frame.

In Chapter 5, we synthesize the key insights from the previous chapters and use them to offer policy recommendations for the U.S. government as a whole and for DoD and the U.S. Army in particular.

Finally, in Appendix A, we provide the details of our framework methodology and data sources, and in Appendix B, we list countries' aggregate scores and their scores for each of the 17 framework indicators.

Limitations of the Scope of This Research

This report harnesses unclassified sources, including analyses, data, public government documents, and media reporting. We do not incorporate classified sources, and our research should not be viewed as a substitute for classified reporting; rather, we leverage unclassified sources to develop a framework to assess what the world may look like in the 2030–2040 time frame. Specifically, we have scoped this report and its findings with the intent of facilitating broader discussions and further analysis of the long-term drivers, locations, and implications of future basing and access locations sought by the PRC.

CHAPTER 2

China's Overseas Interests and Requirements for Global Military Power

The deployment of PLA forces abroad represents a significant change for a country that has for decades resisted foreign basing and access and, until recently, largely lacked the ability to project and sustain military forces beyond its immediate periphery. Beijing's willingness to increase its military operations abroad reflects in large part the reality that its interests and objectives have changed after decades of rapid growth. How will China's situation evolve in the coming decades, and how might this affect PLA operations abroad? Which key structural trends might shape Chinese requirements for overseas military activity? How might Chinese leaders interpret those requirements, and how might they direct the military accordingly?

Our research aims to shed light on such questions. Looking out to the year 2040, we have organized this chapter into three sections. In the first, we consider key strategic trends that we anticipate will continue through the next few decades. These trends provide the most basic incentives for China to increasingly send PLA forces abroad. We then consider relevant aspects of China's national and military strategies that could influence how Beijing chooses to respond to those incentives in the second. We build on the preceding sections in the third to examine how specific Chinese interests and perceived threats posed to them may frame options for future military operations and activities abroad.

Strategic Trends Shaping a More Global PLA

How China's situation evolves in coming years will inform Chinese leaders' calculus on sending more military units and more diverse types of military forces abroad. In this section, we focus on three key trends that we assess will significantly shape demand for PLA activities abroad: the shifting balance of international power, the evolution of the Chinese economy and the global economy, and the nature of intensifying great-power competition. These trends and their implications, discussed in further detail below, are summarized in Table 2.1. We focus on these trends based on our analysis of official Chinese documents and Western and Chinese scholarly literature.

Trend 1. Shifting Balance of Global Power

The coming decades are likely to see the structure of global politics shift as the developing world, with China at the fore, gains more power relative to the developed West, and also as China's power grows vis-à-vis the United States'. Beijing clearly perceives these trends as well: Two 2019 government white papers characterize the international order as shaped by "profound changes unseen in a century," including a more multipolar world with increased economic, information, and cultural diversification.[1] They contrast China's rise, por-

---

[1] State Council Information Office of the People's Republic of China, *China's National Defense in the New Era*, trans., Beijing, July 2019b; State Council Information Office of the People's Republic of China, *China and the World in the New Era*, Beijing,

TABLE 2.1

Key Strategic Trends and Implications for PLA Presence Abroad

Geostrategic Trend	Implications for PLA Presence Abroad
Shifting balance of global power	• Increasing Chinese power could induce more confidence and risk-taking in PLA operations abroad. • Demand will increase for China to prioritize security partnership-building and access with developing countries, especially under the framework of BRI; many of these countries confront a variety of security threats.
Evolution of the Chinese economy and the global economy	• Anticipated economic deceleration and competing social spending demands may constrain the PLA from further or new large force structure increases, but the PLA could probably still afford to continue ongoing modernization efforts. • The growing importance of technology and digital services could elevate the importance of information networks and cyberspace for the global economy. • China may seek more presence and partnerships near vital economic interests located along the Indian Ocean; in South, Southeast, and Central Asia; and in the Middle East, Africa, and Latin America.
Intensifying great-power competition	• Chinese military diplomacy may focus on undercutting U.S. alliances and partnerships in Asia and building its own partnerships, particularly with BRI member countries. • Competition with rivals in Asia could constrain the PLA's ability to field large portions of its military abroad. • While focusing on nontraditional threats that affect some of its BRI partners, China may also seek to deploy more combat-oriented forces abroad.

trayed as achieving mutual benefit for both China and its partners, with "outdated" hegemonic approaches to global leadership. The implication is that while the balance of global power is becoming more multipolar overall, China's changing circumstances are a key driver of that multipolarity. Another key driver is weakening hegemonic powers, given that "pursuing hegemony and militarism will only consume national strength and lead to decline."[2] As the authors of China's 2019 defense white paper also observe, "the realignment of international powers accelerates and the strength of emerging markets and developing countries keeps growing."[3] Continued Chinese economic growth offers more opportunities for China to partner with other countries, particularly developing countries. Overall, the sheer size of China's economy could surpass that of the United States in nominal terms within the next decade, although a declining working population and a rising debt-to-gross domestic product (GDP) ratio may delay that milestone.[4] In either case, the United States will continue to have the world's most powerful, globally distributed military, and its economic strength on a per capita basis will exceed that of China as well. However, the gap in national power will likely continue to narrow.[5]

This trend provides an incentive for China to prioritize the building of bilateral and multilateral security partnerships with other developing countries to help shape an international order that better suits Beijing's needs.[6] To earn their support and realize the economic potential of emerging economies, China may have to help manage a variety of security challenges that affect countries in the developing world. A more powerful PLA could also induce more confidence and risk-taking in operations abroad, including a greater willing-

---

September 27, 2019c.

[2] State Council Information Office of the People's Republic of China, 2019c.

[3] State Council Information Office of the People's Republic of China, 2019b.

[4] Lizzy Burden, "China's Economy Set to Overtake U.S. Earlier Due to Covid Fallout," *Bloomberg*, December 25, 2020; Michael Pettis, "Debt, Not Demographics, Will Determine the Future of China's Economy," *Fortune*, June 17, 2021.

[5] Stephen G. Brooks and William C. Wohlforth, "The Rise and Fall of the Great Powers in the Twenty-First Century," *International Security*, Vol. 40, No. 3, Winter 2015–2016.

[6] State Council Information Office of the People's Republic of China, 2019c.

ness to carry out combat operations. A China focused on cultivating support in the developing world might step up efforts to address security concerns in relevant areas, particularly with developing countries that are BRI members.

Trend 2. Evolution of the Chinese Economy and the Global Economy

Another key driver of PLA operations abroad concerns the anticipated evolution of the Chinese and global economies. China's efforts to protect overseas interests will be informed by the realities of its own economic situation, given its economic growth is expected to decelerate. Prior to and at the outset of the coronavirus disease 2019 (COVID-19) pandemic, economic forecasters predicted that China could maintain a yearly growth rate of between 3.7 to 5.7 percent through 2030, starting higher and then tapering off toward the end of the decade.[7] Over the past several years, China's annual defense budget has remained consistent at 1.5 to 1.6 percent of its GDP, although it is unclear whether this proportion will change as China's economic growth slows and the military faces competing demands for social spending for an aging population.[8] Moreover, the cost of maintaining a professional military that operates a greater proportion of advanced platforms and technologies will likely increase.[9] These trends may constrain the PLA from making further or new large force structure increases, but if we assume that Beijing will continue to peg its defense budget at a similar percentage of GDP as in the past, then the PLA could probably still afford to continue ongoing modernization efforts.[10]

The evolving nature of China's economy could affect its approach to overseas security as well. Chinese leaders have outlined an ambition to transform the economy into a technologically advanced industrial power. Reflecting these ambitions, Beijing has developed a "Made in China 2025" industrial plan and other economic plans aimed at establishing the country's lead in advanced technologies.[11] As the controversy between China and the United States over 5G has shown, Beijing's ambition to overtake the United States in technological leadership could exacerbate rivalry between the two countries.[12] It could also incentivize Beijing to accelerate efforts to build a comprehensive partnership network featuring Chinese-led technologies, trade and investment rules and norms, and security cooperation arrangements. The coming years could also

---

[7] International Monetary Fund, "Report for Selected Countries and Subjects," data set, World Economic Outlook Database, October 2020; Emmanuel Louis Bacani, "S&P: China's GDP Growth to Average 4.6% Through 2030 in 'Inescapable' Slowdown," S&P Global Market Intelligence, August 29, 2019; PricewaterhouseCoopers, *The Long View: How Will the Global Economic Order Change by 2050?* The World in 2050 report, London, February 2017. These reports did not take the COVID-19 pandemic into account. See also "Chinese Economy to Overtake U.S. 'by 2028' Due to Covid," BBC, December 26, 2020.

[8] Jane's, "China Defense Budget Overview," *Sentinel Security Assessment–China and Northeast Asia*, June 8, 2020. Jane's assessment includes the official defense budget and some elements that China does not include in its official budget, such as pensions and civil-military research and development costs. Jane's assessment does not include all the Chinese domestic security organs featured in some other estimates, which would bring the estimate up to roughly 2.5 percent of GDP. Another Western assessment of "off-budget" revenues and expenses found that these nonpublic amounts are likely to decrease over time, indicating that even though China's true defense budget is not made public, it is unlikely to grow faster as a percentage of GDP than the official defense budget. See Phillip C. Saunders, "Hearing on a 'World-Class' Military: Assessing China's Global Military Ambitions," testimony before the U.S.-China Economic and Security Review Commission, Washington, D.C., June 20, 2019.

[9] Adam P. Liff and Andrew S. Erickson, "Demystifying China's Defense Spending: Less Mysterious in the Aggregate," *China Quarterly*, Vol. 216, December 2013.

[10] Jane's, "United States Defense Budget Overview," *Sentinel Security Assessment–North America*, February 20, 2019.

[11] Karen M. Sutter, "'Made in China 2025' Industrial Policies: Issues for Congress," Washington, D.C.: Congressional Research Service, IF10964, August 11, 2020.

[12] Nicol Turner Lee, *Navigating the U.S.-China 5G Competition*, Washington, D.C.: Brookings Institution, April 2020.

see services and the digital trade play a slightly larger role in the Chinese and world economies.[13] The future expansion of China's digital economy is constrained by a large rural workforce that cannot be easily absorbed into the digital economy, but cyberspace will likely remain important for China's economic security.[14] Digital financial transactions and cross-border trade in digital services, therefore, also raise the importance of the PLA's ability to provide cybersecurity.

Chinese authorities argue that the stagnating global economy can be reinvigorated by a new version of globalization centered on BRI, a large-scale Chinese-led effort to link the economies of Eurasia, the Middle East, Africa, and Latin America through infrastructure development, trade, and investment. The BRI has been criticized for promoting "debt traps," facilitating corruption, and, in some cases, facilitating wasteful and economically dubious projects.[15] However, experts acknowledge the need for infrastructure and invest-ment to realize the growth potential of emerging economies. Most authoritative Western experts view BRI as likely to play an important role in realizing this potential.[16] For example, the World Bank estimated that implementation of major BRI projects could increase global trade between 1.7 and 6.2 percent and raise world incomes by 0.7 to 2.9 percent over the next few decades.[17] The anticipated evolution of the global economy in a direction that more prominently features developing countries—many of which are deep-ening partnerships with China under BRI—provides an incentive for China to focus its overseas military activities in those regions, a tendency that could be reinforced by Beijing's ambitions to establish itself as a leader in advanced manufacturing.

Trend 3. Intensifying Great-Power Competition

As the balance of global power shifts, what Beijing views as progress toward achieving a "more balanced" configuration of strategic power will be challenged by growing "international strategic competition."[18] Both Western and Chinese sources anticipate that the coming decades will prominently feature major power or great-power competition, with the primary contenders expected to be China and the United States.[19] The

---

[13] However, much of China's service sector consists of finance, real estate, and low-wage service jobs, with information tech-nology, research and development, health care, and environment-related service jobs collectively comprising about 9 percent of GDP in 2016. Overall, the size of China's digital economy has been slightly smaller than that of Organisation for Economic Co-operation and Development (OECD) countries at around 6 percent of GDP in 2018 (Andrew Mullen, "China's Service Sector: What Is It and Why Is It Important to the Economy?" *South China Morning Post*, March 3, 2021; Alicia Garcia Herrero and Jianwei Xu, "How Big Is China's Digital Economy?" Brussels: Bruegel, Working Paper No. 4, May 17, 2018).

[14] Timothy R. Heath, "The 'Holistic Security Concept': The Securitization of Policy and Increasing Risk of Militarized Crisis," Jamestown Foundation, *China Brief*, Vol. 15, No. 12, June 19, 2015. In particular, a striking feature of China's economy is its dependence on digital payments, which accounted for 40 percent of the world's total and was worth $790 billion U.S. dollars in 2016 (Jonathan Woetzel, Jeongmin Seong, Kevin Wei Wang, James Manyika, Michael Chui, and Wendy Wong, "China's Digital Economy: A Leading Global Force," New York: McKinsey Global Institute, August 2017).

[15] Rafiq Dossani, Jennifer Bouey, and Keren Zhu, *Demystifying the Belt and Road Initiative: A Clarification of Its Key Features, Objectives and Impacts*, Santa Monica, Calif.: RAND Corporation, WR-1338, 2020.

[16] OECD, "The Belt and Road Initiative in the Global Trade, Investment and Finance Landscape," in *OECD Business and Finance Outlook 2018*, Paris: OECD Publishing, p. 7; Hui Lu, Charlene Rohr, Marco Hafner, and Anna Knack, *China Belt and Road Initiative: Measuring the Impact of Improving Transportation Connectivity on Trade in the Region—A Proof-of-Concept Study*, Santa Monica, Calif.: RAND Corporation, RR-2625-RC, 2018.

[17] Michele Ruta, Matias Herrera Dappe, Somik Lall, Chunlin Zhang, Erik Churchill, Cristina Constantinescu, Mathilde Leb-rand, and Alen Mulabdic, *Belt and Road Economics: Opportunities and Risks of Transport Corridors*, Washington, D.C.: Inter-national Bank for Reconstruction and Development, World Bank, 2019.

[18] State Council Information Office of the People's Republic of China, 2019b.

[19] White House, *National Security Strategy of the United States of America*, Washington, D.C., December 2017.

2019 Chinese defense white paper regarded the Asia-Pacific region as "generally stable," but noted "uncertainties" owing to increasing "major power competition."[20] Chinese defense white papers since the early 2000s have similarly observed an "intensifying international competition."[21]

In the post–Cold War era, China's operations abroad have consisted exclusively of noncombat missions. Interactions with the U.S. military outside of Asia have mostly been cooperative, as, for example, has occurred in counterpiracy operations near the Gulf of Aden, as well as in some humanitarian assistance missions.[22] Authoritative Chinese documents indicate a desire to avoid major combat with the United States if possible, and China currently lacks the power-projection capabilities to be able to challenge the United States at substantial distances from China's own shores.[23] However, the intensification of competition with the United States raises the prospect of more antagonistic encounters, even as Beijing remains focused on a variety of traditional and nontraditional threats both along its periphery and abroad. China's determination to establish its primacy in Asia also provides a strong incentive for Beijing to build up its security partnerships and erode U.S. alliances and partnerships.[24]

Although the United States may be China's most formidable rival, China also faces competition from other powers in its region. In particular, Japan and India have the strength and motivation to resist Chinese encroachments. Both also maintain lively feuds with China over disputed territory. Other middle-sized powers may resist China's efforts to assert its primacy in the Indo-Pacific, such as Vietnam. To maintain its claims and prepare for possible contingencies along its periphery with these and other neighbors, China will need to maintain substantial armed forces within and along its borders. Thus, although Chinese leaders may seek to develop combat capabilities to protect their more distant interests, competition with other Asian powers and the persistence of unresolved disputes will likely impose some restraints. An era of great-power competition may also open opportunities for China to build counterbalancing partnerships against the United States in other regions, such as with Russia, Iran, or perhaps with countries in the Americas.[25]

By 2040, the intensification of rivalry with the United States and other countries raises the possibility that PLA operations abroad will include some form of combat, even if primarily indirect. The imperative of protecting against potential threats from Asian rivals will add a further constraint on China's ability to field a large military abroad. The PLA's ability to compete with the United States and other rivals will be further complicated by the imperative to address the variety of security concerns that affect partner nations along BRI routes.

---

[20] State Council Information Office of the People's Republic of China, 2019b.

[21] State Council Information Office of the People's Republic of China, 2015b.

[22] Peter A. Dutton and Ryan D. Martinson, eds., *Beyond the Red Wall: Chinese Far Seas Operations*, Newport, R.I.: U.S. Navy War College, China Maritime Study No. 13, May 2015.

[23] John Vrolyk, "Insurgency, Not War, Is China's Most Likely Course of Action," *War on the Rocks*, December 19, 2019.

[24] Bonny Lin, Michael S. Chase, Jonah Blank, Cortez A. Cooper III, Derek Grossman, Scott W. Harold, Jennifer D. P. Moroney, Lyle J. Morris, Logan Ma, Paul Orner, Alice Shih, and Soo Kim, *U.S. Versus Chinese Powers of Persuasion: Does the United States or China Have More Influence in the Indo-Pacific Region?* Santa Monica, Calif.: RAND Corporation, RB-10137-AF, 2020b.

[25] For a military-focused example, Cuba has reportedly provided access to China for signals intelligence since the 1990s (see Underwood, 2018).

Chinese National Strategy, Foreign Policy, and Military Strategy

Chinese leaders' responses to the trends reviewed above are informed by the priorities and policies that Chinese leaders have set for the nation. In this section, we review key features of China's national and military strategies (summarized in Table 2.2), focusing on the elements most relevant to how the PLA might operate abroad.

National Strategy and Foreign Policy

Chinese leaders have for decades upheld the "rejuvenation of the Chinese nation," which in recent years has been given the moniker of the "China Dream," as the principal goal of their national strategy.[26] The CCP has set the centennial anniversary of the founding of the PRC in 2049 as the desired time frame for achieving this goal. The core of the China Dream consists of a high living standard for all Chinese citizens and the country's revival as a prosperous, great power under CCP rule.[27]

TABLE 2.2

National Strategy, Foreign Policy, and Military Strategy: Implications for PLA Activities Abroad

Directive	Implications for PLA Presence Abroad
National strategy	
Achieve the China Dream	• Prioritize PLA overseas missions to secure resources, markets, and energy to support domestic development objectives • Shape terms of international peace and stability • Maintain forces for contingencies along China's periphery
Foreign policy	
Build network of partnerships	• Focus on countries along BRI routes for military access and security partnerships
Support multilateral security	• Favor military operations under multilateral authority, such as the Shanghai Cooperation Organisation • Provide PLA support to regional multilateral organizations, such as the African Union
Maintain opposition to alliances	• Seek to erode U.S. alliances through military diplomacy • Create alliance-like partnerships to facilitate military basing or access and combined operations
Military strategy	
PLA directed to protect China's overseas interests	• Expand military operations and activities abroad to protect Chinese citizens and their assets abroad, especially along BRI routes
PLA directed to shape a favorable international security order	• Increase military operations and activities to promote stability along BRI routes and strengthen integration of relevant countries into Chinese-led trade and investment networks • Undermine opponents of CCP by using PLA cyber and information operations • Build up PLA to counter U.S. military power as part of great-power competition

SOURCES: Authors' analysis of sources cited in the "National Strategy and Foreign Policy" and "Military Strategy" sections, including Xi, 2017; State Council Information Office of the People's Republic of China, 2019b; State Council Information Office of the People's Republic of China, 2019c; and Yan, 2019.

---

[26] "Xi Thought Leads to China Dream," *China Daily*, January 2, 2018.

[27] Xi, 2017.

While designed primarily to guide the formulation of domestic policy, the China Dream carries important implications for the country's potential deployment of military forces abroad. Most notably, elevating the standard of living for the Chinese populace requires a massive infusion of resources from the international economy. Chinese leaders have linked the domestic end state of a China Dream with that of an international end state that they call the "World Dream."[28] As part of this vision, officials uphold basic aspects of the existing order, such as the United Nations. However, the same officials call for renovating the order to better accommodate Chinese norms and political preferences, including deemphasizing institutions' focus on democratization and existing alliance structures, such as those of the United States.[29] China's leaders have explicitly linked overseas initiatives to PLA roles as well. In January 2019, Xi Jinping called on the central government leadership to establish a "security support system" for BRI.[30] In July 2019, Chinese Minister of Defense Wei Fenghe stated that the PLA would "deepen military exchanges and cooperation" with other countries under the BRI framework.[31] At the same time, both the PLA and the People's Armed Police (China's paramilitary force) are responsible for ensuring the key domestic drivers of the China Dream are not threatened by neighbors or internal pressures. They do so by maintaining forces capable of rapidly responding to a variety of contingencies along China's periphery.[32]

In terms of discrete foreign policy objectives, the pursuit of a China Dream gives rise to three areas of emphases: building new China-led networks of partnerships, supporting multilateral security fora (as opposed to others' unilateral or Western-led initiatives), and seeking to erode established security alliances. On the PLA's role in supporting these efforts, in the post–Cold War period China has maintained that it is opposed in principle to military intervention, but, as recently evidenced by Chinese leaders' statements regarding PLA support for BRI, Beijing is already reevaluating this policy stance in light of changing security needs.[33] Officials and analysts now argue that China's involvement in other countries does not violate the "non-interference" principle if it occurs with the consent—or at the request—of host nations and under certain multilateral conditions.[34] Chinese leaders have particularly favored the United Nations (UN) as a vehicle for international involvement in other countries because this, in theory, suggests that relevant UN operations represent the will of the international community rather than just that of China. This approach also enables

---

[28] Zheng Bijian, "Xi Jinping's Dream for China and the World," *China Daily*, April 13, 2018.

[29] See the discussion by Daniel Tobin (Chapter 2, pp. 9–34) and others in Kamphausen, Lai, and Ma, 2020.

[30] "On January 21, 2019, Xi Jinping Attended the Opening Ceremony of the Seminar on Key Provincial and Ministerial-Level Leading Cadres, Insisting on Bottom Line Thinking, and Focusing on Preventing and Resolving Major Risks, and Delivered an Important Speech" ["习近平2019年1月21日出席省部级主要领导干部坚持底线思维着力防范化解重大风险专题研讨班开班式并发表重要讲话"], Xinhua, January 22, 2019.

[31] "China to Deepen Military Cooperation with Caribbean Countries, Pacific Island Countries: Defense Minister," Xinhua, July 8, 2019.

[32] On the relationship between the PLA and the People's Armed Police and their roles in mitigating internal and external threats, see OSD, 2020, pp. 29, 34, 69–72.

[33] "Commentary: Chinese Military Contributes to World Peace," Xinhua, September 18, 2020. For an earlier discussion of this trend, see Mathieu Duchâtel, Oliver Bräuner, and Zhou Hang, "Protecting China's Overseas Interests: The Slow Shift Away from Non-Interference," Stockholm International Peace Research Institute, SIPRI Policy Paper No. 41, June 2014.

[34] See discussion of consent in State Council Information Office of the People's Republic of China, *China's Armed Forces: 30 Years of UN Peacekeeping Operations*, Beijing, September 2020. On shifting views of non-interference in China, see Jason Li, "Conflict Mediation with Chinese Characteristics: How China Justifies Its Non-Interference Policy as an Arbitrator," Stimson Center, August 27, 2019; and Chen Zheng, "China Debates on the Non-Interference Principle," *Chinese Journal of International Politics*, Vol. 9, No. 3, Autumn 2016.

China to delegitimize military interventions that do not meet Beijing's approval.[35] In addition to Chinese involvement with the UN, officials advocate for international security cooperation under the authority of Chinese-led or Chinese-promoted multilateral entities, such as the Shanghai Cooperation Organisation.[36] In the coming years, PLA advisors could provide assistance and advice to multilateral regional security groups, such as those associated with the African Union.[37] Where multilateral political cover is unavailable, China could consider a broader variety of military operations, including combat operations, so long as a partner nation were to request or consent to China's involvement and thereby help counter potential criticism of China for undertaking unilateral military interventions.

China's advocacy of a position of "non-alignment" and rejection of alliances also reflects both political calculations and historical influences.[38] The criticism of alliances makes a virtue of the fact that China itself lacks any alliances beyond that with North Korea.[39] It also supports China's efforts to contrast itself with Western powers and delegitimize U.S. involvement in any confrontation or clash that might involve China and its neighbors, including Japan, Taiwan, and the Philippines. As the competition with the United States deepens and the need for reliable security partners abroad grows, however, Beijing could rethink these principles. China might choose to build de facto alliances that enable military basing or access and combined operations with host nations' militaries, even if China continues to avoid the label of "alliances" for political reasons.

Military Strategy

According to official documents and military reporting, the military's missions have been largely defined by the "historic mission and tasks" outlined by Hu Jintao in 2004, and we assume that the underlying economic motives that spurred the 2004 policy will remain a key driver to send the PLA abroad in the coming decades.[40] Of the revised missions as articulated in China's 2019 defense white paper, several are especially relevant to potential PLA operations abroad. These include the mission to "provide strategic support for protecting China's overseas interests," which requires the PLA to improve its ability to protect overseas personnel, resources, shipping lanes, and interests. Another relevant mission includes the provision of

---

[35] Wang Yi, "Working Together to Address the New Threat of Terrorism," statement by the Minister of Foreign Affairs of the People's Republic of China at the UN Security Council Summit on Terrorism, New York, September 24, 2014, Ministry of Foreign Affairs of the People's Republic of China, September 25, 2014.

[36] State Council Information Office of the People's Republic of China, *China's Policies on Asia-Pacific Security Cooperation*, Beijing, January 2017a.

[37] Gisela Grieger, "Briefing: China's Growing Role as a Security Actor in Africa," Brussels: European Parliamentary Research Service, October 2019.

[38] On non-alignment, see State Council Information Office of the People's Republic of China, 2015b. The 2019 white paper describes the Shanghai Cooperation Organisation as a "constructive partnership of non-alliance" (State Council Information Office of the People's Republic of China, 2019b).

[39] Anny Boc, "Does China's 'Alliance Treaty' With North Korea Still Matter?" *The Diplomat*, July 26, 2019.

[40] As originally articulated, the PLA's historic mission and tasks are "(1) providing an important guarantee of strength for the party to consolidate its ruling position, (2) providing a strong security guarantee for safeguarding the period of important strategic opportunity for national development, (3) providing a powerful strategic support for safeguarding national interests, and (4) playing an important role in safeguarding world peace and promoting common development" (James Mulvenon, "Chairman Hu and the PLA's 'New Historic Missions,'" *China Leadership Monitor*, No. 27, January 2009). See also Cortez A. Cooper, *The PLA Navy's "New Historic Missions": Expanding Capabilities for a Re-emergent Maritime Power*, Santa Monica, Calif.: RAND Corporation, CT-332, 2009.

"strategic support for promoting world peace and development."[41] Although unstated, this mission also suggests that the PLA could support civilian authorities in their efforts to undermine opponents of the CCP and weaken long-resented norms and values preferred by the West, such as those related to human rights and democracy. The focus on building a favorable security environment also authorizes the PLA to build up a military capability to deter and counter the power of the United States and other rival powers as part of a great-power competition.

Core Interests, Threats, and Strategic Response Options

In this section, we examine more closely the possibilities for Chinese military operations abroad. We do this by assessing how the country's core national interests and Beijing's perception of potential threats to those interests shape its potential response options. We use three overarching interests—secure the homeland, ensure continued economic development, and expand China's international space—to categorize Chinese interests, which we summarize in Table 2.3, including potential threats and possible response options associated with each. We discuss each core interest more fully in subsequent sections.

TABLE 2.3

Chinese Interests, Potential Threats, and Potential PLA Response Options

Chinese Interests	Perceptions of Potential Threats to Interests	Potential PLA Response Options
Secure the homeland		
Preserve CCP rule and domestic stability	• Cyberattacks • Foreign agents	• Cyber operations at home or abroad • SOF activities to counter individual threats overseas in permissive environments
Secure sovereignty and territory	• Separatism • Rival state claims	• Military buildup and preparation to defeat Taiwan, U.S. intervention, land border incursions, terrorism, and air and maritime challenges • Joint island seizure and blockade operations
Protect physical security	• Nuclear attack • Cyberattack on infrastructure • Attacks on space assets	• Strategic deterrence to deter adversaries from preventing China's rise through strong nuclear, cyber, space, conventional defense
Ensure continued economic development		
Ensure access to overseas markets, especially energy and mineral imports	• Loss of escalation control in war • Interdiction of shipping • Maritime piracy	• Patrols to escort merchant shipping • Military assistance to client states • Multilateral counterterrorism operations

---

[41] The revised missions are (1) "provide strategic support for consolidating the leadership position of the CCP and the socialist system"; (2) "provide strategic support for the safeguarding of national sovereignty, unity, and territorial integrity"; (3) "provide strategic support for protecting China's overseas interests"; and (4) "provide strategic support for promoting world peace and development" (Yan, 2019).

Table 2.3—Continued

Chinese Interests	Perceptions of Potential Threats to Interests	Potential PLA Response Options
Provide security for Chinese citizens and investments abroad	• Civil wars • Interstate wars involving Chinese partner nations • Nonstate threats	• Military assistance to client states • Chinese participation in UN PKO • Quick-reaction force to carry out NEO • PLA support to client militaries • Military intervention in civil conflicts
Expand China's international space		
Consolidate Chinese influence on the Asia-Pacific security environment and beyond	• Instability in areas featuring Chinese interests • Competitor actions to undermine Chinese influence	• Military diplomacy to build a network of supportive security partners • International military exercises and assistance to shape security order • Military intervention to support a partner nation
Advance prestige and global governance interests	• Anti-China coalitions • Actions that harm China's prestige • Nontraditional threats to the global commons	• Military diplomacy to support partnership building • Military modernization to build a world-class military to deter war • Military intimidation to pressure states to respect CCP values and interests • Leadership and participation in UN PKO • Patrols and escort missions along shipping routes in Indian Ocean or other SLOCs

NOTE: NEO = noncombatant evacuation operation; PKO = peacekeeping operations; SLOC = sea line of communication; SOF = special operations forces.

Core Interest 1. Secure the Homeland

In this section, we review China's interests in ensuring security for the regime and political system, as well as its sovereignty and territorial and physical security.

Preserve CCP Rule and Domestic Stability

The most essential objective of China's core interests is to maintain the political system and the CCP's monopoly on power. Chinese sources generally judge that there is a relatively low level of domestic threat. The 2019 defense white paper claims that China "continues to enjoy political stability, ethnic unity, and social stability."[42] However, Chinese authorities routinely blame unnamed "external powers," a thinly veiled reference to the United States and other Western countries, for promoting separatism and defiance of CCP rule. For example, the 2019 defense white paper criticizes unnamed "external separatist forces" for "Tibet independence" and in Xinjiang as "threats to China's national security and social stability."[43]

In coming decades, possible threats to this interest could include foreign and domestic nonstate actors who promote political dissent and opposition to CCP rule. The CCP appears to perceive important threats as being transmitted through cyberspace, although the CCP also fears nonstate actors crossing the Chinese border from Central Asia. If China chooses to use the PLA to counter such threats, its options include paramilitary support to law enforcement and military cyber and information warfare operations. SOF could help fight nonstate threats in permissive environments, such as possibly in Central Asia.

---

[42] State Council Information Office of the People's Republic of China, 2019b.

[43] State Council Information Office of the People's Republic of China, 2019b.

Secure Sovereignty and Territory

Beijing seeks to secure its borders and control territories and waters whose ownership is contested by others. The most prominent threats to this group of interests stem from countries and neighbors that contest Chinese control of territory. In particular, the government of Taiwan rejects Beijing's claims of sovereignty over it, and countries such as Japan, the Philippines, India, and Vietnam contest Beijing's control over select land and maritime areas.[44] Beijing additionally views the possibility of U.S. military intervention in a conflict involving China and a rival disputant as a threat to China's control of its claimed territory.

To counter these threats, China has generally relied on whole-of-government and military noncombat actions to consolidate China's position and weaken that of rival claimants. In future years, China could continue to rely on diplomatic, economic, military, cyber, and informational tactics in the gray zone, including military modernization, patrols, reconnaissance, and demonstrations, to intimidate and deter rivals, as well as potential U.S. intervention.[45] If, however, the PLA becomes sufficiently confident of its ability to defeat or deter any U.S. forces sent to intervene, Beijing may take more-aggressive actions, such as setting up blockades or seizing disputed islands or territory.

Protect Physical Security

Interests related to China's physical security are among the most vital to the survival of the nation. These include providing basic protection from catastrophic nuclear attacks and guarding the safety and integrity of the nation's infrastructure and key aspects of its society and economy, including finance and other key functions, many of which rely on cyber and space assets.

There are several threats to this group of interests. First, Beijing perceives that an uncontrolled escalation in war, especially with a nuclear great power like the United States, could doom the country's efforts to achieve national revitalization. Another threat of concern for physical security could be preemptive attacks to undermine and prevent China's rise through the use of nuclear, space, cyber, or other weapons. Cyberattacks by state-backed actors could cripple and destroy core parts of the nation's infrastructure, including power, water, and transportation. State-backed attacks on space assets via kinetic or non-kinetic means could undermine or destroy vital services for the domestic economy and society. To deter potential attacks of any kind, the PLA could expand its military modernization program. It could also strengthen its ability to deter nuclear, cyber, and space attacks with appropriate defensive and offensive capabilities.

Core Interest 2. Ensure Continued Economic Development

Although China's trade dependence peaked in 2006, its economy still relies heavily on overseas markets, resources, and energy sources.[46] Over the next 20 to 30 years, China will continue to remain dependent on the global economy for resources, energy, and markets. In this section, we review two key groups of interests related to access to overseas resources and markets and to the security of Chinese citizens and key assets abroad.

---

[44] State Council Information Office of the People's Republic of China, 2019b.

[45] For more information on China's use of military and nonmilitary gray zone tactics in the Indo-Pacific, see Bonny Lin, Cristina L. Garafola, Bruce McClintock, Jonah Blank, Jeffrey W. Hornung, Karen Schwindt, Jennifer D. P. Moroney, Paul Orner, Dennis Borrman, Sarah W. Denton, and Jason D. Chambers, *Competition in the Gray Zone: Countering PRC Coercion Against U.S. Allies and Partners in the Indo-Pacific*, Santa Monica, Calif.: RAND Corporation, RR-A594-1, 2022.

[46] World Bank, "Trade (% GDP): China," webpage, December 2020.

Ensure Access to Overseas Resources and Markets

An overarching potential threat to China's economy is the possibility that a war involving China could escalate beyond its control, spilling over into multiple regions and affecting various economic sectors. A more discrete threat is the Chinese economy's dependence on imports for about two-thirds of its petroleum and for many of the raw materials that power its economic growth.[47] Roughly 80 percent of these imports must pass through the distant Straits of Malacca before reaching China, making this a strategic chokepoint of great importance to the PLA.[48] In the future, new natural gas pipelines from Russia, gas and oil pipelines through Pakistan and Myanmar, and government policies to wean China off of fossil fuels could reduce the danger of a petroleum blockade.[49] Even so, through 2040, China's economic prosperity will likely remain dependent on petroleum imports from the Middle East and Africa.[50] China's economy is also reliant on foreign markets for its products. Beijing has sought to reduce its dependence on exports, and the share of trade in China's GDP has fallen from about 64 percent in 2006 to about 32 percent in 2019.[51] As with energy imports, many of China's exports must pass through the Straits of Malacca to reach markets in Africa, the Middle East, and especially Europe. Well over half of its exports likewise are sent to other Asian nations or to the Americas.[52] China's interest in finding faster shipping routes to markets in Europe provides a strong incentive for PLA forces to secure shipping lanes through Arctic waters as well.[53]

China's maritime passageways to the Middle East are especially vulnerable to attack or disruption by nonstate actors, such as pirates.[54] If international competition intensifies in the coming decades, Beijing could worry that rival states, such as India, may be tempted to disrupt the shipping lanes along the Indian Ocean. To counter this potential maritime threat, the PLA could expand the overseas presence of military forces capable of protecting merchant shipping through key chokepoints. In Central Asia, small units of PLA counterterrorism specialists could work with partner nations to protect vulnerable pipelines. China might additionally consider establishing access and presence in regions featuring vital resources, including Southeast Asia, Africa, the Middle East, and Latin America.

Provide Security for Chinese Citizens and Investments Abroad

China's overseas interest have expanded in other ways, including its overseas investments, development projects, and the number of its citizens working abroad. According to OECD, in 2019, China's stock of overseas direct investment was as high as $2 trillion U.S. dollars.[55] Most of China's investment is in relatively low-risk,

---

[47] Jeff Barron, "China's Crude Oil Imports Surpassed 10 Million Barrels per Day in 2019," U.S. Energy Information Administration, March 23, 2020.

[48] Timothy R. Heath, *China's Pursuit of Overseas Security*, Santa Monica, Calif.: RAND Corporation, RR-2271-OSD, 2018, p. 7; China Power Team, "How is China's Energy Footprint Changing?" China Power Project, Center for Strategic and International Studies, February 15, 2016, updated March 17, 2022.

[49] Larry Luxner, "What China's March to Net-Zero Emissions Means for the World," Atlantic Council, January 20, 2021.

[50] Michael Lelyveld, "China's Carbon Targets Spark Rift with Russia," Radio Free Asia, November 6, 2020; Heath, 2018, p. 7; China Power Team, 2022; U.S. Energy Information Administration, "China," webpage, September 30, 2020.

[51] Kevin Yao, "China Pursues Economic Self-Reliance as External Risks Grow: Advisers," Reuters, August 4, 2020.

[52] Observatory of Economic Complexity, "China," webpage, 2020.

[53] State Council Information Office of the People's Republic of China, *China's Arctic Policy*, Beijing, January 2018.

[54] Oliver Cuenca, "Ethiopia-Djibouti Line Reports Reduced Revenue Due to Vandalism," *International Railway Journal*, December 16, 2020.

[55] OECD, "FDI Stocks (indicator)," webpage, undated.

developed countries like the United States or Western European nations.[56] However, China also has considerable investments in more-volatile, poorer parts of the world, although these mostly take the form of large, Chinese-funded and -executed construction projects instead of direct investment.[57] Development projects in politically less-stable regions have also put many Chinese citizens in harm's way. As with investment, the majority of China's citizens abroad live either in countries near China or in stable Western countries, but the number of Chinese nationals is growing rapidly in Africa, the Middle East, and other places, some of which face multifaceted security challenges.[58]

Threats to Chinese overseas interests include terrorism, political instability, international crime, and regional conflicts between states.[59] Chinese citizens in Africa, Central Asia, and South Asia have been subject to attacks and kidnapping by militants participating in local non-state and interstate conflicts and by criminals.[60] Thus far, China has often sought to protect its people and investments by cooperating with and providing aid to local government forces, sometimes creating local police or militia units specifically tasked with defending Chinese projects.[61] The PLA and Chinese security contractors can also help safeguard citizens by providing NEO and rescue operations, as the military did in Libya in 2011 and in Yemen in 2015.[62] Leveraging China's influence in the UN, Beijing could continue to advocate for deploying UN-flagged military units in unstable areas with Chinese citizens.

Core Interest 3. Expand China's International Space

Although many experts have focused on the material requirements for the country's revitalization, the intangible requirements of the China Dream merit emphasis as well. We discuss these two groups of interests next.

Consolidate Influence in the Asia-Pacific Region and Beyond

Chinese leaders have emphasized the importance of the region along its borders, or *periphery*, as the geographic foundation for its rise. Since 2012, China has become increasingly active in promoting the region's integration through Chinese-led initiatives, such as BRI, the Asian Infrastructure Investment Bank, and other efforts.[63]

Key potential threats include both regional hot spots and nontraditional sources, including natural disasters and civil conflict. Beijing also perceives competitor actions by the United States or other countries aimed at undermining Chinese influence as potential threats. To support broader Chinese efforts to promote regional stability, the PLA could engage in more military diplomacy by providing such services as humanitarian assistance and disaster relief, support for PKO, and other noncombat missions. To counter the

[56] China Power Team, "Does China Dominate Global Investment?" China Power Project, Center for Strategic and International Studies, September 26, 2016, updated January 28, 2021.

[57] China Power Team, 2021.

[58] Daniel Goodkind, *The Chinese Diaspora: Historical Legacies and Contemporary Trends,* Washington D.C.: U.S. Census Bureau, August 2019, pp. 5–6.

[59] State Council Information Office of the People's Republic of China, 2019c, pp. 31–32; State Council Information Office of the People's Republic of China, 2019b; State Council Information Office of the People's Republic of China, 2017a.

[60] Helena Legarda and Meia Nouwens, "Guardians of the Belt and Road: The Internationalization of China's Private Security Companies," Mercator Institute for China Studies, August 16, 2018.

[61] Legarda and Nouwens, 2018.

[62] Shannon Tiezzi, "Chinese Nationals Evacuate Yemen on PLA Navy Frigate," *The Diplomat*, March 30, 2015.

[63] Xi Jinping, "Working Together for an Asia-Pacific Community with a Shared Future," Ministry of Foreign Affairs of the People's Republic of China, November 20, 2020.

influence-building activities of the United States and other competitors, China could build its own support-ive network of nations.[64] For example, Chinese leaders have prioritized the building of partnerships in the Asia-Pacific, especially in Southeast and South Asia, with BRI members.[65]

Advance Prestige and Global Governance Interests

Chinese leaders have increasingly emphasized the importance of "dignity" for the country, which they have characterized in terms of international "respect" for the nation's interests.[66] Chinese leaders have lodged pro-tests and carried out retaliation against countries that appear to show support for activists hostile to Beijing's policies regarding Taiwan, Hong Kong, Xinjiang, Tibet, and other sensitive issues.[67] Chinese leaders also make clear that Beijing expects to assume a larger role in global governance in the coming decades. Xi Jin-ping has stated on numerous occasions that China intends to expand its role in "global governance" and has directed officials to "inject Chinese voices" into organizations responsible for aspects of global governance, even as he insisted that China upholds the international order.[68]

Potential threats include the formation of an anti-China coalition or coalitions, led most likely by the country that Chinese analysts most often refer to as the "strong enemy" (the United States), which could constrain or block China's freedom of action.[69] Provocations that Beijing sees as flagrantly opposing China's clearly stated preferences, policies, and norms, such as the formal recognition of Taiwan as a country, could also severely harm China's influence and reputation if left unanswered. China's best hope of avoiding the threat of uncontrolled escalation is to avoid a general war with the United States if possible.[70] To undermine the possibility of an anti-China coalition, China could carry out whole-of-government actions to undermine U.S. alliances.[71] The PLA could consider operations to intimidate U.S. allies and partners and, in extreme cases, perhaps even support covert and SOF operations to undermine or overthrow hostile governments. China could also bolster its appeal by stepping up its leadership in UN PKO and other international security efforts.[72] PLA support to partner nations could additionally seek to help build stability in key regions for Chi-nese economic, energy, and other interests.

---

[64] "Xi Eyes More Enabling International Environment for China's Peaceful Development," Xinhua, November 30, 2014.

[65] "Xi Jinping Gives Important Remarks at Central Work Forum on Diplomacy to the Periphery" ["习近平在周边外交工作谈会上发表重要讲话"], Xinhua, October 25, 2013.

[66] Ministry of Foreign Affairs of the People's Republic of China, "State Councilor and Foreign Minister Wang Yi Interview to Xinhua News Agency and China Media Group on International Situation and China's Diplomacy in 2020," Decem-ber 30, 2021.

[67] Elaine Pearson, "China's Bully Tactics Haven't Silenced Australia," Human Rights Watch, December 3, 2020.

[68] "Xi Stresses Need to Improve Global Governance," Xinhua, April 8, 2018; State Council Information Office of the People's Republic of China, "China Ready to Promote Reform of Global Governance System," Xinhua, September 14, 2017b.

[69] Nathan Beauchamp-Mustafaga, "Dare to Face the 'Strong Enemy 强敌': How Xi Jinping Has Made the PLA Talk About the United States," *Sinocism*, March 4, 2021.

[70] Ministry of Foreign Affairs of the People's Republic of China, "Interview on Current China-US Relations Given by State Councilor and Foreign Minister Wang Yi to Xinhua News Agency," August 6, 2020.

[71] State Council Information Office of the People's Republic of China, 2017a. Although this policy does not directly call for an end to U.S. alliances in East Asia, it does indicate that these alliances should not be strengthened, should not focus on China as a threat, should not enable the United States or other nations to aid U.S. allies in any conflict with China, and should be subsumed into a "community of common destiny."

[72] State Council Information Office of the People's Republic of China, 2020; State Council Information Office of the People's Republic of China, 2019c, pp. 31–33.

Implications for China's Pursuit of Overseas Basing and Access

We draw on the above assessment of Beijing's views of global trends, interests, and perceived threats to visualize key elements of China's expanding overseas interests based on current available data focused on China's overseas economic activity, energy imports, and related security concerns in Figure 2.1.

Elements featured in Figure 2.1 include significant destinations of overseas Chinese investments; key energy and sea routes to the Chinese mainland; potential overseas maritime chokepoints; China's top coal, natural gas, and crude oil sources by origin country; and a notional range ring to represent an area of potential threats from an adversary's kinetic fires, such as long-range precision strike weapons. Although the rankings of specific countries based on these data points will likely shift over the 2030–2040 time frame, many countries are likely to remain enduring energy and/or economic partners with China over the coming years. Taken together, these economic, energy, and security interests highlight the importance of the broader Indian Ocean region and Oceania, as well as portions of the Middle East and Africa, for China's emerging overseas military activities and presence.[73]

Conclusion

Given Beijing's assessment that continued economic growth is the engine of CCP legitimacy and an important source of that growth will rely on China's activities abroad, China's overseas interests provide compelling incentives for Chinese leaders to expand the PLA's operational presence abroad, especially in developing countries located along BRI routes. In other words, Beijing's primary motivation for expanding PLA presence abroad is rooted in the desire to protect China's growing economic interests. Beijing's motives are thus fundamentally based on achieving domestic priorities, such as economic growth to sustain the regime's legitimacy, and are, at most, only secondarily about competing with or imposing costs on the United States or any other country. Given China's evolving overseas economic, energy, and security interests, likely priority regions for PLA basing or access include the Middle East, Africa, and the broader Indian Ocean region, including the Indo-Pacific beyond the first island chain.

Expanding PLA presence in these regions could nevertheless affect U.S. interests as China deepens security partnerships with other countries. Our review of China's core interests and how threats could emerge in the coming decades implies a wide range of potential PLA operations and activities abroad, from peacetime military diplomacy and partnership-building activities to potential combat operations with partner nations. Intensifying competition with the United States and other rival Asian powers could additionally motivate the PLA to consider a broader range of operations abroad than the military conducts today, including some form of combat operations. In the following chapter, we build on this assessment to explore where specifically and how the PLA could posture itself overseas to operate abroad.

---

[73] Although some countries in North and South America and Europe are also highly relevant for Chinese objectives and interests, China has a variety of diplomatic, economic, and other tools to advance its interests and preferred policies in those regions, suggesting military basing and access may not be as much a priority in those regions in the 2030–2040 time frame compared with other regions. For more discussion on this subject, see Chapter 3.

FIGURE 2.1

Overseas Chinese Investment, Resources, and Security Interests

SOURCES: American Enterprise Institute (AEI), "China Global Investment Tracker," webpage, undated (see Sheet 1: Dataset 1: Column D: Quantity in Millions); OSD, *Annual Report to Congress: Military and Security Developments Involving the People's Republic of China 2018*, Washington, D.C.: U.S. Department of Defense, May 2018, p. 56; United Nations, "UN Comtrade Database," webpage, 2021; ArcGIS, "Global Shipping Routes," webmap, undated.

NOTE: This figure portrays key dynamics depicted in the PLA literature discussed further in Chapter Three. The investment data comes from AEI's China Global Investment Tracker. Countries shaded in red represent China's cumulative investment from 2005 to 2020 in countries with investments that totaled $5 billion U.S. dollars or higher. Pipeline and energy import route information are taken from the 2018 OSD report on China. China's top energy partners are based on UN Comtrade data from 2019; depicted on the map are China's top coal, natural gas, and crude oil import partners calculated by trade value. All partners listed provide at least 3 percent of China's imports of at least one energy type. Major sea lanes are based on ArcGIS information on global shipping routes. Chokepoint range rings denote a six-hour steaming range (a radius of 275 kilometers [km]) for large PLAN surface combatants to rapidly arrive to a location. The 5,000-kilometer range ring is not mentioned in the literature that we reviewed; it represents the hypothetical range of future ground-based precision fires that would be of key concern for Chinese military planners.

A Framework for Assessing China's Pursuit of Overseas Basing and Access Locations

As we discussed in Chapter 2, a major driver for growing PLA activities abroad over the past two decades stems from senior CCP leader directives for the PLA to develop capabilities that protect China's growing national interests. After senior Chinese leaders issued this mandate to the military in 2004, sustained overseas missions began in earnest in 2008 via deployments of three PLAN ships for counterpiracy patrols in the Gulf of Aden. Over the past 20 years, the PLA has gradually built up a range of overseas activities to further China's broader diplomacy efforts and advance its own operational objectives.[1] Key types of activities include delegations and functional exchanges; PKO; combined bilateral and multilateral exercises; maritime patrols and port calls; intelligence gathering activities; and humanitarian assistance/disaster relief (HA/DR) operations, NEOs, and other nontraditional security operations.

Despite greater emphasis on overseas military presence and capabilities by Chinese leaders and in authoritative military texts since at least 2004, few official Chinese sources detail thinking or planning for future PLA basing or access locations abroad. In this chapter, we provide an approach for conducting a systematic analysis of basing and access options for China's military out to the 2030–2040 time frame. A growing body of literature by Chinese military analysts and academic researchers explores potential criteria for overseas PLA locations, as well as options for prioritizing locations for future PLA basing or access. Building on this discussion, we develop a framework to evaluate which overseas locations could rank highly as future PLA basing and access locations from the perspective of Chinese officials.

We have organized this chapter into four sections. First, we briefly summarize insights from the growing discussion in authoritative Chinese sources of the need for the PLA to protect overseas interests. Growing emphasis on this role over the past 20 years provides broad direction for the PLA, but these sources do not specify where China will pursue overseas access, nor which types of military forces, units, systems, or capabilities may be needed to operate at overseas locations. Second, we leverage research on factors that PLA analysts and Chinese academics see as desirable for potential overseas locations and how they may enable PLA operations to develop our framework dimensions, which evaluate the desirability and feasibility of potential host nations. We note the limitations of our approach and analysis in the third section. In the fourth section, we briefly review the discussion of current and future military capabilities desired for power projection to and operations at overseas locations as the PLA continues to improve its "far seas" and other capabilities beyond the second island chain. This chapter sets the stage for Chapter 4, in which we use the framework to evaluate 108 countries in three priority regions—the Middle East, Africa, and the Indo-Pacific—as potential host nations for PLA basing and access in the 2030–2040 time frame.

---

[1] Kenneth Allen, Phillip C. Saunders, and John Chen, *Chinese Military Diplomacy, 2003-2016: Trends and Implications*, Washington, D.C.: National Defense University Press, China Strategic Perspectives 11, July 2017.

China's Growing Interest in Overseas Military Basing and Access

Despite calls for greater overseas military presence and capabilities by Chinese leaders and authoritative military texts since at least 2004, few official Chinese sources detail thinking or planning for future PLA basing or access locations abroad. In this section, we review the limited high-level guidance available, focusing on China's national defense white paper series and strategic-level PLA texts and supplemented by broader policy announcements from China's leaders. The guidance in these sources shapes more-detailed analysis by PLA and academic researchers on desired attributes of potential host nations for Chinese basing and access.

China's national defense white papers, coordinated among multiple government organizations and reflecting official policy positions, chart the evolution of the PLA's growing focus on overseas operations and key enablers, such as basing and access.[2] The papers' discussion of overseas missions, roles, and capabilities for the PLA reflects the military's lack of focus on overseas operations prior to 2004 and the steady growth in focus on this area following CCP leaders' new guidance in 2004. The white papers prior to 2002 even go so far as to state that "China does not station any troops or set up any military bases in any foreign country."[3] As discussed in Chapter 2, General Secretary Hu Jintao announced a set of "new historic mission and tasks" for the PLA in 2004, which included a growing overseas role for the PLA.[4] White papers since 2004 note the

---

[2] State Council Information Office of the People's Republic of China, *China's National Defense* [中国的国防], Beijing, July 1998a; State Council Information Office of the People's Republic of China, *China's National Defense*, trans., Beijing, July 1998b; State Council Information Office of the People's Republic of China, *China's National Defense in 2000* [2000年中国的国防], Beijing, October 2000a; State Council Information Office of the People's Republic of China, *China's National Defense in 2000, trans.*, Beijing, October 2000b; State Council Information Office of the People's Republic of China, *China's National Defense in 2002* [2002年中国的国防], Beijing, December 2002a; State Council Information Office of the People's Republic of China, *China's National Defense*, trans., Beijing, December 2002b; State Council Information Office of the People's Republic of China, *China's National Defense in 2004* [2004年中国的国防], Beijing, December 2004a; State Council Information Office of the People's Republic of China, *China's National Defense in 2004*, trans., Beijing, December 2004b; State Council Information Office of the People's Republic of China, *China's National Defense in 2006* [2006年中国的国防], Beijing, December 2006a; State Council Information Office of the People's Republic of China, *China's National Defense in 2006*, trans., Beijing, December 2006b; State Council Information Office of the People's Republic of China, *China's National Defense in 2008* [2008年中国的国防], Beijing, January 2009a; State Council Information Office of the People's Republic of China, *China's National Defense in 2008*, trans., Beijing, January 2009b; State Council Information Office of the People's Republic of China, *China's National Defense in 2010*, [2010年中国的国防], Beijing, March 2011a; State Council Information Office of the People's Republic of China, *China's National Defense in 2010*, trans., Beijing, March 2011b; State Council Information Office of the People's Republic of China, *The Diversified Employment of China's Armed Forces* [中国武装量的多样化运用], Beijing, April 2013a; State Council Information Office of the People's Republic of China, *The Diversified Employment of China's Armed Forces*, trans., Beijing, April 2013b; State Council Information Office of the People's Republic of China, *China's Military Strategy* [中国的军事战略], Beijing, May 2015a; State Council Information Office of the People's Republic of China, 2015b; State Council Information Office of the People's Republic of China, *China's National Defense in the New Era* [新时代的中国国防], Beijing, July 2019a; State Council Information Office of the People's Republic of China, 2019b. For the significance of these white papers, see Dennis J. Blasko, "The 2015 Chinese Defense White Paper on Strategy in Perspective: Maritime Missions Require a Change in the PLA Mindset," Jamestown Foundation, *China Brief*, Vol. 15, No. 12, June 19, 2015.

[3] State Council Information Office of the People's Republic of China, 1998a, 1998b, 2000a, 2000b, 2002a, 2002b, 2004a, 2004b, 2006a, 2006b, 2009a, 2009b, 2011a, 2011b, 2013a, 2013b, 2015a, 2015b, 2019a, 2019b. A white paper focused on arms control issued in 1995 and the 1998 and 2000 national defense white papers contain nearly-identical language to this effect (State Council Information Office of the People's Republic of China, *China: Arms Control and Disarmament* [中国的军备控制与裁军], Beijing, November 1995a; State Council Information Office of the People's Republic of China, *China: Arms Control and Disarmament*, trans., Beijing, November 1995b; State Council Information Office of the People's Republic of China, 1998a, 1998b, 2000a, 2000b). The 2002 paper omits this language, perhaps because of ongoing debates regarding China's strategic orientation and its implications for the military that were apparently resolved by the 2004 guidance on the new historic mission and tasks (State Council Information Office of the People's Republic of China, 2002a, 2002b).

[4] As a reminder, the historic mission and tasks are "(1) providing an important guarantee of strength for the party to consolidate its ruling position, (2) providing a strong security guarantee for safeguarding the period of important strategic opportunity for national development, (3) providing a powerful strategic support for safeguarding national interests, and (4) playing

PLA's requirements to increasingly operate overseas, while listing new or ongoing overseas operations.[5] Many white paper and PLA strategy texts frame overseas operations as part of MOOTW, noting that MOOTW can help the PLA carry out the new historic mission and tasks, expand Chinese interests, and contribute to a peaceful security environment.[6]

China's most recent defense white paper from 2019 increases the discussion of the PLA's role in protecting China's overseas interests compared with its 2015 and 2013 predecessors.[7] Reflecting broader adjustments in China's military strategy in the intervening years, the 2019 white paper also revises the 2004 missions to "providing a strategic support for protecting China's overseas interests," which requires the PLA to improve its ability to protect overseas personnel, resources, shipping lanes, and interests. Another relevant mission includes "strategic support for promoting world peace and development."[8] The 2019 white paper describes the need for associated basing or access to support those operations. Specifically, "to address deficiencies in overseas operations and support, [the military] builds far seas forces, develops overseas logistics facilities [海外补给点], and enhances capabilities in accomplishing diversified military tasks."[9] *Far seas* typically refers to waters beyond East Asia extending into the Indian Ocean, the Western Pacific, and farther afield, as contrasted with "near seas" activities in East Asia.[10]

---

an important role in safeguarding world peace and promoting common development" (Mulvenon, 2009). For more information, see Daniel M. Hartnett, "The 'New Historic Missions': Reflections on Hu Jintao's Military Legacy," in Roy Kamphausen, David Lai, and Travis Tanner, eds., *Assessing the People's Liberation Army in the Hu Jintao Era*, Carlisle, Pa.: Strategic Studies Institute, U.S. Army War College Press, April 2014, pp. 31–80.

[5] State Council Information Office of the People's Republic of China, 2004a, 2004b, 2006a, 2006b, 2009a, 2009b, 2011a, 2011b, 2013a, 2013b, 2015a, 2015b, 2019a, 2019b. The 2004 white paper discusses the impact of economic globalization on China's national security and calls on the PLA to defend national development and promote economic development to help China "unceasingly strengthen comprehensive national power" (State Council Information Office of the People's Republic of China, 2004a, 2004b). The 2006 white paper references the historic mission and tasks, calling on the PLA to "foster a security environment conducive to China's peaceful development" (State Council Information Office of the People's Republic of China, 2006a, 2006b). The 2008 white paper builds on its predecessor by listing overseas military operations other than war (MOOTW) tasks such as counterterrorism and peacekeeping, while 2010 adds maritime escort and disaster relief to its list of overseas operations (State Council Information Office of the People's Republic of China, 2009a, 2009b, 2011a, 2011b). Appendixes in some of the white papers also list the PLA's international activities.

[6] For more information on China's use of the term *MOOTW*, see Lin, Garafola, et al., 2022.

[7] State Council Information Office of the People's Republic of China, 2019a, 2019b. The 2013 white paper focuses on the PLA's role in "providing reliable security support for defending China's overseas interests," with sections detailing SLOC protection, NEO efforts, and other operations (State Council Information Office of the People's Republic of China, 2013a, 2013b). The 2015 white paper lists defending overseas interests as one of the PLA's eight strategic tasks, with an emphasis on supporting China's becoming a maritime power. It also states that "in response to the new requirement coming from the country's growing strategic interests, the armed forces will actively participate in both regional and international security cooperation and effectively secure China's overseas interests" (State Council Information Office of the People's Republic of China, 2015a, 2015b).

[8] State Council Information Office of the People's Republic of China, 2019b. As a reminder, the revised missions are more fully explained in a related commentary and are as follows: (1) "provide strategic support for consolidating the leadership position of the CCP and the socialist system"; (2) "provide strategic support for the safeguarding of national sovereignty, unity, and territorial integrity"; (3) "provide strategic support for protecting China's overseas interests"; and (4) "provide strategic support for promoting world peace and development" (Yan, 2019). For more on the evolution of China's overall military strategy, see M. Taylor Fravel, *Active Defense: China's Military Strategy Since 1949*, Princeton, N.J.: Princeton University Press, 2019.

[9] State Council Information Office of the People's Republic of China, 2019a. An official English translation is also available (see State Council Information Office of the People's Republic of China, 2019b).

[10] Kristen Gunness, "The Dawn of an Expeditionary PLA?" in Nadège Rolland, ed., *Securing the Belt and Road Initiative: China's Evolving Military Engagement Along the Silk Road*, Washington: D.C.: National Bureau of Asian Research, September 2019, p. 44.

Discussion of overseas PLA operations and enablers of such operations has also grown in key strategic-level professional military texts for PLA officers, particularly over the past decade. Interest in China developing overseas strategic strongpoints or bases was not mentioned in the *Science of Military Strategy 2001* (hereafter referred to as *SMS 2001*), an update of China's premier strategic-level military text first published in 1987.[11] However, *SMS 2001* notes that overseas bases can be important targets to strike during wartime, implying both the significant benefits to power projection provided by overseas bases and potential vulnerabilities.[12]

The 2013 iteration of *Science of Military Strategy* is the first strategy text to be published following CCP leaders' guidance in 2004 that the PLA should develop capabilities to protect China's growing overseas interests.[13] *SMS 2013* discusses the need for transforming China's defense to "forward edge defense," comprising shifts in the military's strategic layout at home on China's own territory, in the region, and globally in accordance with China's expanding national interests.[14] One component of adjusting its strategic layout is that China must

> build overseas strategic strongpoints [海外战略支点] that rely on the homeland, radiate into the periphery, and venture toward the [Pacific and Indian] Oceans. These sites are to provide support for overseas military operations or act as forward bases for deploying military forces overseas, exerting political and military influence in relevant regions. [China] should form a posture with the homeland strategic layout that takes account of both the interior and the exterior, connects the near with the far, and provides mutual support.[15]

In working with potential security partners, China will "carry out . . . strategic prepositioning beyond [its] borders [境外战略预置] . . . to strengthen the construction of strategic strongpoints [战略支撑点], establish common crisis response mechanisms with the relevant nations, and better expand [its] military's scope for overseas employment."[16] The term *strategic strongpoint* does not have an official definition, but Western ana-

---

[11] *SMS 2001* focuses on historical discussion of base areas [根据地], primarily seizing and operating from terrain within mainland China, a key factor in the PLA's defeat of the Republic of China (ROC) Nationalist forces during the civil war (Peng Guangqian [彭光谦] and Yao Youzhi [姚有志], eds., *Science of Military Strategy* [战略学], Beijing: Academy of Military Science Press, 2001). See Peng Guangqian and Yao Youzhi, eds., *Science of Military Strategy*, trans., Beijing: Academy of Military Science Press, 2005, pp. 108–115, 166, 240, 269–270, 314, for English text. During that conflict, the PLA sought to leverage newly gained territory to conduct ground-centric mobile, positional, and guerilla warfare. For a detailed examination of the PLA's approach during this period and associated operational concepts, see Fravel, 2019, pp. 39–67.

[12] General discussion of striking an opponent's bases is found in *SMS 2001*, pp. 98, 280–281, 328, 331 (Peng and Yao, 2005). In a chapter on the "strategic guidance of high-tech local war," there is a specific reference to striking another country's overseas bases: "Military counterattacks may include . . . attacking the enemy's foreign military bases" (Peng and Yao, 2001, p. 454; Peng and Yao, 2005, p. 426). Broader surveys of PLA writings indicate that Chinese strategists were focused on U.S. power projection by this period, including the United States' ability to leverage overseas bases. For an overview, see Michael S. Chase, Cristina L. Garafola, and Nathan Beauchamp-Mustafaga, "Chinese Perceptions of and Responses to US Conventional Military Power," *Asian Security*, Vol. 14, No. 2, 2018.

[13] Shou, 2013. For an English translation, see China Aerospace Studies Institute, *Science of Military Strategy (2013)*, trans., "In Their Own Words: Foreign Military Thought" series, Montgomery, Ala.: Air University, 2021. For an analysis on the differences between *SMS 2013* and *SMS 2001*, see Joe McReynolds, ed., *China's Evolving Military Strategy*, Washington, D.C.: Jamestown Foundation, 2016.

[14] Shou, 2013, pp. 250–252. The text provides an example of a regional-level strategic layout as the U.S. rebalance to Asia during the Obama administration.

[15] Shou, 2013, p. 254.

[16] Shou, 2013, p. 120.

lysts have tracked its use by Chinese military analysts to describe overseas locations with specific strategic and/or economic value for China, such as ports.[17]

The 2015 National Defense University's edition of the *Science of Military Strategy* and subsequent 2017 and 2020 revisions are key textbooks for PLA officers on the strategic employment and modernization of the Chinese military.[18] In describing the overseas employment of military forces, these texts explain that the PLA can defend the safety of overseas people, resources, and SLOCs; contribute to peace and stability in a way that builds relationships of trust with other governments involved while supporting Chinese companies' continued expansion of overseas activities; and deepen military exchanges to support China's foreign policy priorities.[19] Overseas operations can also improve regional stability, promote China's reputation abroad— particularly (as the authors explain) as more and more countries may view the PLA as a valuable contributor to regional and international security given China's growing role in PKO—and strengthen the PLA's military capabilities.[20] Finally, overseas military operations can "demonstrate strategic capabilities, deter hostile forces, and create an inviolate national image" of strength.[21] In terms of how to support and enable overseas operations, the *SMS* encourages the PLA to expand relations with countries in the Pacific and Indian Ocean regions, "actively explore building overseas resupply points [海外补给点] and support bases [保障基地] with Chinese characteristics"; they should also "sign military cooperation agreements with friendly countries, make advance preparations for military units to use foreign airports, ports, piers," and other infrastructure, and also leverage overseas Chinese commercial entities and personnel.[22] In 2019, after Xi Jinping called for the development of a "security support system" to protect and advance BRI, PLA leaders indicated that China's global military outreach would increase beyond the Pacific and Indian Ocean regions to include countries participating in BRI.[23]

To summarize, authoritative Chinese sources portray the PLA's growing focus on overseas missions and operations, shaped by national-level guidance in 2004 that defending China's overseas interests is a key role for the PLA going forward. Since 2013, strategy texts and China's defense white paper series increasingly call for overseas basing, facilities, or access to support the PLA in carrying out those operations, with a focus on locations in the broader Pacific and Indian Ocean regions. Recent guidance for the PLA to increase engagement with counterparts in support of BRI may foster new or expanded PLA activities beyond the "two oceans" and could drive the PLA to consider access locations even farther afield in the future to support these operations.

---

[17] For more on this term, see Conor Kennedy, "Strategic Strong Points and Chinese Naval Strategy," Jamestown Foundation, *China Brief*, Vol. 19, No. 16, March 22, 2019; Dutton, Kardon, and Kennedy, 2020; and Kardon, 2021.

[18] This *SMS* series is from a separate publisher than the previously mentioned volumes; these are the most recent PLA strategy texts available. See Xiao Tianliang [肖天亮], ed., *Science of Military Strategy* [战略学], Beijing: National Defense University Press [国防大学出版社], 2015; Xiao Tianliang [肖天亮], ed., *Science of Military Strategy* [战略学], Beijing, National Defense University Press [国防大学出版社], 2017; Xiao Tianliang [肖天亮], ed., *Science of Military Strategy* [战略学], Beijing: National Defense University Press [国防大学出版社], 2020.

[19] Xiao, 2020, pp. 313–314.

[20] Xiao, 2020, pp. 314–316.

[21] Xiao, 2020, p. 315.

[22] Xiao, 2020, pp. 325–326. *SMS 2015* includes "sign military agreements. . . piers," but that language is omitted in the 2020 edition (Xiao, 2015, p. 304).

[23] "On January 21, 2019 . . . ," 2019; "China to Deepen Military Cooperation with Caribbean Countries," 2019.

Assessing Potential Future PLA Basing and Access Locations

Although official and authoritative Chinese texts articulate the importance of overseas basing and access for enabling future Chinese military operations, they do not provide specific details on the priorities or desired attributes of overseas facilities, including locations. To help think through how Chinese access and basing priorities may evolve over the next ten to 20 years, we leveraged Chinese sources to construct a framework by which countries can be evaluated as potential host nations for future Chinese basing or access.[24]

Our framework builds on the existing PLAN-centric literature, which typically focuses on analysis at the port level, to incorporate criteria for air and ground forces and assess and rank locations at the country level. We focus on two dimensions of potential host nations from China's perspective: (1) *desirability*, or whether a PLA base, facility, or access in a given country would enable desired power-projection capabilities at tolerable risk; and (2) *feasibility*, or whether China's ability to secure a PLA base, facility, or access in a given country is politically viable in terms of requesting and securing an agreement with a potential host nation. Although we categorize framework indicators as either relevant for desirability or feasibility, indicators across the two dimensions may be correlated, meaning that such a two-dimensional framework may artificially separate non-independent indicators. However, a robustness check comparing the two-dimensional scores in Chapter Four with an alternative scoring system of one overall score demonstrated that some elements of feasibility are important and relevant to consider separately from desirability. Additional details on our methodology, including the data sets that we harnessed for scoring the countries and details on imputed scores, are provided in Appendix A.

Based on our analysis of China's growing overseas interests discussed in Chapter 2 and bolstered by PLA literature on the military's overseas regional focus,[25] our assessment focuses on three identified priority regions for PLA basing and access: the Middle East, Africa, and the Indo-Pacific.[26] We do not assess countries in Europe or in the Western Hemisphere.[27] We also eliminated China and the United States from our assess-

---

[24] We also built on existing Western analyses of Chinese sources, particularly sources focused on potential PLAN bases or access, including key analyses in Kardon, 2021; and Nathan Beauchamp-Mustafaga, "Where to Next?: PLA Considerations for Overseas Base Site Selection," Jamestown Foundation, *China Brief*, Vol. 20, No. 18, October 19, 2020.

[25] PLA analysis focuses on SLOC protection and pursuing basing and access more broadly in the "two oceans" region (the Pacific and Indian Oceans) mentioned in *SMS 2013* (Shou, 2013, p. 254). See also Jiang, Zhang, and Ge, 2017, pp. 504 and 508; and Wang, Qi, and Hai, 2018, pp. 32–33.

[26] Specifically, in our analysis, we group the countries that we assess by the DoD unified combatant command to which they belong: U.S. Africa Command (AFRICOM), U.S. Central Command (CENTCOM), or U.S. Indo-Pacific Command (INDOPACOM). We completed our analysis prior to the realignment of Israel from U.S. European Command to CENTCOM, announced in September 2021, so we have not included Israel in our analysis.

[27] Although the PLA may be interested in pursuing access agreements or mechanisms in or near Europe, Chinese interests and perceived threats in the region can be advanced via a host of diplomatic and economic tools and fora rather than by leveraging the PLA. PLA engagement in Europe is focused on learning from regional militaries—particularly in understanding tactics, techniques, and procedures (TTP) employed by the North Atlantic Treaty Organization—and supporting China's broader foreign policy priorities. See Lucie Béraud-Sudreau and Meia Nouwens, "Sino-European Military Cooperation in the Twenty-First Century: From Friends to 'Frenemies?'" in Roger Cliff and Roy D. Kamphausen, eds., *Enabling a More Externally Focused and Operational PLA: 2020 PLA Conference Papers*, Carlisle Barracks, Pa.: Strategic Studies Institute, U.S. Army War College Press, July 2022. We also did not assess Russia. Although Russia and China have significant aligned geopolitical interests vis-à-vis the United States, Russia is unlikely to welcome Chinese basing or access. Russia has a variety of other mechanisms to strengthen security ties with China, such as bilateral defense exchanges and military exercises, as well as multilateral exercises under the Shanghai Cooperation Organisation. On Russia-China relations, see James Dobbins, Howard J. Shatz, and Ali Wyne, *Russia Is a Rogue, Not a Peer; China Is a Peer, Not a Rogue: Different Challenges, Different Responses*, Santa Monica, Calif.: RAND Corporation, PE-310-A, October 2018; James Dobbins, Howard J. Shatz, and Ali Wyne, "A Warming Trend in China–Russia Relations," *The Diplomat*, April 18, 2019; and Miriam Matthews, Katya Migacheva, and Ryan Andrew Brown,

ment, as well as Taiwan, since Chinese views toward Taiwan are focused on political, economic, and military "reunification" from Beijing's perspective rather than securing basing or access from a host nation.[28]

Our analytical time frame extends from locations that China appears to be pursuing in the near term, such as Cambodia, to the 2030–2040 time frame, given long lead times in requesting, securing, and operationalizing agreements with host nations. Negotiating access agreements and constructing facilities, particularly large-scale formal basing facilities, requires significant investments of the requesting nation's diplomatic attention and endurance, financial resources, and adjustments to military organizations, force structure, training, and personnel processes.[29] For examples, China has a ten-year lease for its base in Djibouti, and construction at the base continued for years following its official opening in 2017. China's potential deal with Cambodia to station PLA forces at Ream Naval Base may include a 30-year lease at that facility.[30]

Desirability

Official and semi-authoritative Chinese sources articulate political, economic, military, and other attributes desirable for a potential host nation for PLA basing or access. Building on insights from these sources, we developed ten measurable indicators to assess the desirability of countries from Beijing's perspective—specifically, whether a PLA base, facility, or access in a given country would enable desired power-projection capabilities at a tolerable risk level. In other words, this dimension of the framework seeks to capture drivers that lead Beijing to value a given location for geostrategic, political, military, economic, or other factors. We weight all the indicators equally. Key themes considered in the desirability portion of our framework include

- **Military utility.** From a strategic and geographic perspective, as well as an operational one, is the host country desirable for military operations and likely PLA missions, now or in the future? Can the PLA rapidly deploy to the country? Can the country's level of development readily support the infrastructure and logistics required for PLA basing or access?

Superspreaders of Malign and Subversive Information on COVID-19: Russian and Chinese Efforts Targeting the United States, Santa Monica, Calif.: RAND Corporation, RR-A112-11, 2021.

The PLA operates a space TT&C station in Argentina. However, compared with the three priority regions of our analysis, we found fewer drivers leading China to prioritize PLA basing and access in the Western Hemisphere in the 2030–2040 timeframe. Our assessment of the Western Hemisphere aligns with recent U.S. Army Training and Doctrine Command analysis on the implications of growing Chinese influence for Army operational environments by 2035, finding via scenario analysis that future Chinese military activities and partnerships are likely to be more significant in the three priority regions of our study than in the Western Hemisphere (Richard B. Burns, Kevin M. Freese, Keith A. French, William C. Hardy, Andrew M. Johnson, Nicole M. Laster, and Anthony E. Mack, *Competition in 2035: Anticipating Chinese Exploitation of Operational Environments,* Fort Leavenworth, Kan.: Operational Environment & Threat Analysis Directorate, U.S. Army Training and Doctrine Command, G-2, August 15, 2019). For more on China's interests in Latin America and the Caribbean, see U.S.-China Economic and Security Revision Commission, "Hearing on 'China in Latin America and the Caribbean,'" transcript, Washington, D.C., May 20, 2021.

[28] On Chinese pressure toward Taiwan, see Lin, Garafola, et al., 2022.

[29] On the U.S. experience in securing and maintaining overseas basing and access, see Stacie L. Pettyjohn and Jennifer Kavanagh, *Access Granted: Political Challenges to the U.S. Overseas Military Presence, 1945–2014,* Santa Monica, Calif.: RAND Corporation, RR-1339-AF, 2016; and Michael J. Lostumbo, Michael J. McNerney, Eric Peltz, Derek Eaton, David R. Frelinger, Victoria A. Greenfield, John Halliday, Patrick Mills, Bruce R. Nardulli, Stacie L. Pettyjohn, Jerry M. Sollinger, and Stephen M. Worman, *Overseas Basing of U.S. Military Forces: An Assessment of Relative Costs and Strategic Benefits,* Santa Monica, Calif.: RAND Corporation, RR-201-OSD, 2013.

[30] China's lease for the Djibouti base reportedly runs until 2026 ("Chinese Ships Drill in Mediterranean en Route to Joint Exercises with Russia," Radio Free Europe/Radio Liberty, July 12, 2017; Page, Lubold, and Taylor, 2019).

- **Utility for protecting China's economic interests.** Is the country relevant and desirable for protecting overseas Chinese citizens and interests and in supporting BRI, as well as other Chinese foreign and economic policies?
- **Low or acceptable political or other risks.** Is the country politically stable, or might political volatility bring about significant changes in political support by the host nation's leaders for PLA basing or access? Could violence in the country lead to significant threats to the base or access itself, including to PLA facilities and units? Is the country prone to natural disasters or extreme weather that might limit the military utility of basing or access, making potential Chinese investment in acquiring basing or access there less useful or riskier in the long term?

Military Utility

Known Chinese Interest in Basing and Access

Demonstrated interest that China has pursued basing or access in a country is the most direct and externally visible indicator that Chinese officials find a potential host nation to be relatively desirable. Although many locations have been rumored to be under consideration, determining the level of official interest that China has expressed in a given country and the recency of Chinese outreach is a difficult task given the lack of public discussion by Chinese officials. We have adopted a conservative approach by using a 2020 DoD report's list of countries for which China has considered or made overtures for PLA basing or access.[31] (Of note, the 2021 edition of the same report did not add any new countries to the DoD's list.)[32] The DoD report reflects insights from the Intelligence Community, indicating that DoD views reporting on these countries as potential host nations for PLA basing or access as credible.[33] PLA sources rarely list specific countries of interest, but two PLA studies have mentioned ten countries as recommended or potential host nations—all of which are among the countries listed in the 2020 DoD report.[34]

---

[31] OSD, 2020, pp. 63, 128–130. DoD lists Myanmar, Thailand, Singapore, Indonesia, Pakistan, Sri Lanka, UAE, Kenya, the Seychelles, Tanzania, Angola, Tajikistan, Namibia, Vanuatu, and the Solomon Islands. We also include Djibouti, given the existing PLA base there; Cambodia, given the report's reference to potential PLA access at Ream Naval Base; and the PLA's space TT&C hosts mentioned in the report—Namibia, Pakistan, and Argentina. We do not assess Argentina, however, because it does not fall within the three priority regions of our analysis. For more information on the potential PLA use of facilities in Cambodia, see Ankit Panda, "Cambodia's Hun Sen Denies Chinese Naval Base Again—but What's Really Happening?" *The Diplomat*, June 2, 2020; and Timothy R. Heath, "The Ramifications of China's Reported Naval Base in Cambodia," *World Politics Review*, August 5, 2019. The 2021 DoD report also states that China is likely considering Cambodia (OSD, 2021, p. 132).

[32] In comparing the 2021 and 2020 DoD reports, we found that DoD instead removed two countries for which China has likely made overtures; the 2020 report lists Namibia, Vanuatu, and the Solomon Islands, but the 2021 report lists only Namibia of these three. Both Vanuatu and the Solomon Islands scored poorly in our analysis, which leveraged the 2020 data, so the 2021 DoD update did not significantly affect their scores nor our overall country ranking (see OSD, 2021, p. 132).

[33] DoD, "Chad Sbragia, Deputy Assistant Secretary of Defense for China Press Briefing on the 2020 China Military Power Report," transcript, August 31, 2020.

[34] We count the PLA analysts' reference to Djibouti as part of DoD's count. In 2014, scholars from the PLAN's Naval Research Institute listed potential locations of "replenishment and support points" [海外补给点和保障点] for PLAN operations, recommending Myanmar, Pakistan, Djibouti, the Seychelles, Sri Lanka, and Tanzania (Li, Chen, and Jin, 2014, pp. 74–75). In 2018, scholars from the PLA's Transportation University stated that "on this foundation . . . of building the first overseas base in Djibouti, in order to better safeguard our growing overseas development interests, our country will step by step plan to build overseas military bases (or overseas strongpoints) [海外军事基地 (或海外保障支撑点)] in Pakistan, the United Arab Emirates, Sri Lanka, Myanmar, Singapore, Indonesia, Kenya, and other countries through various methods such as purchase, leasing, and cooperation, and gradually build and form a networked system for China's overseas logistics support" (Wang, Qi, and Hai, 2018, p. 32). All ten countries listed by these two studies are located in the three priority regions assessed in our study.

We incorporate these insights into our framework by assigning a binary indicator for known Chinese interest in basing or access in a given country. The countries listed in the DoD's reports received a higher score (more desirable), while unmentioned countries received a lower score (less desirable).

Ability to Rapidly Deploy from China to the Potential Host Nation

PLA analysts focus on the ability of potential overseas locations to support a range of time-sensitive MOOTW operations, particularly HA/DR operations and operations to protect Chinese citizens abroad, including NEOs when called on to do so.[35] Researchers from the Dalian Naval Academy view "the usability and timeliness to support military forces" [保障兵力的可用性与时效性] as an important factor in overseas site selection.[36] *SMS 2020* also notes that overseas military operations need to be timely, citing a "golden period" for rescue operations as an example.[37] Although the strategy texts and PLA academic analysis often focus on naval operations, multiple articles by Military Transportation University researchers focus on the need for greater airlift capacity and the use of strategic airlift overseas, particularly the Y-20 military transport aircraft.[38]

We incorporate these insights into our framework by assessing two separate binary indicators for rapid deployment, either via ship or transport aircraft, from mainland China.[39] Because PLA sources do not specify specific time frames for rapid deployments overseas in the case of naval deployments, we evaluate whether the potential host nation has a port in range to rapidly resupply or support major naval or dual-use facilities in the Chinese mainland within one week.[40] For airlift, we evaluate whether the potential host nation falls within the range of a Y-20 transport aircraft carrying a heavy load.[41]

Coastal Country

Multiple PLA sources indicate a preference for potential host nations that could have coastal facilities, particularly near key chokepoints or SLOCs. National University of Defense Technology (NUDT) researchers

---

[35] Li Shougeng [李守耕], Chen Tieqi [陈铁祺], and Wang Feng [王丰], "Research on Pre-positioned Reserves Methods for Combat Readiness Materiel" ["战备物资预置储备模式研究"], *Journal of Military Transportation University* [军事交通学院学报], July 2019, p. 59; Wang, Qi, and Hai, 2019, pp. 32–33. Some of the PLA academic analysis discusses a related important factor of the distance from the potential host location by sea being relatively close to the area being supported. We opted not to assess this at the country level, given the challenge of assessing hundreds of airfields and ports and our lack of insight into which areas the PLA would prioritize supporting in specific operations in addition to major SLOCs. See, for example, Ma Liang [马良], Zhang Lin [张林], and Liu Xinke [刘新科], "Overseas Security Method of Assessing Point Location Based on Rough and Evidence Reasoning Bases" ["基于粗集和证据推理的海外基地保障点选址评估"], *Command Control & Simulation* [指挥控制与仿真], Vol. 36, No. 1, February 2014, p. 91; and Luo Zhaohui [罗朝晖], Wan Jie [万捷], and Li Hongyang [李弘扬], "Research on Factors in Site Selection of Overseas Military Base of Chinese Navy" [我国海军海外基地选址因素研究], *Logistics Technology* [物流技术], June 2019, pp. 141–142.

[36] Ma, Zhang, and Liu, 2014, p. 88.

[37] Xiao, 2020, p. 322.

[38] Wang, Qi, and Hai, 2018, p. 34; Chen Yu [陈瑜], Li Jiansi [李剑肆], and Zeng Yu [曾宇], "Research on the Building of Overseas Strategic Projection Capabilities" ["境外空中战略投送能力建设研究"], *Journal of Military Transportation University* [军事交通学院学报], Vol. 21, No. 2, February 2019, pp. 6–7.

[39] We considered merging these two indicators into one aggregate indicator, but given the emphasis on strategic airlift in the literature, it is possible a host nation could be extremely desirable even if it is beyond the range of a rapid naval deployment from China.

[40] Specifically, we evaluate whether there is a port within 3,024 nautical miles (nm) of steaming distance from two large ports with commercial and military presence in eastern and southern China (Shanghai and Zhanjiang). The distance represents an 18-knot transit time by a large vessel for seven days. More details are provided in Appendix A.

[41] Countries are considered to be within military airlift range of China if they fall fully or partially within 4,500 kilometers of PLA airfields in Qionglai, Kaifeng, or Changji. More details are provided in Appendix A.

viewed SLOC protection missions as a driver to establish overseas bases that provide comprehensive replenishment support.[42] Researchers from the Dalian Naval Academy see the demand for the PLA to protect China's maritime transportation lines as a key driver for overseas base support.[43] Naval engineering researchers assess that an overseas base could more readily provide timely support to flotillas, while a third country's port may not be able to fulfill this role at short notice because of local regulations or other restrictions.[44] Finally, Ministry of National Defense press statements from late 2015 regarding the PLA establishing its base in Djibouti also cite the need for a PLA overseas location to support ongoing naval operations.[45]

We incorporate these insights into our framework by including a binary indicator for coastal countries (more desirable) versus landlocked countries (less desirable). Although landlocked countries may still be valuable potential hosts for PLA ground or air forces, the preponderance of contemporary PLA analysis and discussion regarding overseas locations focuses on coastal access.[46] We assess that this focus is likely to continue through the 2030–2040 time frame or until other significant basing and access agreements are completed for the PLAN.

How Close Is Too Close? Factoring in the Limited Utility of Basing in Very Close Neighbors

While the previous three indicators evince clear benefits for power projection at relatively long ranges, the inverse may also be true. In other words, host nations with potential facilities for China to lease or access that are very close to similar facilities on the Chinese mainland may not rank highly in China's cost-benefit analysis. Such locations may not have significant enough operational utility for Beijing to invest the substantial financial or diplomatic resources in obtaining basing or access there, considering the range of some of the modern PLA's capabilities:

- Aircraft or other systems operating within 200–400 km of China are within range of China's most advanced integrated air defense systems.
- Long-range PLA artillery can strike locations 150 km away.
- Many variants of Chinese combat aircraft can fly at least 800–1,000 km unrefueled before returning to an airfield.
- PLAN ships and submarines can rapidly steam toward the open ocean from bases along China's coast.
- PLAN and People's Liberation Army Air Force (PLAAF) units, along with China's missile forces, can be armed with conventional missiles that range from a few hundred to 1,500-plus kilometers.[47]

Given the PLA's increasing ability to operate as well as the growing frequency of its operations at ranges of 300 to 500 km or greater from China's coast, Beijing may see little incentive in pursuing basing and access

---

[42] Jiang, Zhang, and Ge, 2017, p. 504.

[43] Ma, Zhang, and Liu, 2014, p. 88.

[44] Luo, Wan, and Li, 2019, p. 142.

[45] Ministry of National Defense of the People's Republic of China, 2015a; Ministry of National Defense of the People's Republic of China, 2015b.

[46] See, for example, two articles by both PLAN and non-PLAN military authors, which list only coastal countries as recommended or potential future hosts for the PLA: Li, Chen, and Jin, 2014; and Wang, Qi, and Hai, 2018.

[47] Ranges of Chinese systems are based on OSD, 2020; and Eric Heginbotham, Michael Nixon, Forrest E. Morgan, Jacob L. Heim, Jeff Hagen, Sheng Tao Li, Jeffrey Engstrom, Martin C. Libicki, Paul DeLuca, David A. Shlapak, David R. Frelinger, Burgess Laird, Kyle Brady, and Lyle J. Morris, *The U.S.-China Military Scorecard: Forces, Geography, and the Evolving Balance of Power, 1996–2017*, Santa Monica, Calif.: RAND Corporation, RR-392-AF, 2015. Although China already fields air- and ground-launched missiles that range 1,500 km, OSD assesses that PLAN systems will likely carry long-range antiship cruise missiles, antiship ballistic missiles, and land attack cruise missiles in the future as well (OSD, 2020, pp. 45–47, 59, 78).

within the first island chain between Japan, Taiwan, and edging toward the South China Sea.[48] Basing and access locations in this region also have little utility for augmenting the PLA's existing capability to protect SLOCs or mitigate current maritime chokepoints.

This indicator may also indirectly capture concerns Chinese analysts have about potential reputational costs for basing or sending forces abroad. One PLA study, for example, states that overseas transportation activities are "sensitive, attracting high levels of attention from global public opinion," so the requirements are higher than for domestic activities of the same type.[49] Researchers also discuss the potential for weaponized backlash by host nation, or regional opposition that may damage China's narrative of a "peaceful rise" beneficial for other countries.[50] *SMS 2020* additionally cites concerns about public opinion given greater overseas Chinese military activities.[51]

To implement this indicator, we apply a 500-kilometer penalty based on the proximity of key regions of potential host nations to major PLA facilities. We derive our information on major PLA facilities from a 2020 DoD report on China and a 2019 order of battle map produced by the International Institute for Strategic Studies.[52] This indicator primarily affects North Korea and Vietnam—two countries that are unlikely to host significant Chinese forces in peacetime because of the state of their bilateral relations with China. Previous RAND research on a potential Chinese intervention in a Korean Peninsula contingency indicates that Chinese forces may seek to enter North Korea during crisis or conflict to limit the advance of North Korean forces and refugees into China and conduct other operations, potentially independently of the desires of the North Korean regime.[53] For Vietnam, Hanoi's wariness toward Beijing has only strengthened over the past decade, particularly regarding Chinese military and nonmilitary activities in the South China Sea, on the Indochina Peninsula, and in some instances along or within Vietnam's borders.[54]

Given the lack of direct discussion on this subject in PLA sources, this indicator relies more than the others on an operational assessment of PLA needs and capabilities, and other countries could potentially be affected, too.[55] It is thus possible this indicator indirectly captures other dimensions of desirability that we have not otherwise directly incorporated into our framework.

---

[48] On China's growing overwater air operations, see Edmund J. Burke, Timothy R. Heath, Jeffrey W. Hornung, Logan Ma, Lyle J. Morris, and Michael S. Chase, *China's Military Activities in the East China Sea: Implications for Japan's Air Self-Defense Force*, Santa Monica, Calif.: RAND Corporation, RR-2574-AF, 2018; and Derek Grossman, Nathan Beauchamp-Mustafaga, Logan Ma, and Michael S. Chase, *China's Long-Range Bomber Flights: Drivers and Implications*, Santa Monica, Calif.: RAND Corporation, RR-2567-AF, 2018.

[49] Wang, Qi, and Hai, 2018, p. 33.

[50] Kardon, 2021, pp. 91–92.

[51] Xiao, 2020, p. 320.

[52] OSD, 2020, pp. 98, 103, 106, 109, and 111; International Institute for Strategic Studies, "The 2019 Military Balance Chart: China's Armed Forces," wall chart in *The Military Balance 2019*, Washington, D.C., February 2019.

[53] On China's role in a Korea contingency, see Gian Gentile, Yvonne K. Crane, Dan Madden, Timothy M. Bonds, Bruce W. Bennett, Michael J. Mazarr, and Andrew Scobell, *Four Problems on the Korean Peninsula: North Korea's Expanding Nuclear Capabilities Drive a Complex Set of Problems*, Santa Monica, Calif.: RAND Corporation, TL-271-A, 2019; and Michael J. Mazarr, Gian Gentile, Dan Madden, Stacie L. Pettyjohn, and Yvonne K. Crane, *The Korean Peninsula: Three Dangerous Scenarios*, Santa Monica, Calif.: RAND Corporation, PE-262-A, 2018.

[54] For an overview of Chinese coercion against Vietnam since 2009 and Vietnam's security concerns regarding closer China-Cambodia and China-Laos ties, see Lin, Garafola, et al., 2022.

[55] Because we focus on countries within the first island chain, we considered but did not apply the penalty score to Nepal and Laos. We also did not analyze some countries that scored poorly on feasibility, such as Japan, South Korea, India, and Bhutan, which all received a feasibility score of Tier 4 (bottom 25 percent of all countries scored) and therefore do not rank highly in our overall tiering system regardless. For more information, see Appendix A.

Level of Human Development

The PLA research that we reviewed highlights how conditions within the host nation's economy could impact the overall quality of a location's support to PLA forces. Researchers from the Dalian Naval Academy view the basic infrastructure development level of a host nation as important for supporting potential basing or access, including overall transportation, equipment maintenance, and medical services, as well as local economic conditions near the base or access port.[56] Naval engineering analysts focus on the role of the country's economic policy and local economic situation in shaping basing decisions, including the host nation's economic system (e.g., market economy), level of economic development, economic conditions and growth trajectory, macroeconomic policy, and sector-specific conditions.[57] They also cite the host nation's technology level as relevant for maximizing the utility of a base or access.[58] NUDT researchers have analyzed economic activity at the port level via annual tonnage of port throughput, citing throughput as an indicator of a location's operational capability to support a military base.[59]

We incorporate this emphasis on the impact of the host nation's human development level on the military utility of a potential base or access by assessing economic and human development at the country level. For this, we leverage 2020 data from the World Bank's Human Development Index, which assesses life expectancy, education, and gross national income (GNI) per capita.[60]

Utility for Protecting China's Economic Interests

Level of Chinese Investment

Multiple studies assert that economic factors are relevant to the selection of PLA basing and access locations in terms of proximity to overseas Chinese activities that the military has been directed to protect or secure. A Naval University of Engineering study frames this in terms of supporting China's continued economic development, calling overseas base construction an "important link in [China's] military's strategy . . . to actively promote the country's development."[61] A study by Military Transportation University researchers notes that the base in Djibouti was established not only to protect energy supply lines but also to lower trade risks and ensure the safety of overseas Chinese investments and citizens.[62]

We incorporate these insights into our framework by assessing the cumulative level of investment by China in each country, positing that higher levels of Chinese investment in a country correspond to greater interest and desirability in securing or protecting surrounding locations. Although investment is only one measure of China's economic interests in other countries, overseas investment has been a centerpiece of Chi-

---

[56] The Dalian Naval Academy researchers referenced the local economy's development level and the ability to provide material resources for strategic support (Ma, Zhang, and Liu, 2014, p. 91).

[57] Luo, Wan, and Li, 2019, pp. 142–143.

[58] Luo, Wan, and Li, 2019, pp. 142–143.

[59] Jiang, Zhang, and Ge, 2017, pp. 505–506.

[60] Max Roser, "Human Development Index (HDI)," *Our World in Data*, 2014.

[61] Luo, Wan, and Li, 2019, p. 141.

[62] Li, Chen, and Wang, 2019, p. 59.

na's overall foreign policy since BRI was formally announced in 2013.[63] We draw our data from AEI's China global investment tracker.[64]

BRI Member or Participant

PLA researchers likewise note the PLA's role in supporting BRI, as well as BRI driving demand for the expansion of overseas activities. Military Transportation University researchers state that options for pre-positioning supplies overseas include leveraging Chinese firms that have gone abroad as part of BRI. For example, the PLA could sign a reserve contract with Chinese oil firms operating in the host nation to provide fuel during wartime; firms could also support the military by providing "life services, medical care, environmental protection, greening, cleaning, fire protection, catering and other fields" at overseas bases.[65] Naval engineering analysts state that with the "deepening of the Belt and Road Initiative, overseas security problems are also emerging, [the PLAN's] overseas military operations other than war are increasing, and the demand for providing overseas support is also increasing."[66] A second study by Military Transportation University researchers characterize the PLA's "intensifying construction of overseas support bases/strongpoints" [海外保障基地 or 海外保障支撑点] as advancing BRI while supporting the military's ability to "go out" [走出去] beyond Chinese shores.[67] NUDT analysts also linked the pursuit of overseas bases to growing BRI-related requirements.[68]

We incorporate these insights into our framework by assessing whether countries are BRI members, positing that BRI member countries may be viewed as more desirable both for protecting China's interests and for potentially supporting PLA basing or access. We leverage data sets on known countries that have signed memoranda of understanding (MOU) with Beijing on BRI.[69]

Low or Acceptable Political or Other Risks

Political Stability and the Absence of Violence

PLA analysts raise the stability of the potential host nation as a potential threat to overseas basing and access, and at least one study notes that stable regimes are more valuable types of host nations. Naval University of Engineering researchers cite political stability as a key element within political and legal factors that can shape and restrict overseas base selection.[70] Dalian Naval Academy researchers discuss broad threats to China's interests stemming from regional instability or instability within a country, as well as specific threats

---

[63] We also use levels of Chinese investment as a proxy for the number of Chinese persons and companies and their associated economic activities in the potential host nation (two other factors commonly cited in the PLA literature), because information on Chinese citizens and companies overseas is not readily available at the country level. We considered additionally assessing cumulative construction, but we decided not to because Chinese interests relating to construction end after project completion unless Chinese firms have also invested in the project.

[64] AEI, undated.

[65] Li, Chen, and Wang, 2019, p. 60.

[66] Luo, Wan, and Li, 2019, p. 141.

[67] Wang, Qi, and Hai, 2018, p. 32. On the role of airlift in supporting BRI, see Chen, Li, and Zeng, 2019, pp. 5–6.

[68] Jiang, Zhang, and Ge, 2017, p. 504.

[69] Green Belt and Road Initiative Center, "Countries of the Belt and Road Initiative (BRI)," webpage, March 2020; Jennifer Hillman and David Sacks, *China's Belt and Road: Implications for the United States*, New York: Council on Foreign Relations, Independent Task Force Report No. 79, 2021.

[70] Luo, Wan, and Li, 2019, pp. 142–143.

to air or shipping routes.[71] Military Transportation University researchers list potential threats, including "societal turmoil" within the host country, demonstrations and protests, political or armed factions, violent crime, and terrorism. The same study notes that Djibouti was selected as a base in part because it "has good social security and the regime has maintained long-term stability."[72]

We incorporate this into our framework by assessing political stability, broadly defined at the country level, positing that greater political stability and fewer incidences of violence are more desirable from the perspective of the PLA in prioritizing basing and access locations. Specifically, we leverage the Political Stability and Absence of Violence indicator in the World Bank's worldwide governance indicators (WGI).[73]

Risk of Climate Change

Although some PLA analysts focus on current-day geological, hydrological, and meteorological conditions, other researchers point out that long-term climate conditions will create risks for potential overseas locations.[74] NUDT researchers viewed poor weather as "the most important threat to military base basic facilities and personnel safety during operations."[75] They note that climate change's threat to coastal ports and military facilities cannot be mitigated via current design planning and construction standards. Instead, assessing whether a facility is capable of being protected against natural disasters is an important criterion for weighing the overall merits of a given base. The same study goes on to provide specific indicators of desirable versus undesirable weather and associated climate change conditions, with desirable conditions described as low danger from severe storms, extreme tides and rising sea levels, thick fog, and high temperatures.[76] More-resilient host nations may therefore be especially worth the long-term political and financial investments of securing basing or access.

We incorporate these insights into our framework by including one indicator that assesses a broad measure of climate change impact for countries, focusing on two elements raised by NUDT researchers: rising sea levels and extreme temperatures. Specifically, we look at rising sea levels in the 2050 time frame and extreme temperature days in the 2040–2059 time frame by leveraging data from a 2019 study in *Nature Communications* and the World Bank's climate knowledge portal.[77]

Feasibility

Chinese sources recognize that securing overseas basing or access requires significant host nation buy-in from political leadership, particularly for both PLA presence and operations. Building on insights from these sources, we developed seven measurable indicators to assess the feasibility of countries from Beijing's perspective, specifically whether obtaining a PLA base, facility, or access in a given country is politically feasible

---

[71] Ma, Zhang, and Liu, 2014, p. 88.

[72] Wang, Qi, and Hai, 2018, pp. 32–35.

[73] World Bank, "Worldwide Governance Indicators," webpage, 2021a.

[74] For examples focused on the importance of current-day weather conditions, see Ma, Zhang, and Liu, 2014, pp. 91–93. The NUDT study additionally mentions flat terrain and good vegetation cover as desirable attributes (see Jiang, Zhang, and Ge, 2017, p. 506).

[75] Jiang, Zhang, and Ge, 2017, p. 505.

[76] Jiang, Zhang, and Ge, 2017, pp. 505–506.

[77] Scott A. Kulp and Benjamin H. Strauss, "New Elevation Data Triple Estimates of Global Vulnerability to Sea-Level Rise and Coastal Flooding," *Nature Communications*, No. 10, October 2019; World Bank Group, "Climate Change Knowledge Portal," database, undated.

in terms of both requesting and securing an agreement with a potential host nation. In other words, this dimension of the framework recognizes that a given country may be highly desirable in terms of geostrategic, operational, military, or other reasons, but it may be unrealistic for China to pursue access or basing because of strained bilateral relations, little Chinese influence within the country, or other unfavorable dynamics. We weight all the indicators equally. Key themes considered in the feasibility portion of our framework include

- **Regime alignment with the PRC.** Do the two countries have similar governance systems and associated power structures? Are the two countries' foreign policies relatively aligned? Might China be able to leverage existing patronage networks or other avenues to increase inducements for the country's leaders to agree to a deal?
- **China's influence in the country.** Is political and military engagement frequent between the two countries? Is China a major established or emerging security cooperation partner as demonstrated by significant arms sales?
- **Potential obstacles in China's relationship with the country.** Do long-standing historical tensions or dynamics in bilateral relations create opposition to hosting the Chinese military? Might third countries object to PLA presence in the country, complicating the potential host nation's relations with highly valued partners? Are there significant diplomatic barriers to hosting the PLA, such as a lack of official diplomatic recognition?

It is important to note that Chinese sources are circumspect about addressing these topics in the context of potential basing and access because evaluating feasibility may involve sensitive discussions regarding China's relations with other countries and their leaders, as well as nonpublic information, such as provisions included in basing or access agreements. We include multiple indicators to assess each of the above themes based on measurable data but recognize that we lack detailed insights into how the PLA may evaluate some of these dynamics.

Regime Alignment with the PRC

PLA sources include common interests between China and potential host nations as a potential influence on basing and access decisions. The Dalian Naval Academy study notes that aligned interests and the host's foreign policy are a component of political and foreign policy factors to weigh.[78] Naval University of Engineering researchers describe multiple political and legal factors that can shape overseas base selection, including political stability, as previously mentioned, but also broader measures related to the host nation's government, government actions, and policies demonstrating its willingness to host foreign powers; interest groups; laws and statutes; and potential limitations stemming from international law.[79] Taken together, PLA assessments view a potential host nation regime's domestic governance system and associated power structures, as well as foreign policy outlook, as shaping basing and access dynamics.

We incorporate these insights into our framework by developing three indicators that may lead a country to be more or less feasible for future PLA basing or access. These are summarized below.

Authoritarian Regime

We hypothesize that having a similar regime type is one measure to assess the overall alignment of a potential host nation with the PRC, which may induce security cooperation involving PLA basing or access. Given

---

[78] Ma, Zhang, and Liu, 2014, p. 91.

[79] Luo, Wan, and Li, 2019, pp. 142–143.

that China is an authoritarian regime, we posit that similarly authoritarian regimes are more feasible for future access than democratic regimes, in which citizens have a variety of rights and mechanisms to obtain information from the government about a foreign military's presence on their soil, as well as to oppose hosting the Chinese military via protests, legal challenges, or other methods.[80] To assess regime type, we leverage data from Freedom House's global freedom score, which measures a population's access to political rights and civil liberties.[81]

Aligned Voting with China

External alignment on foreign policy issues may likewise indicate that the governments of potential host nations see common challenges and opportunities as China. They may also be more willing to partner with China bilaterally to address common foreign policy challenges. We posit that countries with relatively aligned foreign policies are more feasible for potential PLA basing and access than relatively unaligned countries, which may oppose elements of China's foreign policy and associated security policy and military activities. To capture one element of foreign policy alignment, we compare country voting records with China's during roll-call votes in the UN General Assembly.[82]

Perceptions of Corruption

We hypothesize that the presence of corruption may improve feasibility in winning over a country's political or other leadership to support PLA presence in a potential host nation. In at least one instance—Cambodia—known Chinese state-backed or state-sponsored support for a regime's leader has become public in a country that is likely to host PLA forces in the future.[83] Corruption may also facilitate infrastructure deals that can be leveraged for potential PLA access. However, it is possible that too much corruption may negatively affect feasibility if host nations' policies toward the presence of foreign military forces become volatile as rent-seeking or other corrupt behaviors increase.

To assess this dynamic, we leverage data from Transparency International's Corruption Perceptions Index, which analyzes perceptions by businesspeople and country experts of the level of corruption in the public sector for each country.[84] Although the index does not measure corruption directly, it assesses the types of corruption perceived to be present within a country's government, potentially offering more options

---

[80] Although China's vision to reshape the international order does not exclude partnering with democracies in a variety of contexts, China seeks to erode portions of the existing order focused on democratic principles, including universal rights and freedoms, to advance principles that support the CCP's and other regimes' continued authoritarian rule (Nadège Rolland, *China's Vision for a New World Order*, Seattle Wash.: National Bureau of Asian Research, NBR Special Report 83, January 2020, pp. 6, 20, 41–49).

[81] Freedom House, "Countries and Territories," webpage, undated.

[82] Erik Voeten, Anton Strezhnev, and Michael Bailey, "United Nations General Assembly Voting Data," data set, Harvard Dataverse, 2021.

[83] As one public example of likely state-backed or -sponsored support for regime leaders in a country likely to host future PLA basing or access, the Cambodian Prime Minister Hun Sen thanked China following his 2018 election win for providing financial support for the election (see Charles Dunst, "In Cambodia, 'Rule of Law' Means Hun Sen Rules," *Foreign Policy*, December 12, 2019; Philip Heijmans, "Hun Sen—and China—Win Cambodia Elections," *Newsweek*, July 29, 2018). For another example, in the Indo-Pacific, Chinese backers have supported President Duterte in the Philippines via Sino-Philippine friendship organizations, campaign donations prior to the 2016 presidential election, large-scale investments, and high-level advisors (Lin, Garafola, et al., 2022). For more on the potential for Chinese state-backed lenders to shape lendees' domestic and foreign policies, see Anna Gelpern, Sebastian Horn, Scott Morris, Brad Parks, and Christoph Trebesch, *How China Lends: A Rare Look into 100 Debt Contracts with Foreign Governments*, Peterson Institute for International Economics, Kiel Institute for the World Economy, Center for Global Development, and AidData at William & Mary, 2021. On the use of Chinese maritime state-owned enterprises (SOEs) to co-opt elites, see Jones and Veit, 2021.

[84] Transparency International, "Corruption Perceptions Index," webpage, 2020.

for China to induce leaders to agree to basing agreements, as well as commercial sectors, which may be relevant for periodic PLA access of large-scale infrastructure, such as ports or airfields.

China's Influence in the Country

As previously mentioned, Chinese military strategy texts, such as *SMS 2020*, state that overseas PLA activities can help build trust with other governments while deepening military exchanges to support China's foreign policy priorities.[85] Dalian Naval Academy researchers assert that overseas bases will "strengthen the two countries' strategic ties and need to be able to influence regional strategic balances."[86] One study focused on developing overseas airlift capability is candid in stating that "[China lacks] overseas strategic strongpoints for aviation due to strong sensitivities in geopolitics." For BRI, the authors note that in addition to promoting economic ties, China also needs to expand political and cultural ties to alleviate countries' misgivings. The authors also advocate for strengthening military security cooperation, exchanges, and mechanisms to obtain the use of overseas aviation bases.[87]

We incorporate these insights into our framework by developing two indicators that may lead a country to be more or less feasible for future PLA basing or access: frequency of bilateral engagements and arms sales or transfers. These are briefly explained below.

Partner Engagement

We posit that countries with more frequent high-level political engagement from Chinese leaders and more frequent military exchanges with the PLA are more feasible potential host nations for PLA basing or access, compared with countries in which China has not invested substantial political or military engagement. We developed one indicator to assess partner engagement, focusing on two elements: total number of senior political exchanges and total number of military exchanges. We combined the two types into one indicator because China views military diplomacy as supporting political, economic, and foreign policy objectives.[88] In that sense, military diplomacy is one component of overall diplomacy, and both should be relatively aligned, although military diplomacy may lag behind or be less comprehensive than other forms of diplomatic engagement.

We leverage data on CCP International Department engagements with foreign countries from a 2020 study published in *International Studies Quarterly* and data on PLA engagements with counterparts from a National Defense University study.[89] Given that some microstates do not have militaries and therefore con-

---

[85] Xiao, 2020, pp. 313–314.

[86] Ma, Zhang, and Liu, 2014, p. 90.

[87] Chen, Li, and Zeng, 2019, pp. 7–8.

[88] We considered having two separate indicators instead of one combined indictor, but authoritative Chinese government and PLA texts frequently state the principle that military diplomacy supports broader policy objectives, so we did not want to overcount or double count a similar dynamic in China's relations with a given country. For example, the 2004 white paper notes that "China's national defense policy is both subordinated to and in service of the country's development and security strategies" (State Council Information Office of the People's Republic of China, 2004). *SMS 2015* states that "political-military tradeoffs . . . must inform use of force overseas, instructing PLA leaders to pause before committing to international action. . . . Diplomacy is no small matter, and the overseas use of military force is far from trivial. Under a given international strategic situation, the determination to deploy forces to conduct peacekeeping, maritime escort, overseas evacuation, or international rescue tasks should proceed from a strategic consideration of national political interests, economic interests, diplomatic interests, and security interests" (Xiao, 2015, p. 299; as quoted in Kardon, 2021, p. 76).

[89] Christine Hackenesch and Julia Bader, "The Struggle for Minds and Influence: The Chinese Communist Party's Global Outreach," *International Studies Quarterly*, Vol. 64, No. 3, September 2020; Allen, Saunders, and Chen, 2017.

duct few or no exchanges with the PLA, it is possible that we undervalue nonmilitary engagement for a small number of countries.

Arms Sales or Transfers

We likewise posit that growing security cooperation partners of China may be more feasible for potential basing and access partnerships. As the Soviet Union case study in the companion report most notably shows, the Soviet Union often provided military aid in the form of equipment, training, advisors, and related support—either in exchange for access to the host nation's military facilities or to establish its own bases on foreign soil.[90] One tangible measure of security cooperation ties is arm sales or transfers; we leverage data on Chinese arms transfers to other countries from the Stockholm International Peace Research Institute's (SIPRI's) arms transfers database.[91]

Potential Obstacles in China's Relationship with the Country

As noted above, the PLA literature discusses the role of common interests and strong ties between countries in facilitating basing or access. In this third component of feasibility, we flip that dynamic to consider strained ties, tensions, or obstacles that may inhibit security partnerships involving PLA basing or access. The PLA literature comments on potential legal or other obstacles, although this discussion is primarily focused on specific laws, statutes, or regulations that can complicate basing.[92]

We developed two indicators that may make a country more or less feasible for future PLA basing or access. These are briefly explained below.

Tensions in Relations

We posit that long-standing historical tensions or dynamics in bilateral relations may limit a potential host nation's willingness to host the Chinese military. Third countries may also object to PLA presence in the country, complicating the potential host's relations with highly valued partners. We developed one indicator to assess tensions in relations that focuses on these two elements: whether a given country has a contiguous border with another major power (specifically, Russia or the United States), and whether a given country has engaged in conflict opposite the PRC.[93] We combined the two dynamics into one indicator because we did not want to weigh either too strongly; attitudes based on neighbors' views or historical tensions may continue to shift for some potential host nations as China's economic power grows.[94] We analyzed geographic borders using ArcGIS and leveraged the Correlates of War Inter-State War Data to conduct this assessment.[95]

---

[90] Watts et al., 2022.

[91] SIPRI, "SIPRI Arms Transfers Database," webpage, undated. Data retrieved on March 15, 2021.

[92] Luo, Wan, and Li, 2019 p. 142; Wang, Qi, and Hai, 2018, p. 35.

[93] Had we evaluated European countries as part of our assessment, we would have additionally considered including the European Union as a major power for this indicator.

[94] For an overview of these dynamics in the Indo-Pacific, see Bonny Lin, Michael S. Chase, Jonah Blank, Cortez A. Cooper III, Derek Grossman, Scott W. Harold, Jennifer D. P. Moroney, Lyle J. Morris, Logan Ma, Paul Orner, Alice Shih, and Soo Kim, *Regional Responses to U.S.-China Competition in the Indo-Pacific: Study Overview and Conclusions*, Santa Monica, Calif.: RAND Corporation, RR-4412-AF, 2020a.

[95] Meredith Reid Sarkees and Frank Wayman, *Resort to War: 1816–2007*, data set, version 4.0, Washington, D.C.: CQ Press, 2010.

Official Recognition of the PRC over the Republic of China (Taiwan)

While the limited PLA literature on potential legal or other obstacles focuses on specific statutes, we opted to incorporate a straightforward example of laws, policies, and regulations that makes it harder for China to formally request and secure overseas military presence in another country, official diplomatic recognition of the ROC, or Taiwan, over mainland China. Compared with other laws or regulations, a high bar exists to formally switch relations from the ROC to the PRC for Taiwan's remaining partners, so this change is not only significant but public and measurable. Our data on Taiwan's official diplomatic partners comes from the ROC's Ministry of Foreign Affairs website.[96]

Table 3.1 summarizes the 17 framework indicators within the two dimensions of desirability and feasibility.

TABLE 3.1

Framework Indicators for Assessing China's Pursuit of Overseas Basing and Access Locations, by Dimension

Theme	Indicator
Desirability	
Military utility	D1. Known Chinese interest in basing and access
	D2. Within rapid steaming distance of China
	D3. Within military airlift range of China
	D4. Coastal country
	D5. Close proximity penalty
	D6. Level of human development
Utility for protecting China's economic interests	D7. Level of Chinese investment
	D8. BRI member or participant
Low or acceptable political or other risks	D9. Political stability and absence of violence
	D10. Risk of climate change
Feasibility	
Regime alignment with the PRC	F1. Authoritarian regime
	F2. Aligned voting with China
	F3. Perceptions of corruption
	F4. Partner engagement
China's influence in the country	F5. Arms sales or transfers
	F6. Tensions in relations
Potential obstacles in China's relationship with the country	F7. Official recognition of the PRC over the ROC (Taiwan)

---

[96] Ministry of Foreign Affairs of the Republic of China (Taiwan), "Diplomatic Allies," webpage, undated.

Limitations of Our Approach

The limitations of our approach in assembling a framework that matches measurable data to complex dynamics shaping countries' decisions are worth noting. We highlight below such limitations in seven areas in particular.

First, our analysis is conducted at the country level rather than on specific locations or infrastructure, such as ports or airfields. Although existing PLA and Chinese academic analyses have often focused on potential naval access or facilities, including ports with Chinese SOE presence, other studies discuss the need for airfields, logistics hubs, and other infrastructure or capabilities that would not necessarily be co-located with ports. Given the PLA's growing interest in both nonnaval and naval access and basing opportunities, as well as the national-level decisionmaking by a host nation in deciding to sign or refuse an agreement to host the Chinese military, we opted to conduct our analysis at the country level.

Second and relatedly, in our assessment of countries, we do not distinguish between future hosts of formal military bases versus future hosts of periodic PLA access or potential arrangements that may involve more frequent or substantial access than a normal access agreement but do not rise to the scale of a large military base. There are likely some potential host nations that are unwilling to support a permanent or long-term PLA presence but may be willing to allow periodic access or a small warehouse-type facility. Likewise, some PLA analysts recognize and discuss various models and levels of access.[97] Given the number and variety of potential hosts that China can pursue, we lacked enough information to separate out desirable attributes of access locations from those of basing locations.

Third, we do not assess the ripple effect of potential interest in a subsequent base or access agreement following the acquisition of any given location. As future PLA basing and access locations are announced and constructed, however, we anticipate that they will shape leaders' decisions regarding the benefits of obtaining additional locations.

Fourth, we focus on measurable indicators for which we could obtain data for all (or, in limited cases, nearly all) 108 countries that we assessed. Given the number of countries involved, we had limited scope to develop criteria or assign qualitative scores to indicators that lacked preexisting data. Some difficult-to-measure factors mentioned in the literature included the following: the degree of specific threats to potential basing or access locations;[98] the number of reserve or alternate bases nearby;[99] and human and cultural factors of potential host nations, such as the orientation of religion, social groups, culture, and values.[100]

Fifth, we decided not to include three other potential indicators for which data are more readily available:

---

[97] For example, at least one PLA study categorized levels of potential basing and access as "strategic strongpoint" [战略支点], "normal base" [普通基地], or "reserve base" [备用基地], implying that strategic strongpoints can be full-fledged PLA bases (i.e., they can provide even greater levels of support and military value than a regular base) but also that lesser forms of access are an option. This study also described different levels of a host country's ability to build and maintain the base depending on the cooperation level of the host nation and foreign country: If "the establishing country fully enjoys jurisdiction over the base," it is high; if countries "share jurisdiction," it is medium; and low is when "the establishing country provides support for the construction of the military base . . . [and] during peacetime the host nation has jurisdiction, and after the eruption of a crisis use it is requisitioned" by the establishing country. This also implies a model in which not all locations are fully operated by the PLA. See Jiang, Zhang, and Ge, 2017, pp. 505–506.

[98] Absent information on the potential threats Chinese analysts assessed for specific locations, we were not able to assess this indicator. See Ma, Zhang, and Liu, 2014, p. 91.

[99] Given that China only has limited long-term overseas presence to date (primarily in or near Djibouti), we could not evaluate this indicator. One source viewed this factor as having a significant impact on disaster mitigation capability. See Jiang, Zhang, and Ge, 2017, pp. 505–506.

[100] The criteria for assigning values to these indicators was not clear, though at least one source viewed inclusive and diverse host nation populaces sharing some affinity (e.g., language, religion) with the requesting nation as desirable. In a case study

- We did not include an indicator for strategic military utility focused on specific geographic locations, such as the distance to certain naval chokepoints or distance to potentially important U.S. targets, such as Hawaii. Although much of the PLA literature focuses on coastal locations, we did not want to overweight coastal countries in our assessment by including an additional indicator related to naval access, particularly given the increasing demand for overseas basing and access for PLAAF and other nonnaval forces. Also, while overseas bases could be tempting locations in the 2030–2040 time frame to base long-range offensive fires in theory, they may pose significant escalation concerns for host nations and prove difficult or distracting for the PLA to defend during a contingency. We discuss in greater detail why this may be an unattractive option for China to pursue in the companion report, *Implications of a Global People's Liberation Army: Historical Lessons for Responding to China's Long-Term Global Basing Ambitions.*

- We considered but opted not to assess the scale of China's investments in a given country on a per-capita basis, instead using an absolute scale. A per-capita assessment would have affected countries with small populations, such as microstates, because microstates may be especially vulnerable to nominal amounts of Chinese economic inducements that would be considered insignificant in larger economies. We decided to use an absolute scale because higher absolute levels of Chinese investment imply greater numbers of Chinese citizens, firms, and projects overseas, leading to more interests for the PLA to protect.

- We considered but ultimately did not include as an indicator whether a country has a constitutional prohibition on foreign basing. Although such a prohibition would be a potential obstacle from Beijing's perspective, constitutional or other legal prohibitions are not an absolute bar because constitutions or laws can be either changed or subverted by pro-PRC regimes. As an example, Cambodia appears to have developed workarounds to enable the PLA access to the Ream Naval Base, despite Cambodia's constitutional ban on hosting foreign military bases.[101] Instead, we opted to include a country's regime type as an indicator, positing that authoritarian regimes may be more likely to subvert or ignore bans than democratic regimes.

Sixth, as mentioned earlier in the chapter, a two-dimensional framework may artificially separate non-independent indicators. As an alternative scoring method, we performed a robustness check by comparing the two-dimensional scores in Chapter 4 with an alternative scoring system of one overall score reflecting all 17 indicators. Although most of the top-scoring countries discussed in Chapter 4 remained high-scorers in this alternative scoring method, we also found that key U.S. allies rose to the top—the Philippines, South Korea, and Japan—even though it is unlikely that U.S. allies would host the PLA, given their strong relationships with the United States and their own tensions with China. Because our two-dimensional scoring method did not result in those countries becoming top-scorers, this exercise demonstrated to us that some elements of feasibility are important and relevant to consider separately from desirability. For more information, see Appendix A.

Finally, our framework does not account for cases in which potential host nations may proactively offer military basing or access that Beijing may not have otherwise prioritized. Similar to bilateral dynamics regarding overseas Chinese investment, countries may be incentivized—through their own political, economic, or security interests—to offer agreements to China (i.e., *push* to China), not just receive China's requests (or *pull*). In other words, while we assess potential basing and access from a Chinese government perspective

---

involving Singapore, those analysts noted that the majority of the population is ethnic Chinese (Luo, Wan, and Li, 2019, pp. 142–143). See also Ma, Zhang, and Liu, 2014, p. 91.

[101] Page, Lubold, and Taylor, 2019.

based on the best information available, we do not incorporate the agency of other countries in changing China's calculus by proactively opening the door to PLA basing or access. However, we might expect potentially eager hosts to either score relatively well in the feasibility dimension of our framework or else to seek to increase opportunities to partner with China along diplomatic, security, or other dimensions in ways that may increase their score for feasibility in the future. We explore this dynamic further in Chapter 4.

Linkages to Desired Overseas Power-Projection Capabilities

During our review of key Chinese sources on desired attributes for overseas basing and access locations, we found that authoritative guidance and PLA analysis also highlight relevant organizational reforms and military operational concepts that will shape the PLA's overseas power projection. We briefly summarize relevant themes from that Chinese literature in this section, supplemented by key Western sources that focus on long-range power-projection trends.[102] PLA analysts also discuss desired forces for operations abroad; we focus here on referenced weapon systems and platforms, as well as key enablers for overseas operations, such as those for command, control, communications, computers, intelligence, surveillance, and reconnaissance.

One difficulty in assessing PLA future capabilities for overseas power projection is that the ratio of forces that China may harness abroad in the 2030–2040 time frame versus those deployed closer to home is not clear. However, we find some key elements relevant for overseas power projection noted in PLA sources, including the need for maritime replenishment and strategic airlift, which inform the desirability dimension of our basing and access assessment framework. PLA analysts also recognize that sending troops overseas will impose greater requirements on networking the force, building overseas logistics capability, coordinating across civilian and military bureaucracies, increasing the level of personnel training and skills, and determining how best to leverage overseas commercial assets. In this section, we briefly review organizational reforms, missions and roles, service-specific elements, and critical enablers for operating in a more global context.

Strategic Guidance and Related Organizational Reforms

A key goal of recent military reforms is to enable the PLA to operate as an integrated joint force in the coming decades.[103] Two of China's national defense white papers capture adjustments to China's military strategic guidelines relevant for power projection. The military strategic guidelines (MSGs) form the foundation of China's military strategy and shape forcewide modernization objectives.[104] The 2004 white paper featured new MSGs that redirected focus from conducting coordinated joint operations (the focus of the previous

---

[102] For additional Western analysis on emerging Chinese military capabilities and gaps that may be relevant for overseas power projection, see Michael S. Chase, Jeffrey Engstrom, Tai Ming Cheung, Kristen Gunness, Scott Warren Harold, Susan Puska, and Samuel K. Berkowitz, *China's Incomplete Military Transformation: Assessing the Weaknesses of the People's Liberation Army (PLA)*, Santa Monica, Calif.: RAND Corporation, RR-893-USCC, 2015; Heginbotham et al., 2015; Saunders et al., 2019; Gunness, 2019; Forrest E. Morgan, Benjamin Boudreaux, Andrew J. Lohn, Mark Ashby, Christian Curriden, Kelly Klima, and Derek Grossman, *Military Applications of Artificial Intelligence: Ethical Concerns in an Uncertain World*, Santa Monica, Calif.: RAND Corporation, RR-3139-1-AF, 2020; Kamphausen, Lai, and Ma, 2020; U.S.-China Economic and Security Review Commission, *2020 Report to Congress of the U.S.-China Economic and Security Review Commission*, Washington, D.C.: U.S. Government Publishing Office, December 2020; and Wuthnow et al., 2021.

[103] Edmund J. Burke, Kristen Gunness, Cortez A. Cooper III, and Mark Cozad, *People's Liberation Army Operational Concepts*, Santa Monica, Calif.: RAND Corporation, RR-A394-1, 2020.

[104] For more information on Chinese MSGs, see Fravel, 2019.

guidance) to unified, *integrated* joint operations across the entire force.[105] The 2004 white paper is also the first to mention the PLAAF's outward-oriented strategic concept, indicating a role for the PLAAF beyond territorial defense of the Chinese mainland.[106] An additional adjustment to the MSGs in the 2014–2015 time frame kept the focus on integrated joint operations but broke with the PLA's ground-centric tradition—and its army-centric bureaucracy. The new MSGs deemphasize the importance of land power to prioritize fighting and winning maritime-related contingencies in China's broader periphery. Accordingly, the 2015 white paper declared "the traditional mentality that the land outweighs the sea must be abandoned."[107]

In order to transition to an integrated joint force with increasing focus on warfighting in the maritime domain, in 2015 and 2016, the PLA initiated major organizational reforms to improve joint operations within China's borders and to project force from the Chinese mainland throughout the Western Pacific, including the establishment of five joint theater commands with dedicated missions in their respective theaters.[108] Other new organizations include the Strategic Support Force, which provides forcewide support for space and cyber missions, as well as a joint logistics force to streamline and improve the responsiveness and effectiveness of logistics support to the joint force.[109] However, the extent to which integrated joint operations and concomitant reforms have reshaped overseas PLA operations is less clear. The following sections note research on the continued limitations of PLA forces in operating abroad, as well as gaps in external analysts' knowledge as the reforms continue to unfold.

Missions and Force Modernization

While the PLA's ongoing force modernization efforts include supporting greater overseas power projection, the desired ratio of forces that may be expected to operate overseas is not known. Drilling down from the strategic guidance mentioned above, however, PLA analysts do discuss specific overseas missions for the PLA, and some writings advocate for the PLA to build new or additional platforms for power projection.

SMS 2013 summarizes the overseas roles and missions for each of the following services:

- **PLAN.** "Safeguarding the state's overseas interests and the rights and interests of citizens and overseas nationals will become a regular strategic mission for the Navy," including support for Chinese institutions and Chinese fishing fleets operating overseas. *SMS 2013* cites the PLAN's role in evacuating Chinese citizens from Libya as an example of an important PLAN mission.[110]
- **PLAAF.** One of the PLAAF's five strategic tasks is to "participate in international military exchange and cooperation," such as "international rescue, peacekeeping activities, escort and evacuation of overseas nationals, and joint military exercises," as well as conduct counterterrorism activities with other countries and international HA/DR. In doing so, the PLAAF needs to become a "reliable strategic force"

---

[105] State Council Information Office of the People's Republic of China, 2004b. On the difference between regular (coordinated) and integrated joint operations, see Fravel, 2019, p. 220.

[106] For more information, see Kenneth W. Allen and Cristina L. Garafola, *70 Years of the PLA Air Force*, Montgomery, Ala.: China Aerospace Studies Institute, 2021.

[107] State Council Information Office of the People's Republic of China, 2015b.

[108] Philip C. Saunders and Joel Wuthnow, "China's Goldwater-Nichols? Assessing PLA Organizational Reforms," *Joint Force Quarterly*, 3rd Quarter 2016, April 2016.

[109] OSD, 2020, pp. 61–67.

[110] Shou, 2013, p. 211.

capable of long-range employment and quickly reacting to changing situations, which includes the ability to "rapidly fly from the homeland to overseas points" to conduct operations.[111]

- **PLA Army (PLAA).** Stated overseas MOOTW missions include peacekeeping, rescue operations, protecting and evacuating overseas nationals, and "protecting foreign assets and strategic thoroughfares." PLAA forces are also expected to guard against the "three evils" of terrorist, secessionist, and religious extremist forces, leveraging the PLAA's strengths in "wide-ranging distribution, abundant force-strength, diversity in the service arms, flexible maneuver, rapid reaction, and forceful control." Additionally, and at times operating at the threshold between peace and the threshold of armed conflict, the PLAA plays a role with other forces such as the People's Armed Police in its operations at China's borders, including during recent border tensions with India in 2020.[112]

SMS 2020 lists similar roles and missions for each service, noting that PKO are the basic overall target or goal of MOOTW operations.[113]

One 2018 study by PLA transportation analysts assesses that the main missions for which overseas PLA bases are responsible include

- providing replenishment support for naval convoys
- supporting China's participation in international peacekeeping and humanitarian relief efforts
- supporting units that are implementing military cooperation, conducting joint exercises and training (*joint* in this context could mean combined activities with other countries), evacuating or protecting overseas Chinese citizens, conducting emergency rescue, or undertaking other overseas MOOTW missions
- protecting the safety of SLOCs and energy supply lines
- securing the military bases themselves.[114]

In terms of specific forces for overseas operations, *SMS 2020* states that PLA medical, transport, engineering, search and rescue, and operational forces are important, although the latter are not described in detail.[115] It also states that the scale of current overseas deployments is typically small and quite tactical, involving few personnel.[116] In the next section, we explore specific forces mentioned by PLA analysts across the sea, air, and land domains, followed by critical enablers of overseas operations.

Maritime Forces

Admiral Philip Davidson, the then–commander of INDOPACOM, observed in late 2019 that the PLAN had deployed overseas more frequently in the previous 30 months than it had in the past 30 years.[117] Many past naval deployments included relatively limited operational activities, such as making foreign port calls to fur-

---

[111] Shou, 2013, pp. 222, 225–227. For more on these five strategic roles, see Allen and Garafola, 2021.

[112] Shou, 2013, pp. 199–200. The authors acknowledge that some border demarcation disputes have not been resolved, and "some border-area nibbling and counter-nibbling, and frictional and counter-frictional struggles" will continue over the long term. On India-China tensions, see Lin, Garafola, et al., 2022.

[113] Xiao, 2020, p. 320.

[114] Wang, Qi, and Hai, 2018, pp. 32–33.

[115] Xiao, 2020, p. 326.

[116] Xiao, 2020, p. 322.

[117] Ronald O'Rourke, *China Naval Modernization: Implications for U.S. Navy Capabilities—Background and Issues for Congress*, Washington, D.C.: Congressional Research Service, March 8, 2022, p. 35.

ther military diplomacy efforts. This is in contrast to how Chinese analysts are portraying PLAN ships and assets as increasingly capable of conducting a wider array of missions abroad. This growing variety of overseas missions may also require more overseas PLA facilities in the future. The Djibouti base political commissar summarized the ongoing transition in a 2019 interview as follows: "[S]upport methods for China's far-seas escorts are gradually adjusting away from a focus on accompanying replenishment ships supplemented by mooring in foreign ports, into a new model focused on overseas base support supplemented by other ports abroad and domestic support."[118]

One PLA lecturer described strategic strongpoints that can support the PLAN and build the Maritime Silk Road by supporting "comprehensive replenishment, naval ship maintenance, intelligence collection, marine monitoring, humanitarian relief, medical assistance, protection of maritime rights and interests" and both MOOTW and other military operations.[119]

In order to improve these capabilities abroad, PLA transportation researchers have called for the building of "an overseas ocean transportation delivery and supply support force" comprising "several ocean transportation and ocean supply groups." Overseas forces would require new military ships, including "semi-submersible ships, fast combat support ships, multi-purpose bomb transport ships, large oil tankers, multi-purpose transport ships, submarine support ships, [and] new integrated supply ships."[120] These forces can also harness large civilian vessels, which the authors suggest during peacetime can support combat training of military vessels for "cross-border" operations.[121] U.S. National Defense University researchers additionally point out that the PLAN could employ its large inventory of mines to conduct blockade or counterblockade activities in SLOCs or other key chokepoints.[122]

Although the PLA articles that we reviewed do not specifically focus on overseas activities by the PLAN Marine Corps (PLANMC), it is important to note its growing overseas role, most notably in supporting PLAN Gulf of Aden patrols, as well as being stationed at China's first overseas base in Djibouti. Western observers have noted a large increase in PLANMC force structure from 10,000 to a projected 30,000-plus personnel, units gaining organic lift and other capabilities, and training in various terrains and climates, as indicators that the PLANMC is expanding its mission set to include expeditionary operations.[123] In addition to the mechanized infantry company stationed in Djibouti, PLANMC SOF have conducted training exchanges with Djiboutian forces and off the coast of the Gulf of Aden aboard PLAN ships.[124] Landing platform/docks

---

[118] "Military Report: Special Report on the 70th Anniversary of the Founding of the People's Navy, Guaranteed to Win, Logistical Forces Extend to the Far Seas" ["军事报道: 人民海军成立70周 年特别报道保障打赢后勤力量向远海大洋延伸"], video, China Central Television, April 19, 2019, quote beginning at minute 5:10 (as cited in and translated by Kardon, 2021, p. 101, fn 50).

[119] This assessment was made by Zheng Chongwei, former PLA engineer and current lecturer at the Dalian Maritime Academy (as cited in Kardon, 2021, p. 79).

[120] Wang, Qi, and Hai, 2018, p. 34.

[121] Wang, Qi, and Hai, 2018, p. 34.

[122] Joel Wuthnow, Phillip C. Saunders, and Ian Burns McCaslin, "PLA Overseas Operations in 2035: Inching Toward a Global Combat Capability," Strategic Forum, No. 309, Washington, D.C.: National Defense University Press, May 2021, p. 9.

[123] Dennis J. Blasko and Roderick Lee, "The Chinese Navy's Marine Corps, Part 1: Expansion and Reorganization," Jamestown Foundation, China Brief, Vol. 19, No. 3, February 1, 2019a; Dennis J. Blasko and Roderick Lee, "The Chinese Navy's Marine Corps, Part 2: Chain-of-Command Reforms and Evolving Training," Jamestown Foundation, China Brief, Vol. 19, No. 4, February 15, 2019b; OSD, 2020, p. 48; OSD, Annual Report to Congress: Military and Security Developments Involving the People's Republic of China 2019, Washington, D.C.: U.S. Department of Defense, May 2019, p. 35.

[124] Li Kexin [李克欣], Qiu Haohan [李克欣], and Zhai Siyu [翟思宇], "A Glimpse of the Strong Military with He Long, Special Warfare Company Commander in a Navy Marine Corps Brigade" ["海军陆战队某旅特战连连长何龙强军精武掠影"], China Military Online, August 11, 2020; Jiang Shan [江山] and Zhang Junsheng [张峻生], "'Jiaolong' Attacks: Overcom-

and landing helicopter assault ships entering the PLAN's inventory may potentially transport PLAN marines over long distances for overseas missions.[125]

Aviation Forces

Analysts' discussion of aviation forces in the articles that we reviewed primarily focused on transport aircraft. PLA analysts clearly identify strategic airlift as a critical weakness in the PLA's overseas power-projection capability; PLAAF logistics researchers even state that strengthening cross-border strategic airlift is "a long-term dynamic process" that is part of the goal of building a "world-class military."[126] One NUDT scholar suggests that with the fielding of the Y-20 transport aircraft, "China's ability to use its air forces to conduct military troop projection, evacuation, and disaster relief overseas will be significantly improved." However, that same researcher notes that China lacks overseas "airport-type strategic strongpoints suitable for air operations. Leasing or joint use methods can be carried out in the future to obtain airport leases or even establish air support bases in critical regions."[127] PLA transportation analysts recommend that the PLA continue to grow its inventories and more frequently employ the Y-20 "as soon as possible . . . to provide new methods for the rapid and three-dimensional aerial delivery of our overseas military bases."[128] Although these articles did not list a role for China's airborne forces, PLA airborne troops have deployed abroad since at least 2011 via PLAAF transport aircraft for competitions and exercises, including combined exercises with a counterterrorism focus.[129]

One major unknown is the role that PLA manned aircraft and unmanned aerial vehicles (UAVs)—whether in the PLAAF or in other services—may play in future overseas PLA operations.[130] China considered employing a UAV for kinetic strikes in another country as early as 2013 to target a wanted drug lord in Myanmar, but a government official stated that China ultimately decided to pursue capturing him alive.[131] Although UAVs with kinetic payloads offer a variety of options for Chinese military planners, UAVs may also be relatively escalatory in terms of securing buy-in from foreign hosts to operate in or near their territory. Accordingly, non-kinetic payloads such as intelligence, surveillance, and reconnaissance (ISR) or other types of UAVs may be more attractive options.

---

ing the Enemy to Achieve Victory Is Inseparable from Hard Work" ["'蛟龙'出击: 克敌制胜,离不开千锤百炼"], *China Military Online*, August 20, 2020.

[125] Blasko and Lee, 2019a; Blasko and Lee, 2019b.

[126] Chen, Li, and Zeng, 2019, p. 8.

[127] Hu Xin [胡欣], "The Expansion of National Interests and the Construction of Overseas Strategic Strong Points" ["国家利益拓展与海外战略支撑点建设"], *Forum of World Economics & Politics* [世界经济与政治论坛], No. 1, 2019, p. 31. As cited in Kardon, 2021, p. 88, fn 85.

[128] Wang, Qi, and Hai, 2018, p. 34.

[129] Cristina L. Garafola and Timothy R. Heath, *The Chinese Air Force's First Steps Toward Becoming an Expeditionary Air Force*, Santa Monica, Calif.: RAND Corporation, RR-2056-AF, 2017, pp. 18–20.

[130] On Chinese military UAVs, see Dan Gettinger, "Drone Databook Update: March 2020," Annandale-on-Hudson, N.Y.: Center for Study of the Drone at Bard College, March 2020; Elsa Kania, *The PLA's Unmanned Aerial System: New Capabilities for a 'New Era' of Chinese Military Power*, Montgomery, Ala.: China Aerospace Studies Institute, August 2018; Ian Burns McCaslin, *Red Drones over Disputed Seas: A Field Guide to Chinese UAVs/UCAVs Operating in the Disputed East and South China Seas*, Arlington, Va.: Project 2049 Institute, August 2017; Kimberly Hsu, Craig Murray, Jeremy Cook, and Amalia Feld, *China's Military Unmanned Aerial Vehicle Industry*, Washington, D.C.: U.S.-China Economic and Security Review Commission, June 13, 2013; Ian Easton and L. C. Russell Hsiao, *The Chinese People's Liberation Army's Unmanned Aerial Vehicle Project: Organizational Capacities and Operational Capabilities*, Arlington, Va.: Project 2049 Institute, March 11, 2013.

[131] Ernest Kao, "China Considered Using Drone in Myanmar to Kill Wanted Drug Lord," *South China Morning Post*, February 20, 2013.

Like UAVs, manned aircraft with kinetic payloads may also be viewed as escalatory unless the host nation were to secure a commitment from China to employ them in direct support of the host nation. Until the PLAAF fields significant quantities of a high-capacity aerial tanker (one based on the Y-20 is in development), the PLA's ability to carry out long-range or overseas combat aircraft deployments in general will be limited.

Although we did not see these systems discussed in the PLA's overseas basing literature that we reviewed, ground-based air defense systems, such as surface-to-air missile systems, may also be of interest for stationing abroad.[132]

Ground Forces

As part of ongoing reforms, the PLA is reorganizing its ground forces to a combined arms brigade structure, which will be more capable of rapid organic mobility and helicopter-assisted air assault. Most of the articles that we reviewed do not focus on potential PLAA activities abroad, but one article by logistics engineering researchers notes the need for overseas petroleum, oils, and lubricants support bases, including to support MOOTW activities, such as PKO and potential counterterrorism operations. The authors additionally discuss the role of land-based engineering and other units for petroleum, oil, and lubricants support to PLAN forces.[133] PLAA SOF and their counterparts in the People's Armed Police, China's paramilitary force, may also have a role in counterterrorism operations or protecting overseas citizens.[134]

Desired Improvements in Key Enablers

This section summarizes themes raised regarding an increasingly *informatized* or networked force, a key goal for the Chinese military, as well as other important enablers for overseas power projection, including logistics, personnel training and skills, coordination across the Chinese bureaucracy, and leveraging commercial infrastructure for military purposes.

Informatization and Intelligence

The PLA is in the midst of upgrading its equipment and weapons to feature real-time data-networked command capabilities, a process it calls *informatization*. China's goal is to have the force fully equipped with such information technologies by 2035. Chinese sources also indicate that the PLA is simultaneously seeking to advance to a new form of warfare featuring a higher degree of integration with artificial intelligence (AI), a process officials call *intelligentization*. The incorporation of AI into all combat and combat support functions could significantly improve the lethality and effectiveness of PLA combat forces. In the long term, PLA forces operating abroad could be equipped with AI-enhanced weapons, platforms, and equipment.[135] However, in the near term, at least one authoritative Chinese source mentions that informatized capabilities are lacking; *SMS 2020* assesses that overseas "reconnaissance measures are limited, reconnaissance strength is weak, and intelligence support is difficult."[136] A Western assessment finds that China does not have a global command

---

[132] For an overview of these systems, see Bonny Lin and Cristina L. Garafola, *Training the People's Liberation Army Air Force Surface-to-Air Missile (SAM) Forces*, Santa Monica, Calif.: RAND Corporation, RR-1414-AF, 2016.

[133] Zhou Huaqi [周华奇], Li Shaoming [李少鸣], Zhang Hengyang [张恒洋], and Wang Xufei [王旭飞], "Thinking on Our Army Building Oil Support Bases Overseas" ["我军在境外建立油料保障基地的思考"], *Logistics Sci-Tech* [物流科技], No. 2, 2013.

[134] Wuthnow, Saunders, and McCaslin, 2021, p. 6; OSD, 2020, p. 70.

[135] OSD, 2020, p. 118.

[136] Xiao, 2020, p. 319.

and control network capable of supporting large-scale joint operations.[137] Overseas bases, especially on continents farther afield from China, would also bolster the PLA's ISR capabilities beyond China's periphery, including the PLA's ability to monitor U.S. and its ally and partner military activities.

Organizationally, a joint space and cyber branch established in 2016, the PLA SSF, will likely support overseas ISR activities in addition to reconnaissance operations by ships and aircraft increasingly far away from Chinese shores. Beyond the SSF's ground stations and support to space missions, however, its overseas activities are not currently well understood.[138]

Logistics

As part of organizational reforms, the PLA established the Joint Logistics Support Force (JLSF) in 2016.[139] However, the JLSF does not currently operate overseas; whether the JLSF will evolve to have this role in the future is a key question.[140] One PLA analyst writing on prepositioned reserves overseas notes that there are three options for the PLA: It can build warehouses (the Djibouti model), it can develop a joint model with firms and enterprises as part of BRI, or it can rent warehouses.[141] PLA transportation researchers state that overseas bases require specific infrastructure for ships and aircraft, such as runway aprons. Also, given the high consumption of weapons and equipment, ammunition, fuel, and other materiel, the PLA will need a mix of items sent from China and procured locally, which "imposes higher requirements on transport and delivery capability."[142]

In the companion report, one commonality that we found in our historical research on French, Soviet, and Russian pursuits of overseas basing is that, in contrast to China, all three basing nations benefited from compatible military standards, including parts and other enablers used by their hosts: This was due either to prior colonization or to large quantities of arms transfers to host nations.[143] In contrast, the PLA may not benefit to the same degree from its future hosts. China's arms sales and transfers continue to grow, and some of its equipment was either built or reverse-engineered to Russian standards that many potential host nations may share. However, Chinese sources have complained in the past about the difficulty of bringing extra equipment overseas and adapting incompatible equipment to ensure operational success, even for an exercise in Russia.[144]

Human Talent

PLA sources acknowledge that the overseas operating environment presents significant challenges for its personnel and that the PLA needs to increase personnel skills so troops can cope with unexpected or new situations. *SMS 2020* notes that in addition to political credentials and military expertise and technical skills,

---

[137] Wuthnow, Saunders, and McCaslin, 2021, p. 5.

[138] For an overview of the SSF, see John Costello and Joe McReynolds, *China's Strategic Support Force: A Force for a New Era*, Washington, D.C.: National Defense University Press, China Strategic Perspectives 13, October 2018; and Elsa B. Kania and John Costello, "Seizing the Commanding Heights: the PLA Strategic Support Force in Chinese Military Power," *Journal of Strategic Studies*, Vol. 44, No. 2, 2021 pp. 218–264.

[139] Joel Wuthnow, "A New Era for Chinese Military Logistics," *Asian Security*, February 2021; Peltier, Nurkin, and O'Connor, 2020.

[140] Wuthnow, 2021; LeighAnn Luce and Erin Richter, "Handling Logistics in a Reformed PLA: The Long March Toward Joint Logistics," in Saunders et al., 2019, pp. 257–292.

[141] Li, Chen, and Wang, 2019, pp. 59–60.

[142] Wang, Qi, and Hai, 2018, p. 33.

[143] Watts et al., 2022.

[144] Garafola and Heath, 2017, pp. 31–32.

personnel need to have legal and diplomatic training.[145] Some PLA transportation analysts conclude that to carry out transportation operations at overseas military bases, "it is necessary to select and dispatch additional crews and organizational commanders with rich experience, strong sense of responsibility, and strong combat effectiveness."[146] Western researchers also note the need for joint training, foreign language skills, and cultural acumen for troops deploying abroad.[147]

Coordination Across the Chinese Government and Military

Overseas operations require endorsement by senior leaders and coordination across the PRC bureaucracy. *SMS 2020* advises that it is a "political decision to prudently decide whether to . . . send in military forces to defend the country's political and economic interests."[148] At the operational level, *SMS 2020* also notes the need for the PLA to coordinate with other domestic departments on overseas operations.[149] A PLA study by transportation researchers echoes the importance of coordination, highlighting the involvement of multiple "military and local organizations" [单位] in operations abroad, such as "foreign affairs departments, transportation departments, commodity inspection departments, banks, customs organizations," and others. The researchers further specify the following military organizations as having coordinating roles for overseas operations:

- The International Military Cooperation Office is responsible for conducting exchanges with foreign militaries and overseeing the PLA's foreign affairs work.
- The Joint Staff Department (JSD) is in charge of command and control, as well as combat command support, strategy, planning, and readiness. The JSD also links the military high command to China's five theater commands.
- The Logistics Support Department oversees logistics support, funds, and management, as well as the administration of PLA hospitals.
- The PLAN will presumably prepare and deploy PLAN assets abroad.
- The PLAAF will likely undertake similar activities for PLAAF assets.[150]

This discussion implies two dynamics related to overseas power projection that PLA and civilian bureaucracies may still be working to refine. First, as Western researchers have noted, there does not yet appear to be an established mechanism by which relevant military and civilian agencies regularly coordinate, indicating that some elements of coordination remain ad hoc.[151] Second, involvement of PLAN and PLAAF leadership indicates that the services maintain some operational or command role in the deployment of assets overseas; this is different from their domestic role, which since 2016 has been to man, train, and equip the force while the five theater commands have operational command over forces and units.[152] As a side note, the absence of the PLAA from the authors' list of military organizations may either indicate that the study was focused

---

[145] Xiao, 2020, p. 319.

[146] Wang, Qi, and Hai, 2018, p. 34.

[147] Wuthnow, Saunders, and McCaslin, 2021, p. 11.

[148] Xiao, 2020, p. 321.

[149] Xiao, 2020, p. 324.

[150] Wang, Qi, and Hai, 2018, p. 33. Military office and department roles are taken from Saunders et al., 2019, appendix.

[151] Wuthnow, 2021.

[152] For more information on this relationship and the reforms writ large, see Cristina L. Garafola, "Will the PLA Reforms Succeed?" *China Analysis*, European Council on Foreign Relations, March 2016.

on long-range power-projection platforms or that ongoing overseas deployments involving the PLAA use a different process for UN-related missions or, potentially, counterterrorism-related missions along China's periphery. For counterterrorism missions, coordination may also involve China's paramilitary force, the People's Armed Police.

Leveraging Commercial Assets and Enterprises

As both PLA and Western analysts have explored, not every future overseas PLA location may be a formal base. *SMS 2020* observes that the PLA is innovating with new overseas support methods that leverage commercial assets, including those for reconnaissance, replenishment, and other support.[153] In terms of how to support and enable overseas operations, *SMS 2020* states that the PLA should "make advance preparations for military units to use foreign airports, ports, piers," and other infrastructure and also leverage overseas Chinese commercial entities and personnel.[154]

Isaac Kardon's review of the Chinese literature on strategic strongpoints discusses the benefits of leveraging dual-use facilities to harness commercial support for the PLA.[155] Such benefits include the relatively low cost and ready access to a wide variety of facilities owned or operated by Chinese SOEs (typically ports); some analysts view this option as much preferable to the expense of a formal military base, characterized by one assessment as a "money-burning machine."[156] Additionally, the PLA can potentially obtain preferential access to ports due to the presence of Chinese firms, while helping to protect SOE investments, provided that government authorities play a coordinating role in the latter. Finally, some of a given facility's infrastructure can potentially be built to military standards according to provisions within the 2017 National Defense Transportation Law.[157] In synthesizing this literature, however, Kardon concludes that if the PLA seeks the ability to conduct higher-end missions, such as leveraging significant air and sealift or conducting high operating tempo and/or large-scale operations, dual-use strongpoints will be insufficient and some "overtly militarized bases" will be needed.[158]

PLA transportation analysts advocate for harnessing nonmilitary assets to conduct joint activities, including by "establishing an incentive and compensation mechanism for expropriation by overseas Chinese-funded enterprises." These analysts also argue that for MOOTW missions, "a commercial model can be used to purchase local materials to implement transportation and supply support; when performing war tasks, a certain amount of materials can be stored in the host country or neighboring countries as needed."[159] However, another study by naval engineering researchers reports drawbacks to relying on an overseas purchasing model that leverages Chinese enterprises for resupply (framed as part of the PLAN's current approach in 2019). This method was described as still relatively expensive because the firms' activities were not optimized to support the PLA; thus, purchasing efforts were restricted, and because the PLA sometimes need to quickly

---

[153] Xiao, 2020, p. 325.

[154] Xiao, 2020, pp. 325–326. *SMS 2015* includes "sign military agreements . . . piers," but that language is omitted in *SMS 2020* (see Xiao, 2015, p. 304).

[155] Kardon, 2021, pp. 81–91.

[156] Li Qingsi [李庆四] and Chen Chunyu [陈春雨], "Analysis of China's Overseas Port Chain Basing Strategy" ["试析中国的海外港链基地战略"], *Regional and Global Development* [区域与全球 发展], No. 2, 2019, p. 129. As cited in Kardon, 2021, p. 82, fn 56.

[157] Kardon, 2021, pp. 81–85.

[158] Kardon, 2021, pp. 87–93.

[159] Wang, Qi, and Hai, 2018, pp. 34–35.

find a provisioning merchant, costs remained high. A base, the researchers conclude, could provision commercial goods by leveraging long-term cooperation with suppliers, ensure quality, and lower costs.[160]

In the air domain, *SMS 2015* explains the utility of leveraging overseas Chinese firms given the PLA's limited ability to conduct support and replenish missions abroad, particularly for evacuating overseas personnel.[161] PLAAF logistics researchers have likewise discussed integrating civilian airlift into overseas power-projection capabilities.[162] This integration would presumably build on existing models because the PLA has frequently used chartered aircraft or leveraged partnerships with civilian airlines for a variety of noncombat missions overseas, such as flying injured peacekeepers home from South Sudan.[163]

Conclusion

In this chapter, we lay the groundwork for a systematic analysis of basing and access options for China's military out to the 2030–2040 time frame. A growing body of literature by Chinese military analysts and academic researchers explores potential criteria for overseas PLA locations, as well as options for prioritizing locations for future PLA basing or access. Building on this discussion, we develop a framework comprising 17 indicators to assess countries across two dimensions: *desirability*, or a country's utility for overseas Chinese military operations; and *feasibility*, or China's ability to obtain basing or access in a given country. Key themes in the desirability portion of our framework include the military utility of a potential host nation, its utility for protecting China's economic interests, and low or acceptable political or other risks to China of basing forces in the country. The feasibility portion of our framework focuses on the potential host nation regime's alignment with the PRC, China's influence in the country, and potential obstacles in China's relationship with the country.

Although Chinese officials and authoritative sources do not explicitly lay out future roles or missions that PLA forces may be called on to conduct overseas, we find some key elements relevant for overseas power projection noted in PLA sources, including the need for maritime replenishment and strategic airlift. PLA analysts also recognize that sending troops overseas will impose greater requirements on networking the force, building overseas logistics capability, coordinating across civilian and military bureaucracies, increasing the level of personnel training and skills, and determining how best to leverage overseas commercial assets. As China's leaders and the PLA continue to work through these challenges, external observers will gain a more detailed understanding of the organizational structure, key missions, and key forces that will operate abroad.

---

[160] Luo, Wan, and Li, 2019, p. 142.

[161] Xiao, ed., 2015, p. 302.

[162] Chen, Li, and Zeng, 2019, pp. 6–8.

[163] Garafola and Heath, 2017, pp. 25–26.

CHAPTER 4

Evaluating Potential Host Nations as Future Chinese Basing and Access Locations

Building on the framework developed in Chapter 3, we evaluate 108 countries in three regions—the Middle East, Africa, and the Indo-Pacific—as potential host nations for Chinese basing or access. We first present the results of that assessment.[1] We find that a variety of potential partners in the Middle East—given their proximity to key SLOCs and counterterrorism concerns, their source of energy exports to China, and their willingness to increase investment and, potentially, security ties with Beijing—and relatively developed coastal countries ranked favorably across both framework dimensions.

Second, we analyze the results by key themes, highlighting regional dynamics and implications, given potential host nations' agency to shape the feasibility dimension of our framework.

Third, we report on additional analysis that we conducted to understand the influence of one indicator of desirability—demonstrated Chinese interest in specific countries for military basing and access—on countries' scores. The results of that analysis suggest that despite information on where China is pursuing overseas basing and access being difficult to obtain or otherwise unavailable, our framework still captures relevant insights on attributes that Beijing would view as desirable for potential host nations.

For additional details on these results, Appendix A provides more information on our framework methodology and data sources, and Appendix B lists both aggregate scores and individual scores for all 17 indicators for the evaluated countries.

Results of Framework Analysis

After scoring each country across the indicators, we developed aggregate scores for desirability and feasibility and ranked the countries across these two dimensions. We then sorted the 108 countries into four quartiles of 27 countries based on each country's aggregate scores for both dimensions. Figure 4.1 depicts the countries whose scores placed them in the top three quartiles or tiers: Tier 1 consists of countries that scored in the top quartile of all 108 countries' scores across both dimensions, Tier 2 consists of countries that scored in the top 50 percent across both dimensions but lower than the Tier 1 countries, and Tier 3 consists of countries that scored in the top 75 percent across both dimensions, but lower than the Tier 2 countries. For the full list of aggregate and indicator scores, see Appendix B.

We do not depict the countries that scored in the bottom 25 percent of either dimension, reflecting the lowest level of either desirability or feasibility (or both). Fifty-one of the 108 countries that we assessed fell into this lowest tier.

---

[1] In the few cases in which data were missing (usually for microstates or failed states), we used a combination of expert judgment and analogous cases to generate categorical scores. Because values were typically only imputed for one or two of the 17 indicators for a given country, they very rarely influence a country's overall ranking.

FIGURE 4.1

Assessed Desirability and Feasibility of Potential PLA Basing and Access Locations

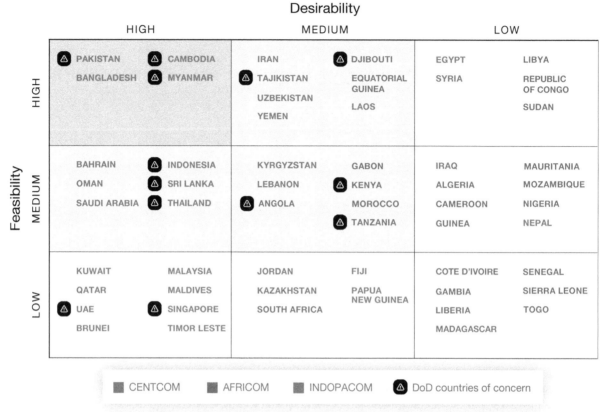

NOTE: Countries are listed in alphabetical order based on their location within the respective U.S. combatant commands' areas of responsibility (AORs). *DoD countries of concern* are listed in the DoD's 2020 annual report to Congress on China as countries in which China is interested in obtaining basing or access (OSD, 2020). We scored Djibouti along with the other countries even though China has already established a base there. The top-left shaded rectangle, Tier 1, consists of countries that scored in the top quartile of all 108 countries' scores across both dimensions. The surrounding three rectangles, Tier 2, consists of countries that scored in the top 50 percent across both dimensions but lower than the Tier 1 countries. The five unshaded rectangles, Tier 3, consists of countries that scored in the top 75 percent across both dimensions, but lower than the Tier 2 countries. We do not depict the countries whose scores placed them in Tier 4, which is the bottom 25 percent of either dimension, reflecting countries with the lowest level of either desirability or feasibility (or both). Fifty-one of the 108 countries that we assessed fell into this lowest tier.

Four countries scored highly in both dimensions (shown in the top-left rectangle of Figure 4.1): Pakistan, Bangladesh, Cambodia, and Myanmar. Moving downward in the figure, six countries scored highly for desirability but medium for feasibility: Bahrain, Oman, Saudi Arabia, Indonesia, Sri Lanka, and Thailand. The top-middle rectangle contains seven countries with medium desirability scores but high for feasibility: Iran, Tajikistan, Uzbekistan, Yemen, Djibouti, Equatorial Guinea, and Laos. Seven countries that received medium scores for both desirability and feasibility sit in the center of the figure: Kyrgyzstan, Lebanon, Angola, Gabon, Kenya, Morocco, and Tanzania. Together, these 24 countries comprise the top-scorers of the 108 countries that we assessed.

Building on Figure 2.1 in Chapter 2 of China's overseas economic, energy, and security interests, Figure 4.2 highlights these 24 countries. Figure 4.2 depicts the top-scoring countries with flag icons in three colors. First, China's inaugural host nation of overseas forces, Djibouti, is depicted with a black flag icon. Although Djibouti already hosts PLA forces, we opted to evaluate it to see how Djibouti would score based on our framework. Djibouti's score of medium desirability and high feasibility reflects analysis by some PLA researchers that Djibouti is a highly feasible location to secure military presence given its willingness to host foreign troops from multiple countries. However, these researchers view some of Djibouti's desirable

FIGURE 4.2

Top Potential PLA Basing and Access Locations Visualized

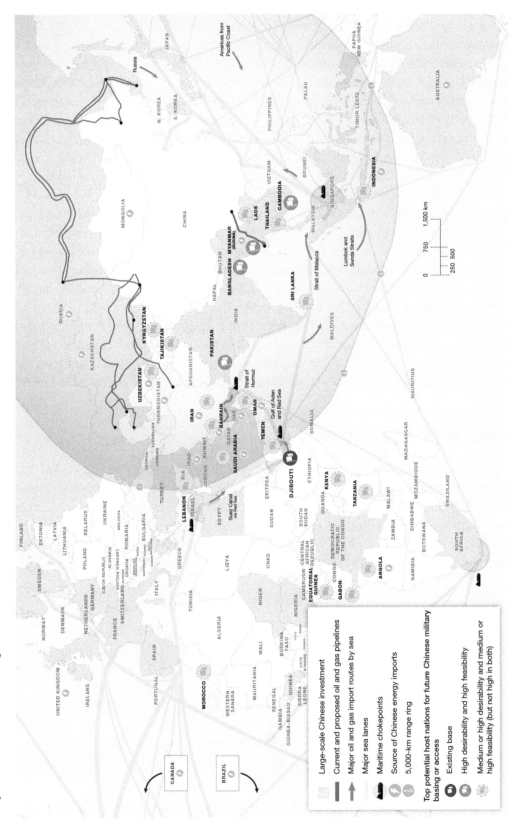

NOTE: Flag icons represent Tier 1 and Tier 2 countries. Tier 1 consists of countries that scored in the top quartile (high) of all 108 countries' scores across both dimensions. Tier 2 consists of countries that scored in the top 50 percent (high or medium) across both dimensions but lower than the Tier 1 countries. Icon placement is approximate and does not reflect specific potential basing or access locations within these countries.

attributes as counterbalanced by its relatively low level of economic development.[2] In other words, Djibouti's receptiveness to hosting another military (as basing is a key sector for its economy) may have made Djibouti a compelling option for Beijing more than the overall utility of a base there for the PLA.

Second, countries that scored highly across both desirability and feasibility are depicted with red flag icons. These four countries—Pakistan, Bangladesh, Cambodia, and Myanmar—have attracted significant attention in both PLA and Western analyses as potential Chinese basing or access locations. Pakistan and Myanmar have been listed in PLA studies as promising potential host nations.[3] Key sites of interest in Pakistan include the ports of Gwadar and Karachi and surrounding areas; for Myanmar, analysts focus on the ports of Sittwe and nearby Kyaukpyu, because Kyaukpyu is the origin of a major oil and natural gas pipeline that flows to China's Yunnan Province.[4] In a detailed study of Gwadar, U.S. Naval War College analysts assessed in 2020 that Gwadar "may one day serve as a major platform for China's economic, diplomatic, and military interactions across the northern Indian Ocean region," though it is both "underdeveloped and underutilized."[5] In Bangladesh, scrutiny has focused on the port of Chittagong. China is also building a submarine base nearby and will provide training for personnel to operate the base and two submarines that Bangladesh purchased from China in 2016, although Bangladeshi officials have stated the base is for Bangladeshi military use only.[6] For Cambodia, attention on Ream Naval Base has been further spurred by the government's recent announcement that China is building facilities there, but Western reporting has also noted Chinese interest in leveraging a separate facility with an airfield.[7]

Third, 19 countries that scored either high or medium in both desirability and feasibility, but not high for both dimensions, are depicted with orange flag icons.[8] These countries include various countries in the Middle East that could become strategic partners, particularly on counterterrorism issues for countries on China's periphery; coastal African countries in three regions; and various countries in the Indo-Pacific.

Key Themes in Country Scoring

Overall, we found a variety of potential partners in the Middle East, given their proximity to key SLOCs and counterterrorism concerns, their source of energy exports to China, and their willingness to increase investment and, potentially, security ties with Beijing; and relatively developed coastal countries ranked favorably across both dimensions of desirability and feasibility. Detailed findings are organized by region, divided among the AORs to which countries belong (CENTCOM, AFRICOM, and INDOPACOM). We focus first on the top overall scorers and then discuss the dynamics related to countries that did not rank as highly.

---

[2] Luo, Wan, and Li, 2019, p. 143. See also Beauchamp-Mustafaga, 2020.

[3] Li, Chen, and Jin, 2014; Wang, Qi, and Hai, 2018.

[4] Kardon, Kennedy, and Dutton, 2020; Peltier, Nurkin, and O'Connor, 2020; Thorpe and Spevack, 2018.

[5] Kardon, Kennedy, and Dutton, 2020, p. 2.

[6] Peltier, Nurkin, and O'Connor, 2020; Thorpe and Spevack, 2018; "China to Help Bangladesh Build Submarine Base, Senior Official Says," Radio Free Asia, September 12, 2019. A 2015 article republished by Xinhua on the benefits of leveraging overseas commercial ports for dual-use roles lists Chittagong among desirable locations (Song Zhongping [宋忠平], "The Dream and Reality of China's Overseas Bases" ["中国海外基地的梦想与现实"], Xinhua, July 8, 2015.

[7] Narin, 2021; Drake Long, "Cambodia, China and the Dara Sakor Problem," *The Diplomat*, October 21, 2020; Peltier, Nurkin, and O'Connor, 2020; Page, Lubold, and Taylor, 2019; Thorpe and Spevack, 2018.

[8] Djibouti also scored in this range, for a total of 20 countries.

Among the Top Overall Scorers, CENTCOM Countries Ranked Most Favorably

In terms of regional variation, Figure 4.3 depicts the proportion of the top-scoring 24 countries in each region: countries that scored either high or medium in desirability and either high or medium in feasibility.

We found that CENTCOM countries ranked the most favorably among the 24 top-scoring countries, both as a proportion of total countries in each AOR that scored highly and in absolute terms, compared with the other two regions. As Figure 4.3 shows, ten of the 24 top-scoring countries (over 40 percent) are located in the CENTCOM AOR, indicating that one or more basing or access facilities in this region may be especially appealing to Beijing. Looking at the AOR as a whole, ten out of 20 countries in CENTCOM made the cut, implying that around 50 percent of CENTCOM countries may be viewed relatively favorably from Beijiing's perspective. By comparison, seven countries in both the INDOPACOM and AFRICOM AORs scored highly, or roughly 29 percent of the total top-scorers. Among 35 total countries in the Indo-Pacific region, 20 percent of INDOPACOM countries were top scorers. AFRICOM, which covers 53 total countries, contained only 13 percent of the top-scoring countries.

CENTCOM Countries Present Compelling Options and Variety for Chinese Basing and Access

Of the 24 top-scoring countries, CENTCOM countries overall ranked highly as both desirable and feasible options for strengthening security partnerships. Given strong diplomatic, economic, and security relations between Beijing and Islamabad, as well as China's deteriorating ties with India, Pakistan may be a particularly sought-after potential host nation.[9] Chinese presence in Pakistan may serve an additionally strategic benefit from Beijing's perspective as Chinese leaders continue to focus on counterterrorism efforts and linked policies of domestic repression in Xinjiang. Operationally, standing up a military presence in Pakistan could serve as a "key peacetime replenishment or transfer point for PLA equipment and personnel," particularly if an airfield or a port were available because Pakistan falls within the operational range of the Y-20 transport aircraft.[10] One Western analyst assessed that "Chinese firms' extensive presence in Pakistan, and the percep-

FIGURE 4.3

Top-Scoring 24 Potential Host Nations, by U.S. Combatant Command

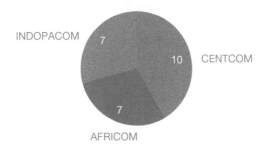

---

[9] On China-Pakistan relations, see Andrew Small, *The China-Pakistan Axis: Asia's New Geopolitics*, London: C. Hurst & Co. (Publishers) Ltd., 2015. On bilateral economic ties and the China-Pakistan Economic Corridor, see Erica Downs, *China-Pakistan Economic Corridor Power Projects: Insights into Environmental and Debt Sustainability*, New York: Columbia University, October 2019. On China's recent frictions with India, see Lin, Garafola, et al., 2022.

[10] On this point, as well as on Xinjiang, see Kardon, Kennedy, and Dutton, 2020, p. 2.

tion of an open invitation from the Pakistani government to augment China's military presence, makes that country a most likely test case for limited use of force in the event of a terrorist incident."[11]

Other CENTCOM countries may be natural partners to pursue given their proximity to key SLOCs and counterterrorism concerns, their source of energy exports to China, and their willingness to increase investment and, potentially, security ties with Beijing. South and Central Asian countries that scored well (Kyrgyzstan, Tajikistan, and Uzbekistan) may be willing to share information or collaborate on terrorism concerns. Iran is a key regional power that shares a similar outlook on some foreign policy issues with Beijing and has expanded its security relations with China.[12] Countries on or near the Arabian Peninsula offer close proximity to SLOCs and could potentially serve as key locations for PLAAF airlift operations, both into the region itself and as a waypoint to Africa and other points west.

Favorable Coastal Regions Stand Out Among AFRICOM Countries

Although no AFRICOM countries scored in the highest tier for desirability, meaning that they did not score in the top 25 percent of countries, coastal countries in the Gulf of Guinea (Angola, Equatorial Guinea, and Gabon); in East Africa along the Indian Ocean (Djibouti, Kenya, and Tanzania); and one country along the Mediterranean (Morocco) scored relatively favorably. Although China already has a base in Djibouti, Djibouti nevertheless scored more highly on feasibility (high) than on desirability (medium), which provides some evidence in support of feasibility as an important consideration for Chinese basing and access locations.[13] Military basing or access south of Djibouti could serve as a favorable transit point on the way toward the southern tip of Africa, while potential locations in the Gulf of Guinea or near the Mediterranean would increase the ability to operate in the Atlantic or near Europe. All three regions could provide options as potential hubs for regional security cooperation or strategic airlift and port operations.

INDOPACOM Countries Provide Options Beyond the Second Island Chain

Top-scorers in this region highlight the utility of basing and access locations that would augment the PLA's ability to project power beyond potential chokepoints between mainland China and the second island chain. These include countries in mainland and maritime Southeast Asia (Cambodia, Indonesia, Laos, Myanmar, and Thailand) and two potential South Asian hosts that border India (Bangladesh and Sri Lanka). With the exception of Cambodia and Laos, all seven countries provide options for increasing maritime or air presence near SLOCs in the Bay of Bengal or in the broader Indian Ocean. Cambodia and Laos may offer attractive options given that Chinese efforts appear to be moving ahead at Ream Naval Base, the two share a border, and China has significant investment in the Laotian high-speed railway system, a project that is valued at roughly a third of Laos's GDP.[14] There is also some evidence to suggest that the PLA prefers to ship supplies to the northern Indochina Peninsula by leveraging shared borders; during COVID-19 diplomacy efforts in early 2020, for example, the PLA dispatched PLAAF aircraft loaded with medical supplies to over 20 countries but opted to send the same materials to Vietnam's military by shipping them to the Vietnamese border.[15]

---

[11] Kardon, 2021, p. 88. See also the Chinese discussion on p. 103, fn 89.

[12] On China-Iran relations, see Will Green and Taylore Roth, *China-Iran Relations: A Limited but Enduring Strategic Partnership*, Washington, D.C.: U.S.-China Economic and Security Review Commission, June 28, 2021.

[13] This aligns with analysis in Beauchamp-Mustafaga, 2020.

[14] Zsombor Peter, "Laos Braces for Promise, Peril of China's High-Speed Railway," Voice of America, March 4, 2021.

[15] "PLA Donates Anti-Epidemic Supplies to Vietnamese Military," *China Military Online*, April 29, 2020.

Potential Host Nations Have Agency in Shaping Feasibility

As we discussed in Chapter 3, potential host nations may be incentivized, because of their own political, economic, or security interests, to offer basing or access agreements to China. Although we might expect some potentially eager host nations to score relatively well in the feasibility dimension of our framework based on data available as of this writing in 2021, other countries' trajectories may evolve toward greater security collaboration with China by the 2030–2040 time frame. This highlights a dynamic apparent in our framework: Countries' current scores for feasibility could rise if they decide to partner with China along diplomatic, security, or other dimensions in the future. Figure 4.4 illustrates the potential host nations that may become options for PLA basing and access were countries with high or medium desirability scores to improve their low feasibility scores, such as by taking actions that would significantly increase their engagement with China or align their policy actions with Beijing's.

The 24 top-scoring countries, from Figure 4.2, are shown again here, but all with black markers. The eight countries depicted with red markers—Kuwait, Qatar, and UAE in the Middle East; and Brunei, Malaysia, the Maldives, Singapore, and Timor Leste in the Indo-Pacific—scored in the top 25 percent of all countries for desirability, but relatively low (only in the top 75 percent of all countries) for feasibility. The five countries shown with the orange markers—Jordan, Kazakhstan, South Africa, Fiji, and Papua New Guinea—scored in the top 50 percent for desirability but only in the top 75 percent for feasibility. Were leaders in any of these 13 countries to decide to establish close security ties with Beijing, they would become significant options for overseas PLA basing and access over the long term.

This dynamic may be especially true in the CENTCOM AOR, which could add up to an additional five countries to the ten that already scored favorably based on our framework. Were China or a potential host nation to improve the feasibility of those countries, up to 75 percent of countries in the CENTCOM AOR may be especially sought after from Beijing's perspective for hosting PLA forces in some capacity. Among AFRICOM countries, South Africa would also be a significant PLA basing or access location given its proximity to major SLOCs and access to the Atlantic Ocean.

In the INDOPACOM AOR, improved feasibility could create additional options for Chinese basing or access in some countries, but it appears to have a higher ceiling in other countries. China could shift existing regional dynamics by obtaining basing, facilities, or access in the seven Indo-Pacific countries shown on Figure 4.4 prior to 2040.[16] On the other hand, most U.S. treaty allies in INDOPACOM, including Japan, South Korea, and Australia, as well as New Zealand, which is not a treaty ally but has substantially increased security ties with Washington over the past decade, are extremely desirable partners theoretically, but they scored in the bottom 25 percent of all countries for feasibility.[17] Dynamics in China's relationships with these countries are unlikely to lead to military basing or access agreements within the 2030–2040 time frame.

Although China's pursuit of basing or access in Oceania may raise concerns for the United States and other countries in the Indo-Pacific, only three Pacific Island Countries (PICs)—Papua New Guinea, Fiji, and Timor Leste—did not score extremely poorly in terms of feasibility. Apart from moderate to high levels of corruption, which may provide incentives for leaders to move forward with a potential offer from Beijing, specific scores that were unfavorable (i.e., indicating low feasibility) for many PICs included

- low voting alignment with China in the UN General Assembly
- relatively infrequent engagement with Chinese political and military leaders

---

[16] On U.S. versus Chinese influence in Indo-Pacific countries, see Lin, Chase, et al., 2020a, 2020b.

[17] Michael S. Chase and Jennifer D. P. Moroney, *Regional Responses to U.S.-China Competition in the Indo-Pacific: Australia and New Zealand*, Santa Monica, Calif.: RAND Corporation, RR-4412/1-AF, 2020.

FIGURE 4.4

Top Potential PLA Basing and Access Locations Visualized with Improved Feasibility

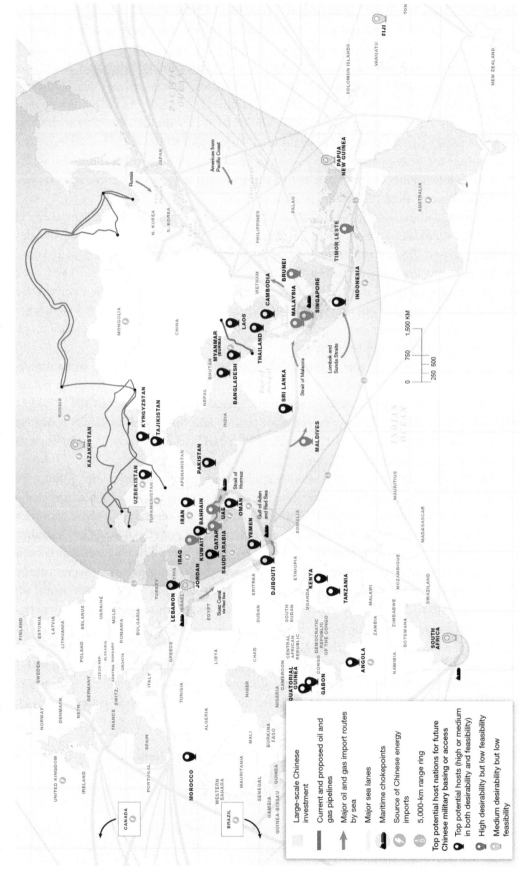

NOTE: Rankings are based on countries' scores from our 2020 assessment. Black icons represent Tier 1 and Tier 2 countries, or countries that scored in the top 50th percentile in both desirability and feasibility dimensions. Icon placement is approximate and does not reflect specific potential basing or access locations within these countries.

- low levels of arms sales or transfers (which overall impacted most INDOPACOM countries except for Bangladesh)
- relatively few authoritarian regimes
- some countries' continued official diplomatic recognition of Taiwan (four PICs).

These scores may imply that while China has agency to increase engagement with countries and pressure Taiwan's remaining official diplomatic partners in the region, the United States and its allies and partners nevertheless potentially retain significant advantages if they continue to maintain or deepen engagement in this region.[18] However, the opportunities and challenges faced by the PICs do not rule out the possibility of China achieving an outsized impact with relatively low levels of diplomatic capital, economic inducements or initiatives, or other tools, particularly for microstates that struggle to improve economic opportunities or increase their levels of development more broadly.

Examining Rankings Independently of Demonstrated Chinese Interest

Finally, we wanted to conduct additional analysis of country scores to understand the influence of one indicator of desirability: demonstrated Chinese interest in specific countries for military basing and access. Given that our framework incorporates demonstrated Chinese interest based on sources available as of 2020, our results may overly focus on countries that external sources assess China as pursuing in the near term, to the detriment of countries that may be of greater interest in the 2030–2040 time frame. To examine the effect of this indicator on countries' scores, we reranked the 108 country scores after excluding this indicator. We find that while excluding demonstrated Chinese interest resulted in some shuffling among the top-scoring countries' rankings for desirability, no top-scorers moved to the lowest tier (bottom 25 percent of all countries scored), nor did any of the lowest-scoring countries jump up to higher tiers of desirability.

Figure 4.5 depicts countries' scores without factoring in demonstrated Chinese interest. Compared with Figure 4.1, some countries move left or right, but none of the countries fall off the grid to join the 51 lowest-scoring countries. Specifically, Iran, Lebanon, Algeria, and Republic of Congo moved one column left to become relatively more desirable, while Angola, Djibouti, Kenya, Tanzania, and Pakistan moved one column right, scoring relatively less desirable. These findings suggest that even if information on where China is pursuing overseas basing and access is difficult to obtain or otherwise not available, our framework still captures relevant insights on attributes that Beijing views as desirable for potential host nations.

---

[18] For related discussion, see Derek Grossman, Michael S. Chase, Gerard Finin, Wallace Gregson, Jeffrey W. Hornung, Logan Ma, Jordan R. Reimer, and Alice Shih, *America's Pacific Island Allies: The Freely Associated States and Chinese Influence*, Santa Monica, Calif.: RAND Corporation, RR-2973-OSD, 2019.

FIGURE 4.5

Alternative Assessment of Potential PLA Basing and Access Locations (Without Demonstrated Chinese Interest Indicator Scores)

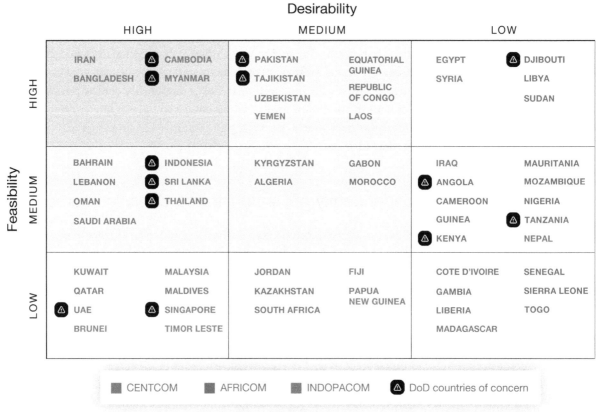

NOTE: Countries are listed in alphabetical order based on their location within the respective U.S. combatant commands' AORs. *DoD countries of concern* are listed in the DoD's 2020 annual report to Congress on China as countries in which China is interested in obtaining basing or access (OSD, 2020). We scored Djibouti along with the other countries, even though China has already established a base there. The top-left shaded rectangle, Tier 1, consists of countries that scored in the top quartile of all 108 countries scored across both dimensions. The surrounding three rectangles, Tier 2, represent countries that scored in the top 50 percent across both dimensions, but lower than the Tier 1 countries. The five unshaded rectangles, Tier 3, represent countries that scored in the top 75 percent across both dimensions, but lower than the Tier 2 countries

Conclusion

After scoring 108 countries in three regions across both dimensions of desirability and feasibility, four countries in the Middle East and Indo-Pacific scored in the top 25 percent of all countries in both dimensions: Pakistan, Bangladesh, Cambodia, and Myanmar. Another 20 countries scored in the top 50 percent of both dimensions, including countries in all three regions (the Middle East, the Indo-Pacific, and Africa). Overall, we found a variety of potential partners in the Middle East, given their proximity to key SLOCs and counterterrorism concerns, their source of energy exports to China, and their willingness to increase investment and, potentially, security ties with Beijing; and relatively developed coastal countries ranked favorably across both dimensions. Among the 24 overall top-scorers, CENTCOM countries ranked especially favorably compared with countries in the AFRICOM and INDOPACOM AORs. CENTCOM countries appear to present especially compelling options and variety for PLA basing and access. In the AFRICOM AOR, three coastal countries ranked highly, while in the INDOPACOM AOR, top-scoring countries provide the PLA with options to better project power beyond the second island chain. Because potential host nations also have agency in shaping feasibility over the 2030–2040 time frame of our study, 13 additional countries that scored relatively poorly in terms of feasibility may offer additional options for

Beijing, depending on future decisions made by those countries' leaders. When we reviewed an alternative ranking for desirability (see Figure 4.5), our framework still captured relevant insights on attributes that Beijing views as desirable for potential host nations.

In terms of potential operational implications for the U.S. armed forces in general and the U.S. Army in particular, these findings suggest many plausible locations for Chinese basing and access that are not especially close to currently deployed U.S. forces; however, Chinese forces operating out of countries in the CENTCOM AOR or expanding China's operations from Djibouti could have the clearest overlap with ongoing or future U.S. activities. Although it is not yet clear how U.S. policy toward Pakistan—one of the highest-scoring countries based on our framework assessment—will evolve following the U.S. withdrawal from Afghanistan in August 2021, a Pakistan more closely aligned with China could potentially pose a greater challenge to India, as well as increase risks for U.S. forces transiting between the INDOPACOM and CENTCOM regions in the event of a conflict. To the extent that the United States continues its counterterrorism missions in South and Central Asia, U.S.-Pakistan security ties will remain important.

If the United States continues to support deployments to Kuwait and missions in Iraq and Syria against the Islamic State, the presence of PLA forces in Saudi Arabia, the Gulf States, or Iran, or to a lesser extent in Central Asia—with countries that scored a mix of high and medium feasibility and desirability—could complicate operations to set the theater in the CENTCOM AOR. Port operations; reception, staging, onward-movement and integration; medical operations; support to other services; and air and missile defense are examples of ongoing missions in the CENTCOM AOR. A considerably expanded PLA presence in Djibouti could also complicate U.S. counterterrorism operations based in Camp Lemonnier. However, if the PLA were to consider high-intensity combat operations, some of the fundamental limitations of the PLA's base in Djibouti may require further expansion and access to a military airbase or deployment of an aircraft carrier with its associated escorts and support vessels, or both.

CHAPTER 5

Synthesis of Findings and Recommendations

In this chapter, we synthesize findings from previous chapters, and drawing on those findings, we offer recommendations for the U.S. government, DoD policymakers, and the U.S. Army. As more information becomes available regarding China's pursuit and prioritization of overseas military basing and access locations, additional dynamics in China's engagement with potential host nations may become important to consider in the future. We therefore include a final section covering a short list of topics for further research and consideration.

China's Expanding Interests Drive Requirements for Overseas Military Power

Since 2004, senior Chinese leaders have directed that the PLA will need to be increasingly capable of operating overseas because of China's expanding interests and Chinese leaders' ensuing commitments to protect them (as outlined in Chapter 2). This direction is shaping China's long-term pursuit of overseas basing and access locations. Beijing's primary motivation for expanding PLA presence abroad is rooted in the desire to protect its growing economic interests. Its motives are thus fundamentally based on achieving domestic priorities, such as economic growth to sustain the regime's legitimacy, and are, at most, only secondarily about competing with or imposing costs on the United States or any other country. However, intensifying competition with the United States and other rival Asian powers could motivate the PLA to consider a broader range of operations abroad than the military conducts today, including some form of combat operations. More broadly, as we explore in the companion report, *Implications of a Global People's Liberation Army*, the Soviet Union's expansion of overseas basing and access from 1955 to 1975 demonstrates the speed at which a determined power can obtain an array of overseas military presence and capabilities.[1] Although China's approach may or may not evolve as rapidly, evaluating potential host nations for both the desirability and feasibility of obtaining overseas military facilities from Beijing's perspective presents several options across the Middle East, Africa, and the broader Indo-Pacific.

A Mix of Factors Shapes China's Pursuit of Overseas Locations

A growing body of literature by Chinese military analysts and academic researchers explores potential criteria for overseas PLA locations, as well as options for prioritizing locations for future PLA basing or access. Building on this discussion, we developed a framework comprising 17 indicators to assess potential host nations across two dimensions with a focus on the 2030–2040 time frame: *desirability*, or the country's utility for overseas Chinese military operations, and *feasibility*, or China's ability to obtain basing or access in a

---

[1] Watts et al., 2022.

given country. Key themes in the desirability portion of our framework include the military utility of a potential host nation, its utility for protecting China's economic interests, and low or acceptable political or other risks to China of basing forces in the country. The feasibility portion of our framework focuses on the potential host nation regime's alignment with the PRC, China's influence in the country, and potential obstacles in China's relationship with the country.

Although Chinese officials and authoritative sources do not explicitly lay out the roles and missions that PLA forces may be called on to conduct overseas, we find some key elements relevant for overseas power projection noted in PLA sources, including the need for maritime replenishment and strategic airlift. This literature suggests that the pursuit of overseas basing and access is likely to diversify beyond the PLAN to encompass other services and a wide array of forces and units. PLA analysts also recognize that sending troops overseas will also impose greater requirements on networking the force, building overseas logistics capability, coordinating across civilian and military bureaucracies, increasing the level of personnel training and skills, and determining how best to leverage overseas commercial assets.

Potential Host Nations for Future Chinese Basing and Access Locations

Our framework identified 24 countries that may be especially well suited to China's pursuit of basing and access, although targeting some collective groupings of countries or a subset of countries in each of the three regions that we evaluated may be more appealing to Beijing than pursuing many locations independent of one another. Based on indicator scores for the two framework dimensions of desirability and feasibility, top-scoring countries included various CENTCOM countries, given their proximity to key SLOCs and counterterrorism concerns, their source of energy exports to China, and their willingness to increase investment and, potentially, security ties with Beijing; and relatively developed coastal countries in multiple regions. Four countries in the Middle East and Indo-Pacific scored in the top 25 percent of all countries in both dimensions: Pakistan, Bangladesh, Cambodia, and Myanmar. Another 20 countries in all three regions evaluated scored in the top 50 percent in both dimensions. Among the 24 overall top-scorers, CENTCOM countries appear to present especially compelling options and variety for PLA basing and access. In the AFRICOM AOR, three coastal countries ranked highly, while in the INDOPACOM AOR, top-scoring countries provide the PLA with options to better project power beyond the second island chain. Because potential host nations also have agency in shaping feasibility over the 2030–2040 time frame of our study, 13 additional countries that scored relatively poorly in terms of feasibility may offer additional options for Beijing depending on future decisions made by those countries' leaders.

Policy Recommendations

As this research indicates, growing overseas PLA presence is not a matter of if, but when. In the immediate future, for example, there are strong indications that Djibouti will not remain China's sole overseas naval facility; Cambodia could be the most likely to next join these ranks based on ongoing Chinese activities at Ream Naval Base. In the long term, China's growing overseas interests are driving Beijing to examine various locations abroad. However, key questions remain regarding the extent of China's future global presence and the types of power-projection activities that it will undertake by leveraging overseas basing and access.

We offer recommendations for policymakers based on the framework assessment that we developed in this report. These recommendations focus on further understanding China's plans for additional overseas basing and access and prioritizing risk to U.S. forces. In the companion report, *Implications of a Global People's Liberation Army*, we compare China's growing overseas military presence with historical case studies to understand the implications for and offer additional recommendations to U.S. policymakers, DoD, and the Army.

Recommendation for the U.S. Government and Department of Defense
Develop Indications and Warning for New Overseas PLA Locations

The primary purpose of our analysis was to understand Beijing's likely long-term aspirations for overseas basing and access. Our framework might be adapted, however, to help develop a set of I&W for China's future pursuit of access and basing in specific locations. Such a framework might be used to inform U.S. diplomatic and other initiatives intended to deny China military access in key states, impose additional costs on China if its military expansion appears threatening, and slow its rate of advance.

In thinking through a potential I&W framework, analysts should be aware that some of the indicators in our existing framework are relatively slow to change given that countries' economies and domestic and foreign policies evolve over many years or even decades. However, other indicators might change more rapidly (such as within one year) depending on the behavior of China and/or potential host nations, meaning that more frequent reassessment could alert policymakers to new opportunities for Chinese basing or access. Table 5.1 summarizes the speed at which our 17 indicators could change. Because our study focused on

TABLE 5.1
Speed at Which Framework Indicators May Change, by Dimension

ID	Indicator	Speed of Change
Desirability		
D1	Known Chinese interest in basing and access	Could change quickly; Beijing or host nation could make overtures
D2	Within rapid steaming distance of China	Slow to change
D3	Within military airlift range of China	Slow to change
D4	Coastal country	Very slow or unlikely to change
D5	Close proximity penalty	Very slow or unlikely to change
D6	Level of human development	Slow to change
D7	Level of Chinese investment	Could change quickly; Beijing and host nation could ramp up deals
D8	BRI member or participant	Could change quickly; Beijing and host nation could sign MOU
D9	Political stability and absence of violence	Could change quickly because of repression, revolution, invasion, etc., in host nation
D10	Risk of climate change	Slow to change
Feasibility		
F1	Authoritarian regime	Could change quickly because of repression, revolution, invasion, etc., in host nation
F2	Aligned voting with China	Slow to change
F3	Perceptions of corruption	Slow to change
F4	Partner engagement	Could change quickly; Beijing and host nation could ramp up visits

Table 5.1—Continued

ID	Indicator	Speed of Change
F5	Arms sales or transfers	Could change quickly; arms transfers may greatly vary each year
F6	Tensions in relations	Slow to change
F7	Official recognition of the PRC over the ROC (Taiwan)	Could change quickly; may be accompanied by economic deals

SOURCES: Matthew Southerland, "As Chinese Pressure on Taiwan Grows, Beijing Turns Away from Cross-Strait 'Diplomatic Truce,'" Washington, D.C.: U.S.-China Economic and Security Review Commission, February 9, 2017; Freedom House, "All Data, FIW 2013–2021," data file, 2021; authors' analysis of sources cited in Chapter 3 and Appendix A.

NOTE: We assessed the speed of potential change by reviewing the underlying time series data for each indicator in our country data set. The speed of change corresponds to the color coding as follows: red ("could change quickly") = warning: large changes in scores observed from year to year in the historical data; yellow ("slow to change") = large changes in scores observed over roughly five years; and green ("very slow or unlikely to change") = static scores.

assessing potential host nations in the long-term future, we did not include very short-term indicators that may change over a few weeks or months in our framework.

Table 5.1 suggests that nine of our indicators are relatively slow-moving, but eight indicators have the potential to change more quickly, including four desirability indicators and four feasibility indicators. For six of those indicators (D1, D7, D8, F4, F5, and F7), China and the potential host nation could seek to rapidly increase the scale or scope of their engagement. Two other indicators (D9 and F1) may be affected by domestic conditions within the country, such as regime change or civil unrest, as well as broader regional instability or conflict. Given their potential to change more quickly, these eight indicators might require more frequent assessment to identify shifts in potential host countries' scores for desirability and feasibility.

An I&W framework could also include indicators with even shorter time frames, such as weeks or months, and could benefit from other indicators that we were not able to assess based on available information. Although developing a full I&W framework was beyond the scope of this study, Table 5.2 summarizes other potential longer-term and shorter-term indicators that a country could become a host nation for Chinese military basing or access. As more information becomes available, analysts could use these indicators to augment the framework assessment discussed in Chapter 3 to produce more-refined assessments of highly favorable locations from Beijing's perspective.

Additional potential indicators may be worth assessing for a subset of countries or PLA forces, such as proximity to specific maritime chokepoints (most relevant for potential PLAN facilities), or analogous indicators identified for air and ground forces as new overseas missions and roles are identified. We briefly discuss each potential indicator below.

Frequency and Recency of China's or a Potential Host Nation's Request

As with other Chinese foreign policy and other initiatives, such as BRI, understanding the details for specific bilateral deals to the extent such information becomes available, including the level of effort that Beijing puts forward in making the request to a potential host nation, will be valuable. Also, as we noted in Chapter Three and explain in greater detail in the companion report, *Implications of a Global People's Liberation Army*, a potential host nation's leaders may have their own incentives to proactively offer to host the PLA. This indictor would support an I&W framework by incorporating frequency and recency, as well as including host nation requests in addition to China's.

Scale and Scope of BRI Partnership with the Potential Host Nation

Although China's leaders have directed the PLA to increase engagement under the BRI framework, not all BRI partners are created equal. A reluctant or token partner with limited areas of cooperation with China

TABLE 5.2

Additional Potential Indicators of China's Pursuit of Basing and Access Locations

Potential Indicator	Speed of Change
Frequency and recency of China's or a potential host nation's request	Could change quickly; Beijing or host nation could make overtures
Scale and scope of BRI partnership with the potential host nation	Slow to change
Presence of Chinese equipment and technology that is heavily integrated into China's military-civil fusion (MCF) strategy	Slow to change
Chinese assessments and reactions to ongoing geopolitical shifts	Slow to change
Increasing PLA engagement with multilateral organizations	Slow to change
PLA visits to or engagement with countries that are not leveraged for propaganda effect	Could change very quickly or relatively quickly based on individual operations or activities
Breakdown of foreign policy consensus among potential host nation elites	Could change quickly because of repression, revolution, invasion, etc. in host nation
Risk of revolutionary change in the potential host nation's government	Could change quickly because of repression, revolution, invasion, etc. in host nation
Emergence of acute security needs unmet by the United States or other Western governments	Could change quickly because of repression, revolution, invasion, etc. in host nation

SOURCE: Watts et al., 2022; We assessed the speed of potential change by leveraging insights from the indicators in Table 5.1, from sources cited in the following discussion, and from Watts et al., 2022.

NOTE: Red and orange warn of an indicator that could change quickly or very quickly, respectively, while indicators that are slower to change are shown in yellow.

under BRI may be less inclined to move forward with hosting the PLA on its territory.[2] Further understanding the scale and scope of a host nation's evolving partnership with China under BRI may help policymakers evaluate bilateral security and other ties that may lead a country to more favorably consider a request to host Chinese forces. This indictor would build on our original framework by moving beyond a signed MOU or potentially short-term changes in Chinese investment to assess the complexity and trajectory of long-term economic, digital, space, and other partnerships under BRI. One challenge in assessing this indicator today is a lack of comprehensive information available at the country level on China's partnerships under BRI, as well as a lack of transparency surrounding some projects or initiatives that may be aligned with BRI objectives but that are not officially labeled as such.[3]

---

[2] Vietnam is one example of a limited BRI partner. See Lin, Garafola, et al., 2022.

[3] This data collection could build on available studies and databases, including Gelpern et al., 2021; Reconnecting Asia Project, "Reconnecting Asia Project Database," Center for Strategic and International Studies, December 2020; AEI, undated; Sebastian Horn, Carmen Reinhart and Christoph Trebesch, "China's Overseas Lending," Kiel, Germany: Kiel Institute for the World Economy, Kiel Working Paper No. 2132, June 2019; AidData, "AidData's Global Chinese Official Finance Dataset, 2000–2014, Version 1.0," webpage, October 11, 2017; Rebecca Ray, Kevin P. Gallagher, William Kring, Joshua Pitts, and B. Alexander Simmons, "Chinese Overseas Development Finance: Geospatial Data for Analysis of Biodiversity and Indigenous Lands," database, Boston University Global Development Policy Center, 2019; and Mercator Institute for China Studies, "MERICS BRI Tracker: Database and Project Design," database, September 18, 2019.

Presence of Chinese Equipment and Technology That Is Heavily Integrated into China's Military-Civil Fusion Strategy

One aim of China's MCF strategy is to improve operational and other benefits for the PLA by leveraging technological development and equipment from civilian sources. As China increasingly exports MCF-related technologies and products overseas, equipment built to Chinese standards that the PLA leverages for operations at home may facilitate partnerships abroad. One example of potentially relevant equipment is the components that increase a potential host nation's public surveillance capability, which China exports via "smart cities" or "safe cities" programs.[4] In addition to concerns about illicit access that equipment may serve in providing non-kinetic exploits into a target country's government, commercial, and critical infrastructure networks, it is possible that successful law enforcement or technology integration partnerships could increase the attractiveness for a host nation to partner with China in broader security contexts, such as counterterrorism, ISR, or information-sharing. On China's side, the presence of Chinese equipment and a broader technology ecosystem in the host nation may improve the ease of sharing information, particularly with regard to systems that play a key role in MCF for the PLA. This ecosystem may alleviate some of the challenges mentioned in Chapter 3 that PLA units have raised in preparing for or conducting operations overseas.

Chinese Assessments and Reactions to Ongoing Geopolitical Shifts

These assessments may be particularly applicable for geopolitical developments that affect Beijing's perceptions of threats related to potential host nations or their neighbors in the region. For example, the U.S. withdrawal from Afghanistan may lead Chinese leaders to seek deeper counterterrorism partnerships with countries on Afghanistan's periphery. If competition with the United States and other rival Asian powers intensifies, Beijing's assessments of the trajectory of competition, particularly U.S.-China competition, could also potentially motivate China to consider a broader range of operations abroad than its military conducts today, including some form of combat operations.

Increasing PLA Engagement with Multilateral Organizations

In addition to PLA bilateral activities with host nations, new or deepening partnerships with other regional or multilateral fora may increase opportunities for Chinese presence in a given region. Examples may include the African Union or other fora with which the PLA has had limited touchpoints to date.

PLA Visits to or Engagement with Countries That Are Not Leveraged for Propaganda Effect

Particularly in the era of "COVID diplomacy," in which the China has harnessed the PLA's growing airlift capabilities to rapidly deliver supplies to other countries, overseas military activities are typically leveraged for public messaging that China is a net provider of both regional and global stability and peace.[5] When activities are not publicly messaged, it is possible that the PLA is undertaking engagements that Beijing wishes to keep under the radar, such as sensitive discussions or operational activities with other countries. This indicator is by no means definitive, given details regarding specific incidents may not be available, but it could be paired with other indicators to provide a better understanding of Chinese outreach to other coun-

---

[4] Huawei promotional materials state that its components are part of at least 120 smart cities in more than 40 countries; a Brookings survey found Chinese surveillance and public security technology platforms have been adopted in over 80 countries since 2008 (Huawei, "Huawei Smart City Brochure," July 27, 2017; Huawei, "Huawei Smart City Overview Presentation," June 10, 2018; Sheena Chestnut Greitens, "Dealing with Demand for China's Global Surveillance Exports," Washington, D.C.: Brookings Institution, April 2020). See, also, Carnegie Endowment for International Peace, "AI Global Surveillance Technology," website, undated; Alice Ekman, *China's Smart Cities: The New Geopolitical Battleground*, Paris: French Institute of International Relations (IFRI), December 2019; and Jonathan E. Hillman and Maesea McCalpin, "Watching China's 'Safe Cities,'" Washington, D.C.: Center for Strategic and International Studies, November 2019.

[5] Meia Nouwens, "The Evolving Nature of China's Military Diplomacy: From Visits to Vaccines," London: International Institute for Strategic Studies, May 2021.

tries. It may also be especially short term (i.e., only a few weeks or months in advance of news on a basing or access agreement) based on operational details of specific visits.

Breakdown of Foreign Policy Consensus Among Potential Host Nation Elites

Building on findings from the companion report, *Implications of a Global People's Liberation Army*, we found that dramatic shifts in a country's foreign policy, whether exacerbated by regional tensions or other dynamics, can open or close opportunities for Beijing. As one ongoing example in the economic realm involving China and the Maldives shows, volatile or split policy objectives among elites can shift countries' willingness to partner deeply with Beijing. When the current administration took power in the Maldives in a 2018 election, it ordered a review into the previous administration's financial dealings, including the extent of debt to China and the opaque conditions tied to Chinese lending estimated at roughly one-third of the country's GDP. At least one project during the prior administration was sponsored on the Maldivian side by a then-sitting parliamentary member. The investigation is ongoing, but the current administration seeks to renegotiate some terms with China.[6]

Risk of Revolutionary Change in the Potential Host Nation's Government

Relatedly, severe power struggles for control in a potential host nation's government may result in new leaders or embattled leaders hanging onto power who seek out deeper economic and security partnerships with other countries to further their rule. An indicator focused on the potential for revolutionary change could help incorporate the influence of internal regime dynamics into an I&W framework.

Emergence of Acute Security Needs Unmet by the United States or Other Western Governments

Finally, *Implications of a Global People's Liberation Army* provides historical examples of cases in which countries sought to expand security ties with a large power, such as Somalia approaching the United States during the 1960s and 1970s and then quickly turning to the Soviet Union for aid when the Somali government determined that U.S. support was insufficient.[7] China could potentially become a security partner of choice for countries by the 2030–2040 time frame if the PLA builds a positive reputation in carrying out overseas operations, particularly if potential host nations face limited alternatives. As we discussed in Chapter 3, PLA authors already assess that more countries may come to view the PLA as a valuable contributor to regional and international security given its greater role abroad, such as in carrying out PKO.[8]

Recommendation for the U.S. Army

As we discussed in Chapter 4, many plausible locations for Chinese basing and access are not particularly close to currently deployed U.S. forces, although the greatest overlap may occur in the CENTCOM AOR. Were China to pursue a rapid basing and access expansion overseas and if it decided to deploy and employ offensive systems at its bases, U.S. joint platforms capable of long-range strikes (including combat aircraft, surface vessels, and submarines) that are optimized for high-end conflict would have significant advantages in overcoming defenses at Chinese bases located at great distance from the Chinese mainland. However, in the event of a conflict with China, Army units could be better placed in some regions or contexts to defeat targets if doing so would permit other high demand assets—such as submarines, bombers, and aircraft

---

[6] Aishath Hanaan Hussain Rasheed, "Work of Asset Recovery Commission Ongoing: Gov't Spokesperson," *Raajje*, February 11, 2021; Anbarasan Ethirajan, "China Debt Dogs Maldives' 'Bridge to Prosperity,'" BBC, September 17, 2020; Alasdair Pal and Devjyot Ghoshal, "Report on Alleged Chinese Corruption in Maldives Due by June: Minister," Reuters, January 16, 2020; Marwaan Macan-Markar, "China Debt Trap Fear Haunts Maldives Government," *Nikkei Asia*, September 15, 2020.

[7] Watts et al., 2022.

[8] Xiao, 2020, pp. 314–316.

carriers—to carry out other wartime missions. As we find in the companion report, given the potential for regional instability in locations that China may pursue, gaining and maintaining familiarity with likely Chinese weapon systems and TTP may also help the Army prepare for potential contingencies involving Chinese partners or proxy forces in key regions.[9]

Prioritize Countries of Concern for Army Organizations and Forces

The Army could perform country-level or facility-level risk assessments based on the countries identified in the framework as priority host nations for China basing and access along with additional government assessments. Army assessments could focus on specific mission sets that the Army currently conducts and those it may be called on to conduct in the future, during periods of both crisis and competition. Two additional lenses may be beneficial: (1) the Army's ability to conduct Army-specific missions and roles, and (2) the Army's ability to conduct missions and roles that support broader joint force missions and activities. Areas of emphases in assessments should include the risk to U.S. forces if China were to establish significant presence and conduct various military activities, as well as general threats to force protection or other challenges posed by Chinese forces present in close proximity to U.S. forces, such as counterintelligence issues and operations security considerations. These reviews would identify options to mitigate near-term or less-severe risks, as well as gaps in concepts, capabilities, equipment, personnel expertise, training, or posture, which addressing could help increase mission success in a more complex operating environment. For example, we note in the companion report that retaining capabilities for lower intensity conflict and increasing capabilities to rapidly respond to crises may be valuable in countries hosting or near PLA forces.[10]

Areas for Future Research

There were two additional areas that we sought to incorporate in this research but lacked the relevant information to do so. As more information becomes available, research on both topics would prove valuable in further understanding the role that China's military forces will play overseas.

Risks China May Incur in Expanding Its Operations Overseas

Although PLA analysts acknowledge the tactical challenges of operating overseas and reputational concerns that China may face, we did not find any detailed discussion of broader operational challenges with an eye toward future operational concepts that may leverage multiple overseas bases or points of access. Potential risks include the difficulty of conducting force protection missions in insecure regions and potential counterintelligence risks. Then there are the challenges of conducting expeditionary warfare operations far from home, including stresses and strains on the PLA's nascent joint command structure, as well as the logistics requirements of sustaining facilities and forces abroad. Although PLA discussion of difficulties encountered during China's limited overseas operations to date provides some foundation for understanding these dynamics, the increasing variety of missions and forces abroad will continue to expand the range of new operational challenges and vulnerabilities.[11]

---

[9] Watts et al., 2022. See also Stephen Watts, Bryan Frederick, Nathan Chandler, Mark Toukan, Christian Curriden, Erik E. Mueller, Edward Geist, Ariane M. Tabatabai, Sara Plana, Brandon Corbin, and Jeffrey Martini, *Proxy Warfare as a Tool of Strategic Competition: State Motivations and Future Trends*, Santa Monica, Calif.: RAND Corporation, RR-A307-2, forthcoming.

[10] Watts et al., 2022.

[11] For examples of past efforts by the PLAAF to overcome these challenges, see Garafola and Heath, 2017, pp. 29–32.

The Role of Private Military Contractors in Supporting Overseas Basing and Access

A variety of Chinese private security contractors (PSCs) or private military contractors operate overseas, particularly in Africa, but whether they will support the PLA's growing presence abroad is unclear.[12] Unlike Russia's Wagner Group, these groups appear to be commercially oriented, but it is possible that Chinese PSCs could expand their services to indirectly support PLA operations, bolstered by some PSC founders' or leaders' linkages to the PLA. Given that Chinese PSC operations abroad are likely to continue to grow, future analysis could explore whether links emerge with overseas PLA facilities and forces. A case study in the companion report notes that Russian PSCs operate in Syria, where Russia has a naval base and has also deployed air and ground forces.

---

[12] Heath, 2018; Legarda and Nouwens, 2020.

Methodology for Basing and Access Framework

Caveats Regarding Our Methodology

Our analysis is conducted at the country level rather than on specific locations or infrastructure, such as ports or airfields.[1] We scored 108 countries in the three priority regions—the Middle East, Africa, and the broader Indo-Pacific.[2] Country scores for some indicators may exhibit correlation because of underlying inputs, such as GDP.

In the few cases where data were missing (usually for microstates or failed states), we used a combination of expert judgment and analogous cases to generate categorical scores. Because values were typically only imputed for one or two of the 17 indicators for a given country, they very rarely influence a country's overall ranking.

Scoring Method

We matched the identified themes and criteria in the Chinese literature to publicly available quantitative and qualitative data to develop 17 indicators, of which ten assess desirability and seven assess feasibility. Scores for each indicator are weighted equally and added up to obtain a composite desirability score and a composite feasibility score. Absent more-detailed information on CCP and PLA leaders' priorities for basing and access, we adopted this most-straightforward weighting scheme rather than make additional assumptions to favor some indicators over others.

We have categorized the indicators as either relevant for desirability or feasibility, but indicators across the two dimensions may be correlated, meaning that a two-dimensional framework may artificially separate non-independent indicators. To examine an alternative scoring method that could reduce potential distortions caused by our two-dimensional framework, we performed a robustness check by comparing the two-dimensional scores in Chapter 4 with an alternative scoring system of one overall score based on all 17 indicators. We then reviewed the 24 top-scorers using this alternate method. We found that 14 of the 24 top-scoring countries discussed in Chapter 4 remained high-scorers with the one-score approach. Another seven were among the 13 countries that we identified as potential options for China if those countries undertook

---

[1] Some indicators, such as human development and climate risk, could vary within a given country. The data sets that we used assessed both indicators at the country level. Likewise, airlift and ship steaming range could include some ports and airfields or airports and not others in a given country, but we scored a country as "within range" at the country level if *any* ports or airfields fell within the ranges that we specified between the country and China.

[2] We eliminated China and the United States from our assessment, as well as Taiwan, because PRC views toward Taiwan are focused on political, economic, and military "reunification" from Beijing's perspective rather than securing basing or access from a host nation.

active outreach to Beijing on hosting PLA forces (i.e., highly desirable but currently low in terms of feasibility), indicating that our two-dimensional framework offers relevant insights about this group of countries as well. However, we also found that three key U.S. allies joined the ranks of the 24 top-scorers—the Philippines, South Korea, and Japan—even though it is unlikely U.S. allies would host the PLA, given their strong relations with the United States and their own tensions with China. Because those countries did not become top-scorers through our two-dimensional scoring method, this exercise demonstrated to us that some elements of feasibility in our framework are important and relevant to consider separately from desirability.

Finally, we sorted the 108 countries into four quartiles of 27 countries each based on their aggregate scores for each of the two dimensions.

Desirability Indicators

Building on insights from official and semi-authoritative Chinese sources on valuable attributes for overseas basing and access, we assessed the desirability of countries for Chinese basing and access.[3] Specifically, we focused on whether a PLA base, facility, or access in a given country would enable desired power-projection capabilities at tolerable risk. Desirability is assessed using a composite score of the ten indicators listed in Table A.1.[4] The table shows the lowest and highest scores possible for each indicator.[5]

D1. Known Chinese Interest in Basing and Access

This indicator shows a higher level of desirability based upon publicly known PRC interest in military basing or access within a given country. This value is based on information provided in the DoD's *Military and Security Developments Involving the People's Republic of China 2020: Annual Report to Congress*. DoD lists countries in which China has demonstrated interest in locating military logistics facilities, countries that China has engaged to discuss basing or access options, and countries that have already established PLA bases or may do so in the near future.[6] The report also includes countries in which the PLA Strategic Support Force operates TT&C stations.

How countries are scored: This is a binary indicator. Countries scored higher (more desirable) if they were listed by DoD in its 2020 annual report. For example, Kenya was listed by DoD and received a score of 1 (more desirable), while Yemen was not listed by DoD and received a score of 0 (less desirable).

Source: *Military and Security Developments Involving the People's Republic of China 2020: Annual Report to Congress.*[7]

---

[3] For more information on these sources, see Chapter 3.

[4] The calculation for desirability is the sum of scores for D1 through D10. Because two indicators are inverted (meaning 0 is more desirable and 1 is less desirable), the highest possible score is 8 (i.e., most desirable from Beijing's perspective).

[5] For normalized scores, we use $z = (x_i - min(x))/(max(x) - min(x))$. The minimum (min) and maximum (max) are based on the subset of countries that we assess, which are the 108 countries in the three priority regions.

[6] In comparing the 2021 and 2020 reports, we found that DoD removed two countries from the list for which China has likely made overtures: Vanuatu and the Solomon Islands. DoD also clarified that China is likely considering Cambodia (OSD, 2021, p. 132). Both Vanuatu and the Solomon Islands scored poorly, so the 2021 DoD update would not have significantly affected these countries' scores or our overall ranking.

[7] OSD, 2020, pp. 63, 128–130.

TABLE A.1

Desirability Indicator Values

ID	Indicator	Score Value	Score Type
D1	Known Chinese interest in basing and access	0 or 1	Binary
D2	Within rapid steaming distance of China	0 or 1	Binary
D3	Within military airlift range of China	0 or 1	Binary
D4	Coastal country	0 or 1	Binary
D5	Close proximity penalty	−3 to 0	Penalty applied to specific countries based on their combined score for D4, D5, and D6
D6	Level of human development	0 to 1	Scale (normalized)
D7	Level of Chinese investment	0 to 1	Scale (normalized)
D8	BRI member or participant	0 or 1	Binary
D9	Political stability and absence of violence	0 to 1	Scale (normalized)
D10	Risk of climate change	−1 to 0	Scale (normalized)

D2. Within Rapid Steaming Distance of China

This indicator provides a binary value for countries within 3,024 nm of steaming distance from large ports with commercial presence and proximity to naval forces in East and South China (Shanghai and Zhanjiang). The distance represents an 18-knot transit time by a large vessel for seven days and denotes the potential ability to rapidly resupply or support a naval or dual-use facility from the Chinese mainland within one week. This is consistent with previous RAND research examining potential operations by another sophisticated military actor, Russia; that research assessed four to seven days for Russian naval response times to various crisis scenarios.[8]

How countries are scored: This is a binary indicator. Countries scored higher (more desirable) if a major port within those countries was located within 3,024 nm of either of the two Chinese ports. For example, Papua New Guinea fell within the specified range and received a score of 1 (more desirable), while Ghana did not and received a score of 0 (less desirable).[9]

Source: Authors' calculations using a sea and port distances online tool.[10]

D3. Within Military Airlift Range of China

Countries are considered within military airlift range of China if they fall fully or partially within 4,500 km of PLA airfields at Qionglai, Kaifeng, or Changji. The specific distance is based on Chinese state media discussion that Y-20 aircraft can "deliver a heavy equipment division 4,500 km away."[11] Qionglai and Kaifeng

---

[8] Ben Connable, Abby Doll, Alyssa Demus, Dara Massicot, Clint Reach, Anthony Atler, William Mackenzie, Matthew Povlock, and Lauren Skrabala, *Russia's Limit of Advance: Analysis of Russian Ground Force Deployment Capabilities and Limitations*, Santa Monica, Calif.: RAND Corporation, RR-2563-A, 2020, p. xv.

[9] Because the Marshall Islands' Port of Majuro is oriented very near the outer ring of steaming distance, inclusion varies dependent on calculating tools. For the purposes of this analysis, we have included the Marshall Islands as within rapid steaming distance.

[10] "Sea Distances/Port Distances," Sea-Distances.org, undated. Calculations were performed in 2021.

[11] "By 2020, the Chinese Air Force Will Be Equipped with 40 Y-20s That Can Deliver a Division Long Distances" ["2020年中国空军将装备40架运-20 可远程投送1个师"], Xinhua [新华网], July 13, 2018. The Xinhua article cited Western

airfields are PLAAF Y-20 bases; we also included Changji because it is a major Western Theater Command base that could potentially provide support for Y-20 missions to Western locations and regions.

How countries are scored: This is a binary indicator. Countries scored higher (more desirable) if they partially or completely fell within 4,500 km of the three specified airfields. For example, Iran fell within the range and received a score of 1 (more desirable), while Morocco fell outside the range and received a score of 0 (less desirable).

Source: Authors' calculations using ArcGIS.

D4. Coastal Country

This indicator shows whether the country is coastal or landlocked.

How countries are scored: This is a binary indicator. Countries scored higher (more desirable) if they are coastal. For example, coastal Japan received a score of 1 (more desirable), and landlocked Afghanistan received a score of 0 (less desirable).

Source: U.S. Central Intelligence Agency's (CIA's) *The World Factbook*.[12]

D5. Close Proximity Penalty

This indicator takes into account the limited military utility for China of potential host nations that are within extremely close range of major PLA bases within mainland China. When considering overseas military access or basing, China's close neighbors—those within a few hours of flying time or roughly a day of steaming time to the mainland—provide limited added value for PLA operations. We focused in particular on countries within the first island chain between Japan, Taiwan, and edging toward the South China Sea.

How countries are scored: Countries within the first island chain with locations that China could use for military purposes (e.g., near key cities leveraging major transportation or port infrastructure) and that are located within 500 km of major PLA facilities in China received a "penalty" on their steaming range (D2), military airlift range (D3), and coastal score (D4). This penalty removes the advantage given to coastal countries within steaming and airlift range that are nonetheless of limited utility to China given their close proximity to PLA facilities. We defined *major PLA facilities* as multiple PLAA, PLAN, and/or PLAAF bases or headquarters locations either co-located or located in close proximity to mainland China.

For example, both North Korea and Vietnam fall well within 500 km of major PLA facilities (less desirable) and received this penalty.[13] This means that these countries received a –1 for each of the three indicators in which they had scored a 1 for close proximity to China (D2, D3, and D4), resulting in a total score of –3 (less desirable), which we added to their composite score for desirability. In contrast, countries that lie

---

media for the 4,500 km range; other Chinese sources list similar ranges, with discussions of 5,000–5,200 km ranges for Y-20s carrying "normal" equipment loads. We opt for the more conservative 4,500 km range, which may provide flexible options for flight paths, enable heavier loads, or accommodate other unexpected situations during airlift operations. See "normal equipment load exceeds 5,000 km" in Huang Zijuan [黄子娟], "How Many Y-20s Does Our Military Require? Experts Teach You How to Calculate" ["我军需要多少运-20? 专家教你计算"], *China Military Online* [中国军网], June 8, 2016. For other Chinese sources listing 5,200 km, see "Russian Media: Y-20 About to Enter Service with the Chinese Air Force; Will Be More Important Than the J-20" ["俄媒: 运-20即将列装中国空军 比歼-20更重要"], Xinhua [新华网], June 10, 2016; and "British Media Says the Y-20 Has Been Delivered to the Chinese Air Force in Batches; 1,000 Aircraft Needed to Fulfill Strategic Air Delivery Requirements" ["英媒称运20已批量交付中国空军 满足战略空运1000架"], Xinhua [新华网], January 14, 2018.

[12] CIA, "Field Listing–Coastline," *The World Factbook*, undated.

[13] The distance between Dalian, China (home to a major PLAN facility, as well as PLAAF and other units) to Nampo and other locations in northern North Korea is under 500 km, as is the distance from Hainan, China (home to multiple PLAA and PLAN units) to Haiphong and other locations in northern Vietnam.

beyond 500 km, such as the Philippines, received a score of 0 (more desirable).[14] Like risk of climate change (D10), this indicator is inverted, meaning that a higher score is less desirable (in other words, the score value is subtracted from the composite score for desirability).

Sources: *Military and Security Developments Involving the People's Republic of China 2020: Annual Report to Congress* and the International Institute for Strategic Studies' 2019 "China's Armed Forces" map.[15]

D6. Level of Human Development

This indicator measures three dimensions of human development: life expectancy, access to education (measured by two metrics—access to education and mean years of schooling), and standard of living (measured by GNI per capita.) The score is drawn from the most recent year available (2019) of the United Nations Development Programme's (UNDP's) HDI. The index first normalizes each of the four metrics to a value between 0 and 1 based on the upper and lower limits of the given metric. HDI is calculated as the geometric mean (equally weighted) of life expectancy, education, and GNI per capita.

How countries are scored: Countries scored higher (more desirable) if they had high HDI scores. For example, Malaysia had higher HDI levels and received a score of 0.80 (more desirable), while South Sudan had lower HDI levels and received a score of 0.39 (less desirable).

Source: UNDP's *Our World in Data*, Human Development Index.[16] We imputed the following values through analysis and RAND subject-matter expertise because HDI data for the these countries were unavailable:[17]

- Somalia: 0.00[18]

---

[14] Based on our assessment, locations in countries (near or bordering China) with major infrastructure that do not fall within 500 km of significant PLA facilities include the Philippines, Thailand, Myanmar, Bangladesh, Pakistan, Kyrgyzstan, Uzbekistan, and Tajikistan. Because we focused on countries within the first island chain, we considered but did not apply the penalty to Nepal and Laos. We also did not analyze some countries that scored poorly on feasibility, such as Japan, South Korea, India, and Bhutan, which all placed in Tier 4 (bottom 25 percent of countries) for feasibility, and therefore, they did not rank highly overall regardless.

[15] OSD, 2020, pp. 98, 103, 106, 109, 111; International Institute for Strategic Studies, 2019.

[16] Roser, 2014.

[17] For Nauru, North Korea, Tuvalu, and Somalia, RAND staff with expertise on Northeast Asia, the PICs, and Africa rated each country as very low (0.00), low (0.33), high (0.66), or very high (1.00) based on a review of quantitative and qualitative information on the relevant country. These estimated scores were then imputed *after* the raw data had been normalized in order to avoid skewing the normalized scale.

[18] To estimate Somalia's development level, we considered different sources for each of the three components of the HDI score: GNI per capita, life expectancy, and expected/average years of schooling. Economically, the World Bank does not publish data for Somalia on GNI per capita (the HDI metric used), but it does publish statistics for GDP per capita at purchasing power parity (PPP, current international $). In 2020, Somalia scored among the world's lowest countries along these metrics ($875), with scores comparable to the countries with normalized HDI scores near 0.0, including Niger (HDI: 0.0, GDP per capita, PPP: $1,263), Central African Republic (HDI: 0.2, GDP per capita, PPP: $980), and Chad (HDI: 0.9, GDP per capita, PPP: $1,603). In terms of life expectancy from birth, Somalia also scores among the very worst in the world at 57.4 years, according to the World Bank's world development indicators (WDI; World Bank, "World Development Indicators," webpage, undated-b. Data accessed on August 16, 2021). Again, this figure is similar to that of the four "very low" comparators with HDI scores of less than 0.1: Central African Republic (53.3 years), Chad (54.2 years), South Sudan (57.8 years), and Niger (62.4 years). Finally, while reliable data is not available on expected and average years of schooling in Somalia, we qualitatively assessed the country to also be among the worst in the world. For instance, according to the U.S. Agency for International Development, "the educational deficit in Somalia is one of the most acute in the world," with about 3 million out of the 5 million school-aged children not even enrolled in school, including almost 1 million children directly displaced by conflict (U.S. Agency for International Development, "Somalia: Education," webpage, March 19, 2021). Similarly, the World Bank notes that Somalia's estimated primary gross enrollment rate of 20 percent (ages 5–14 years) is "significantly below sub-Saharan Africa, low income coun-

- North Korea: 0.33[19]
- Tuvalu: 0.33[20]
- Nauru: 0.66.[21]

---

tries, and fragile-and-conflict-affected countries" (World Bank, "Somalia Education for Human Capital Development Project (P172434): Project Information Document (PID)," Washington, D.C., PIDA28885, March 10, 2021b). According to estimates by the Education Policy Data Center, 79 and 72 percent of primary-aged and secondary-aged school kids, respectively, are not enrolled—and these numbers are far worse for females (Education Policy and Data Center, "Somalia: National Education Profile, 2018 Update," Washington, D.C., 2018). These figures again are similar to or worse than the World Bank's data on primary completion rate for the aforementioned comparators (Central African Republic, Chad, Niger, and South Sudan), which generally are in the 20 percent to 60 percent range. For these reasons, we estimated Somalia to have an imputed HDI score of 0.00, equal to Niger.

[19] Imputing North Korea's value was slightly more challenging. The World Bank does not provide either GDP or GNI per capita data; instead, we referred to the CIA *World Factbook*'s 2015 estimate of a real GDP per capita of $1,700 (in 2015 U.S. dollars), which also aligned closely with the Heritage Foundation's estimate of $1,800. This "low" (rather than "very low") economic level was roughly similar to at least 11 of the other 12 comparators with normalized HDI scores between 0.30 and 0.40. With the exception of Syria, for which data was missing, these countries' real GDP per capita all ranged from about $1,100 to $2,600 (in 2020 U.S. dollars), including Angola, Cambodia, Cameroon, Myanmar, Nepal, Nigeria, Pakistan, Papua New Guinea, Solomon Islands, Tanzania, and Zimbabwe. In terms of life expectancy, the World Bank's WDI and CIA's *World Factbook* supply similar estimates for North Korea: 72.3 years and 71.7 years, respectively. According to the CIA, this ranks 162nd in the world (compared with, for instance, Somalia's ranking of 225th at 53.0 years). Relative to the 12 comparators with normalized HDI scores between 0.30 and 0.40, this slightly above the cohort's average of 66 years, aligning most closely with Nepal (70.8 years), Syria (72.7 years), and the Solomon Islands (73.0 years). Finally, in terms of education, the CIA's *World Factbook* estimates about 100 percent literacy and that 11 years of school is the expectancy from primary to tertiary. Similarly, in 2008, the last year that data are available, WDI estimated a 99 percent literacy rate for ages 15 and up. In short, we assess North Korea to have a "low" GDP per capita, a well below-average life expectancy, and a relatively "high" educational access and attainment score. Cumulatively, we assessed North Korea to be closer to a normalized HDI score of 0.33 rather than 0.00 or 0.66. (We accessed data on August 16, 2021 from the following sources: CIA, "The World Factbook," webpage, August 18, 2022; Heritage Foundation, "Explore the Data: All Index Data," data set, 2021; World Bank, undated-b.) See also UNDP, *Human Development Report 1998*, New York: Oxford University Press, 1998, p. 21; UNDP, "PRK–Human Development Indicators," undated; and Bertelsmann Stiftung, *BTI 2020 Country Report—North Korea*, Gütersloh, 2020.

[20] We adjudicated at length over whether to score Tuvalu as a 0.33 or 0.66. There were several pieces of key evidence considered. First, UNDP's 2020 index does not assign Tuvalu an aggregate score, but it does provide data on GNI per capita, measured in 2017 PPP ($6,132) and on expected years of schooling (12.3 years). By a similar economic metric, the World Bank estimates Tuvalu's real GDP per capita at PPP to be $4,653 in 2020 (current international $), which is similar to WDI's estimates for at least 11 of the 12 aforementioned countries with normalized HDIs between 0.3 and 0.4 (again, excluding Syria, for which GDP data is not available). In 2020 international dollars, these countries' relatively "low" GDP per capita (PPP) ranged from $2,619 (Solomon Islands) to $6,538 (Angola), with the closest comparator being Papua New Guinea ($4,326), Cambodia ($4,422), Myanmar ($4,794), and Pakistan ($4,877). Second, ranking 181st worldwide according to CIA estimates, Tuvalu's relatively "low" life expectancy (68.1 years) was close to the mean of the previously identified 12 "low" comparators (65.6 years). Finally, UNDP's 2020 index estimates expected years of schooling to be 12.3 years, while WDI data on primary school completion rates in Tuvalu typically ranged from a high 70s to low 90s percent. Although not a perfect proxy for UNDP's averaged mean/expected years of schooling, Tuvalu's score appears to be higher than or equal to most of the 12 "low" comparators. For these collective reasons—low GDP per capita, PPP; low life expectancy; and moderate-to-high educational completion rates—we estimated Tuvalu's normalized HDI value to be closer to 0.33 than to either 0.00 or 0.66. (We accessed data on August 16, 2021 from the following sources: CIA, 2022; Heritage Foundation, 2021; World Bank, undated-b.)

[21] Nauru was the most difficult of the four values to estimate. Economically, Nauru's GDP per capita (PPP) of $14,099 (in 2019 current dollars) is very similar to countries like Fiji ($14,263), Mongolia ($12,838), Algeria ($11,136), Thailand ($19,234), and Sri Lanka ($13,635)—which have normalized HDI scores of 0.66, 0.66, 0.68, 0.69, 0.71, respectively. In terms of life expectancy, however, Nauru's place is among less-developed comparators, ranking 184th worldwide according to CIA estimates (67.6 years), similar to Tuvalu's "low" imputed score. Indeed, the UN assesses Nauru has "the shortest life expectancy of any country in the Pacific." Finally, Nauru's primary school completion rates are relatively high (typically in the 90s) according to WDI data, and CIA estimates an expectancy rate of nine years of schooling between primary to tertiary education levels. Altogether, because of Nauru's moderate per capita income level, relatively low life expectancy, and moderate-to-high educational attainment rates, we estimated Nauru's normalized HDI value to be closer to 0.66 than to either 0.33 or 1.00. (We accessed data on August 16, 2021 from the following sources: CIA, 2022; Heritage Foundation, 2021; World Bank, undated-b; United

D7. Level of Chinese Investment

This indicator provides a normalized value for investment based on spending data on Chinese investment in the given country from 2005–2020 in millions of U.S. dollars.

How countries are scored: We normalized these scores to a scale of 0.00 to 1.00 based on the highest and lowest dollar values of investment in the 108 countries that we scored. Countries scored higher (more desirable) if they had greater values of Chinese investment. For example, with around $36 billion in cumulative investment, Singapore had more Chinese investment than Malaysia's $19 billion; Singapore received a 0.36 normalized score compared with Malaysia's 0.19 normalized score.[22]

Source: AEI's China Global Investment Tracker.[23]

D8. BRI Member or Participant

This indicator provides a binary value indicating whether a country has a BRI MOU with China as of January 2021. Seven countries have "unknown" values in the data source, which indicates that there is conflicting information on the existence of MOUs. We have listed these countries as "no MOU" for the purposes of our analysis.[24]

How countries are scored: This is a binary indicator. Countries scored higher (more desirable) if they have a known BRI MOU with China. For example, Brunei has an MOU with China on BRI and received a score of 1 (more desirable), while Jordan does not and received a score of 0 (less desirable).

Source: Green Belt and Road Initiative Center, "Countries of the Belt and Road Initiative" webpage.[25]

D9. Political Stability and the Absence of Violence

This indicator measures perceptions of the likelihood of political instability and/or politically motivated violence, including terrorism. The normalized metric provides a mean score for each country for the years 2015–2019. The composite indicator includes measures of orderly transfers, armed conflict, violent demonstrations, social unrest, international tensions and terrorist threats, political terror scales, security risk ratings, intensity of internal conflicts, intensity of violent activities, intensity of social conflicts, government stability, internal conflict, external conflict, ethnic tensions, protests and riots, terrorism, interstate war, and civil war. Data are drawn from the Political Stability and Absence of Violence indicator in the World

---

Nations Pacific, "Nauru," webpage, 2021; Illana Gordon, "Welcome to Nauru, the Most Corrupt Country You've Never Heard Of," *Dose*, Medium, April 18, 2017.)

[22] The maximum value in our subset of 108 countries was 101,180 ($101.18 billion in Australia) and the minimum value was 0 (for 35 countries). Singapore had 36,200 in Chinese investment, which translated to a 0.36 normalized score. Malaysia had 19,270 in Chinese investment, which translated to a 0.19 normalized score.

[23] AEI, 2021 (data accessed on February 19, 2021). The data run through the end of the 2020 calendar year.

[24] The countries with conflicting information are Austria, Benin, Comoros, Democratic Republic of Congo, Dominica, Niger, and Russia.

[25] Green Belt and Road Initiative Center, 2020. We cross-checked this data set with a 2021 CFR report, which cited the Green Belt and Road Initiative Center list and the Chinese government's BRI website. However, the Chinese government's website does not consistently list countries with MOUs (Government of the People's Republic of China, "One Belt, One Road Portal" ["中国一带一路网"], webpage, undated; we provide the link to the English-language portal in the bibliographic entry). See also Hillman and Sacks, 2021, p. 14.

Bank's WGI, which range from approximately –2.8 (weak governance performance) to 2.0 (strong governance performance).[26]

How countries are scored: We normalized the World Bank's scores on the –2.5 to 2.5 scale to a scale of 0.00 to 1.00 based on the highest and lowest values of the 108 countries that we scored. Countries scored higher (more desirable) if they were more politically stable and saw less violence. For examples, Singapore had few incidents or perceptions of political instability and violence and scored a 1.49 over the specified period, equating to a normalized score of 0.99 (more desirable), while Syria had high scores for instability and violence and scored –2.79 over the same period, equating to a normalized score of 0.01 (less desirable). Indonesia received a –0.50 score from the World Bank, equating to a 0.53 normalized score; Tonga received a 0.92 score from the World Bank, resulting in a 0.86 normalized score.[27]

Source: World Bank's WGI, Political Stability and Absence of Violence indicator.[28]

D10. Risk of Climate Change

Risk of climate change for each country is measured as a composite variable that includes the projected percentage of a population occupying land vulnerable to sea level rise in 2050 and the projected annual number of days over 35 degrees Celsius in the 2040–2059 time frame. The value for a population occupying land vulnerable to sea level rise is created using a model with a moderate emissions scenario, which predicts a 2-degree Celsius temperature rise and a stable Arctic (sea model K14). The score indicates the percentage of the population living below the future-predicted local high tide line. The measure for annual number of days over 35 degrees Celsius (*hot temperature days*) uses the median projected value from up to 35 medium-low emission models.

How countries are scored: A 2019 *Nature Communications* study projects the percentage of the country's population occupying land vulnerable to sea level rise, and the World Bank's climate knowledge data predict the number of days per year of hot temperature days. We normalized the scores for both sea level rise and hot temperature days to a scale of 0.00 to 1.00 based on the highest and lowest values of the 108 countries that we scored. Then we calculated the average of the two scores for the final climate risk score. Countries scored lower risk (more desirable) if they had low scores and worse or more risky (less desirable) if they had high scores, which represent a higher projected percentage of a country's population occupying land vulnerable to sea level rise and a higher number of hot temperature days.

- Examples for sea level rise: Mongolia scored favorably with 0 percent of its population projected in the study to be vulnerable to sea level rise, receiving a 0.00 (more desirable) normalized score, while the Marshall Islands scored relatively poorly with 70 percent of its population projected to be vulnerable to sea level rise, receiving a 1.00 (less desirable) score. Relatively landlocked Iraq was projected to have 8 percent of its population vulnerable, receiving a 0.11 normalized score, while coastal Vietnam was projected to have 23 percent of its population vulnerable, receiving a 0.33 normalized score.[29]
- Examples for hot temperature days: Somalia scored the highest (less desirable) with 69.6 hot temperature days and received a score of 1.00. Japan is projected to have less than one hot temperature day, so

---

[26] Highest and lowest scores vary over time; we note recent ranges here, but the World Bank typically describes the range as –2.5 to 2.5.

[27] For this indicator, the maximum value in our subset of 108 countries was 1.54, and the minimum value was –2.84.

[28] World Bank, 2021a.

[29] For sea level rise vulnerability, the maximum value in our subset of 108 countries was 70 percent of the population projected to be vulnerable (Marshall Islands), and the minimum value was 0 percent projected to be vulnerable (for 31 countries).

its normalized score was 0.00 (more desirable). Egypt had 22 hot temperature days projected, receiving a 0.32 normalized score, while Kenya had 42 hot temperature days projected, receiving a 0.60 normalized score.[30]

Compared with some of the other indicators, a higher risk of climate change value indicates greater potential instability and risk and has a negative impact on desirability.

Sources: 2019 study in *Nature Communications* and the World Bank's climate knowledge portal.[31]

As noted above, the sea level rise score is 50 percent of a country's total score for climate risk. Because of missing data for projected sea level rise from the World Bank's climate knowledge portal, we imputed the following values through subject-matter expertise and analysis:[32]

- Democratic Republic of the Congo (DRC): 0.00[33]
- Yemen: 0.00.[34]

Feasibility Indicators

We also assessed the feasibility of countries for Chinese basing and access after reviewing official and semi-authoritative Chinese sources, which recognize that securing overseas basing or access requires significant host nation buy-in and support for both PLA presence and operations.[35] Specifically, we focused on whether China's ability to secure a PLA base, facility, or access in a given country is more or less politically feasible in terms of both requesting and securing a deal with a potential host nation to grant access. Feasibility is assessed using a composite score of the seven indicators listed in Table A.2.[36] The table illustrates the lowest and highest scores possible for each indicator.

---

[30] For number of hot temperature days, the maximum value in our subset of 108 countries was 69.6 days (Somalia), and the minimum value was 0 days (for 18 countries).

[31] Kulp and Strauss, 2019; World Bank Group, 2021.

[32] For DRC and Yemen, RAND staff with expertise on climate change and on Africa and the Middle East rated each country as "very low" (0.00), "low" (0.33), "high" (0.66), or "very high" (1.00) based on a review of quantitative and qualitative information on each relevant country. Consistent with the methodology used to impute unknown values for other variables (e.g., human development), these estimated scores have been applied to the raw data after they were normalized to a 0.00 to 1.00 scale.

[33] Our pre-normalized assessment for the DRC is a score of ~1.0 or less, corresponding to very low risk for sea level rise because of its small coastal population (less than 1 percent) and primarily landlocked borders. Indeed, the combined population of the country's two main ports, Matadi and Boma, is only about 343,000, or 0.04 percent of its total population of 86 million. Finally, we also considered the scores of several adjacent states along the West African coast. Neighboring Congo, which also lacks much coastline, scored 0 percent, while in nearby Namibia, Angola, and Gabon—adjacent countries on the western seaboard with much longer coastlines—an estimated 1 percent, 4 percent, and 4.5 percent of their populations, respectively, are at risk of sea level rise under moderate climate change scenarios through 2050. For these reasons, we judged that far less than 1 percent of DRC's population is at risk. We have thus imputed a normalized score of 0.00 for sea level rise risk for the DRC, although the real value of this probability is likely slightly higher than an absolute zero.

[34] Our pre-normalized assessment for Yemen is a score of ~1.0 or less, corresponding to very low risk for sea level rise. We based this score primarily on that of neighboring Oman (0.84) because of the two countries' similar geographic location and coastline. Moreover, Oman's capital of Muscat is closer to the coast than Yemen's capital of Sanaa, which is inland—potentially implying a lower per capita risk of sea level rise in Yemen than in Oman. We have thus imputed a normalized score of 0.00 for sea level rise risk for Yemen, although the real value of this probability is surely slightly higher than an absolute zero.

[35] For more information on these sources, see Chapter 3.

[36] The calculation for feasibility is the sum of scores for F1 through F7. The highest possible score is 3 (i.e., most feasible from China's perspective).

TABLE A.2
Feasibility Indicator Values

ID	Indicator	Score Value	Score Type
F1	Authoritarian regime	–1 to 0	Scale (normalized)
F2	Aligned voting with China	0 to 1	Scale (normalized)
F3	Perceptions of corruption	–1 to 0	Scale (normalized)
F4	Partner engagement	0 to 1	Scale (normalized)
F5	Arms sales or transfers	0 to 1	Scale (normalized)
F6	Tensions in relations	–1, –0.5, or 0	Value
F7	Official recognition of the PRC over the ROC (Taiwan)	–1 or 0	Binary

F1. Authoritarian Regime

For this indicator, we used 2021 global freedom score values, which measure a population's access to political rights and civil liberties. A country or territory is awarded 0 to 4 points for each of ten political rights indicators, which take the form of questions related to electoral process, political pluralism and participation, and functioning government. Similarly, a country is awarded a score of 0 to 4 on 15 civil liberties indicators, which include questions of freedom of expression and belief, associational and organizational rights, rule of law, and personal autonomy and individual rights. The highest possible score is 100 (40 for political rights and 60 for civil rights), which was then normalized to a score from 0.00–1.00.

How countries are scored: Countries scored better (more feasible) if they were more authoritarian. A higher indicator value indicates that the population has greater access to political rights and civil liberties, which has a negative impact on feasibility. For example, Saudi Arabia received a global freedom score of 7, equating to a normalized score of 0.07 (more feasible), while Australia received a global freedom score of 97, equating to a normalized score of 0.98 (less feasible). Burkina Faso received a global freedom score of 54, equating to a normalized score of 0.54, while Mozambique received a global freedom score of 43, equating to a normalized score of 0.43.[37]

Source: Freedom House's 2021 global freedom scores.[38]

F2. Aligned Voting with China

This indicator measures the alignment between a given country and China during roll-call votes in the UN General Assembly between 2011–2020. Values indicate the percentage of times in which a given country's votes aligned with those of China during this period.

How countries are scored: Countries scored higher (more feasible) if their voting records were more aligned with China's. For examples, Turkmenistan's averaged ten-year voting record aligned with China's 91 percent of the time, receiving a normalized score of 1.00 (more feasible), while Palau's voting record aligned with China's 52 percent of the time, receiving a normalized score of 0.18 (less feasible). Malaysia's voting aligned 87 percent of the time, corresponding to a 0.91 normalized score, while Japan's voting aligned 69 percent of the time, corresponding to a 0.54 normalized score.[39]

Source: UN General Assembly voting data.[40]

---

[37] The maximum value in our subset of 108 countries was 99 (New Zealand), and the minimum value was 1 (Syria).

[38] Freedom House, undated.

[39] For this indicator, the maximum value in our subset of 108 countries was 91-percent alignment (Turkmenistan), and the minimum value was 43-percent alignment (Micronesia).

[40] Voeten, Strezhnev, and Bailey, 2021.

F3. Perceptions of Corruption

This indicator provides a score using aggregated data from 13 sources on perceptions by businesspeople and country experts of the level of corruption in the public sector for each country. The sources include indices, assessments, and surveys that evaluate corruption based on perceptions of levels of bribery, diversion of public funds, use of public office for private gain, nepotism in the civil service, and state capture, as well as the strength of institutions and mechanisms intended to mitigate corruption. Each of the 13 sources is standardized to a 0 to 100 scale, then aggregated into a single Corruption Perception Index (CPI) score.

How countries are scored: Countries scored better (more feasible) if they were perceived to be more corrupt. We used the most recently available data at the time of this writing, which cover corruption between 2018–2020. A higher indicator value reflects low perceptions of corruption and has a negative impact on feasibility. For examples, Tajikistan scored a 25 on the CPI, equating to a normalized score of 0.17 or more perceptions of corruption (more feasible), while New Zealand scored an 88 on the CPI, equating to a 1.00 normalized score or very few perceptions of corruption (less feasible). Bangladesh scored a 26 on the CPI, equating to a normalized score of 0.18, while Ghana scored a 43 on the CPI, equating to a 0.41 normalized score.[41]

Source: Transparency International's CPI.[42]

Because of missing data in the CPI, we imputed the following values through subject-matter expertise and analysis:[43]

- Fiji: 0.33[44]
- Kiribati: 0.33[45]

---

[41] The maximum CPI value in our subset of 108 countries was 88 (New Zealand), and the minimum CPI value was 12 (Somalia and South Sudan).

[42] Transparency International, 2020.

[43] For the eight PICs and one African country listed here, RAND staff with expertise on PICs rated each country as "very high" perceptions of corruption (0.00), "high" perceptions of corruption (0.33), "low" perceptions of corruption (0.66), or "very low" perceptions of corruption (1.00) based on a review of qualitative information on each relevant country. For all nine countries, our analysis easily eliminated scores on the far ranges of corruption (0.00 and 1.00), and we assessed that all the PICs probably fell somewhere between 0.33 and 0.66 on the normalized scale. We note, however, that in several instance it was not clear whether to impute a 0.33 or 0.66. Consistent with the methodology that we used to impute unknown values for other variables (e.g., D7 human development), these estimated scores have been applied to the raw data set from Transparency International *after* it was normalized to a 0.00 to 1.00 scale.

[44] Our estimated score for Fiji is 0.33, corresponding to relatively high perceptions of corruption. This score is in part based on Freedom House's assessment that "safeguards against corruption are limited in their effectiveness" and "corruption remains a serious problem" in Fiji, including political corruption and corruption within the police force. It is also based on Transparency International's assessment that there exists high levels of bribery, nepotism, and cronyism, particularly in appointments and advancements in civil service positions and SOEs. That said, new anticorruption measures have been taken, particularly since the country's most recent coup in 2006. The Heritage Foundation also scores Fiji's "government integrity" on the slightly lower side (46.8 out of 100 possible), while the World Bank's WGI project scores Fiji as slightly strong in its "control of corruption" metric (scoring 0.56 on a scale of –2.5 = weak control to 2.5 = strong control). The following sources informed this analysis: Freedom House, "Fiji: Freedom in the World 2020," webpage, 2020a; Jorum Duri and Kaunain Rahman, "Pacific Island Countries: Overview of Corruption and Anti-Corruption," Bergen, Norway: CMI U4 Anti-Corruption Resource Centre and Transparency International, August 28, 2020; Heritage Foundation, 2021 (Index of Economic Freedom, "Government Integrity" indicator data); United Nations Office on Drugs and Crime, "Tackling Corruption, a Key to Recover with Integrity," December 9, 2020; U.S. Department of State, "2020 Country Reports on Human Rights Practices: Fiji," March 30, 2021a; World Bank, "Worldwide Governance Indicators," interactive data access tool, undated-c.

[45] Our estimated score for Kiribati is 0.33, corresponding to high perceptions of corruption. This score is in part based on the International Monetary Fund's assessment that "addressing governance deficiencies in budget outcomes and institutions would help improve efficiency and reduce vulnerabilities to corruption." The U.S. Department of State also noted that "officials sometimes engaged in corrupt practices with impunity." Transparency International assessed that "official corruption,

- Marshall Islands: 0.33[46]
- Nauru: 0.33[47]
- Palau: 0.33[48]
- Samoa: 0.33[49]
- Micronesia: 0.33[50]

nepotism, favouritism and other abuses of privilege, based on tribal and church ties, are major issues . . . [which are] exacerbated by poorly resourced oversight bodies that fail to carry out their anti-corruption mandates." The Heritage Foundation scores Kiribati's "government integrity" on the lower side (27.9 out of 100 possible), while the World Bank's Country Policy and Institutional Assessment (CPIA) index on transparency, accountability, and corruption in the public sector also ranks Kiribati relatively poorly (with a score of 3.5, where 1 = low corruption and 6 = high corruption). The World Bank's WGI project scores Kiribati somewhat more positively in its "control of corruption" metric (scoring 0.37 on a scale of –2.5 = weak control to 2.5 = strong control). The following sources informed this analysis: International Monetary Fund, "Kiribati: Staff Concluding Statement of the 2021 Article IV Mission," March 2, 2021; U.S. Department of State, "2020 Country Reports on Human Rights Practices: Kiribati," March 30, 2021b; Transparency International, 2020; Heritage Foundation, 2021; World Bank, "Country Policy and Institutional Assessment," webpage, undated-a; Duri and Rahman, 2020; Freedom House, "Kiribati: Freedom in the World 2020," webpage, 2020b; World Bank, undated-c.

[46] Our estimated score for the Marshall Islands is 0.33, corresponding to high perceptions of corruption. This score is in part based on the Freedom House's and the State Department's assessment that corruption is a "chronic problem." The World Bank's WGI scores the Marshall Islands as somewhat weak in its "control of corruption" metric (scoring –0.04 on a scale of –2.5 = weak control to 2.5 = strong control). The World Bank's CPIA index on transparency, accountability, and corruption in the public sector ranks the Marshall Islands relatively poorly (with a score of 3.5, where 1 = low corruption and 6 = high corruption). The following sources informed this analysis: Freedom House, "Marshall Islands: Freedom in the World 2020," webpage, 2020c; U.S. Department of State, "2020 Country Reports on Human Rights Practices: Marshall Islands," March 30, 2021c; World Bank, undated-c.

[47] Our estimated score for Nauru is 0.33, corresponding to high perceptions of corruption. This score is in part based on reporting regarding misuse of the funds from Nauru's Trust Fund and allegations regarding detention camps that Nauru hosts for Australia. It is also based on Freedom House's and Transparency International's assessment that "corruption is a persistent issue in the country." The World Bank's WGI project scores Nauru around the bottom third of countries worldwide in its "control of corruption" metric (scoring –0.45 on a scale of –2.5 = weak control to 2.5 = strong control). The following sources informed this analysis: Gordon, 2017; Peter Dauvergne, "A Dark History of the World's Smallest Island Nation," *MIT Press Reader*, July 22, 2019. See also Kaufmann and Kraay, 2020; U.S. Department of State, "2020 Country Reports on Human Rights Practices: Nauru," March 30, 2021e; Duri and Rahman, 2020.

[48] Our estimated score for Palau is 0.33, corresponding to high perceptions of corruption. This score is in part based on the U.S. Department of State's assessment that "government corruption was a problem, and the government took some steps to address it." The World Bank's WGI project scores Palau around the bottom third of countries worldwide in its "control of corruption" metric (scoring –0.45 on a scale of –2.5 = weak control to 2.5 = strong control). The following sources informed this analysis: U.S. Department of State, "2020 Country Reports on Human Rights Practices: Palau," March 30, 2021f; World Bank, undated-c; Freedom House, "Palau: Freedom in the World 2020," webpage, 2020e.

[49] Our estimated score for Samoa is 0.33, corresponding to high perceptions of corruption. This score is in part based on Freedom House's assessment that "corruption remains a problem and a cause of public discontent, and the government has at times resisted calls for a stronger response." It is also based on the Heritage Foundation's and Transparency International's assessment that "official corruption is still a major cause of public concern," particularly over abuse of public funds and resources. The Heritage Foundation also scores Samoa's "government integrity" on the lower side (32.7 out of 100 possible), while the World Bank's CPIA index on transparency, accountability, and corruption in the public sector also ranks Samoa relatively poorly (with a score of 4.0, where 1 = low corruption and 6 = high corruption). The World Bank's WGI project scores Samoa somewhat more positively in its "control of corruption" metric (scoring 0.56 on a scale of –2.5 = weak control to 2.5 = strong control). The following sources informed this analysis: Freedom House, "Samoa: Freedom in the World 2020," webpage, 2020f; Duri and Rahman, 2020; Heritage Foundation, 2021 (Index of Economic Freedom, "Government Integrity" indicator data); U.S. Department of State, "2020 Country Reports on Human Rights Practices: Samoa," March 30, 2021g; World Bank, undated-a; and World Bank, undated-c.

[50] Our estimated score for Micronesia is 0.33, corresponding to high perceptions of corruption. This score is in part based on Freedom House's assessment that "official corruption is a problem and a source of public discontent. Complaints about misuse of public resources are frequent." The Heritage Foundation also scores Micronesia's "government integrity" on the

- Tonga: 0.33[51]
- Tuvalu: 0.66.[52]

F4. Partner Engagement

This indicator provides a composite value that includes measures of the frequency of meetings between the CCP International Department and officials in other countries, as well as the number of military engagements that a country has participated in with China. Meetings with CCP leaders is a normalized value drawn from a data set capturing the 2002–2017 period. Military engagement is a normalized value drawn from 2009–2019 data and includes military exercises, naval ports of call, and senior level visits between PLA and partner country officials.

How countries are scored: The studies tallied the number of political and military engagements per country, respectively. We normalized the scores for both to a scale of 0.00 to 1.00 based on the highest and lowest values of the 108 countries that we scored. Then we calculated the average of the two scores for the final partner engagement score. Countries scored higher (more feasible) if they have held a higher number of meetings with CCP International Department and foreign representatives. Countries scored higher (more feasible) if they conducted more military exercises, naval ports of call, and senior level visits with the PLA.

- Examples for political engagement: Cambodia had 83 engagements during the specified period and scored a 0.61 on the normalized scale (more feasible), while Kuwait had zero engagements during the

---

lower side (25 out of 100 possible), while the World Bank's CPIA index on transparency, accountability, and corruption in the public sector also ranks Micronesia relatively poorly (with a score of 3.5, where 1 = low corruption and 6 = high corruption). The World Bank's WGI project scores Micronesia somewhat more positively in its "control of corruption" metric (scoring 0.75 on a scale of –2.5 = weak control to 2.5 = strong control). The following sources informed this analysis: Freedom House, "Micronesia: Freedom in the World 2020," webpage, 2020d; Heritage Foundation, 2021 (Index of Economic Freedom, "Government Integrity" indicator data); U.S. Department of State, "2020 Country Reports on Human Rights Practices: Micronesia," March 30, 2021d; World Bank, undated-c.

[51] Our estimated score for Tonga is 0.33, corresponding to high perceptions of corruption. This score is in part based on Freedom House's assessment that "corruption and abuse of office are serious problems. While public officials and leaders of state-owned companies are sometimes held to account for bribery and other malfeasance, anticorruption mechanisms are generally weak and lacking in resources." It is also based on the Heritage Foundation's and the U.S. Department of State's assessment that "corruption and abuse of office are major issues in the country." The World Bank's WGI project scores Tonga around the 42nd percentile of countries worldwide in its "control of corruption" metric (scoring –0.35 on a scale of –2.5 = weak control to 2.5 = strong control). The Heritage Foundation also scores Tonga's "government integrity" on the lower side (44.6 out of 100 possible), while the World Bank's CPIA index on transparency, accountability, and corruption in the public sector also ranks Tonga relatively poorly (with a score of 3.5, where 1 = low corruption and 6 = high corruption). The following sources informed this analysis: Freedom House, "Tonga: Freedom in the World 2020," webpage, 2020g; Duri and Rahman, 2020; World Bank, undated-c; Heritage Foundation, 2021 (Index of Economic Freedom, "Government Integrity" indicator data); U.S. Department of State, "2020 Country Reports on Human Rights Practices: Tonga," undated-a; World Bank, 2020.

[52] Our estimated score for Tuvalu is 0.66, corresponding to low perceptions of corruption. This score is in part based the U.S. Department of State's assessment that "the law provides criminal penalties for some forms of corruption by officials such as theft, and the government generally implemented the law effectively. There were no reports of government corruption during the year." It is also based on Freedom House's and Transparency International's assessment that "corruption is not a significant challenge on the island." The World Bank's WGI project scores Tuvalu somewhat positively in its "control of corruption" metric (scoring 0.41 on a scale of –2.5 = weak control to 2.5 = strong control). However, the World Bank's CPIA index on transparency, accountability, and corruption in the public sector ranks Tuvalu more poorly (with a score of 3.5, where 1 = low corruption and 6 = high corruption). The following sources informed this analysis: U.S. Department of State, "2020 Country Reports on Human Rights Practices: Tuvalu," undated-b; Duri and Rahman, 2020; Freedom House, "Tuvalu: Freedom in the World 2020," webpage, 2020h.

same period and scored a 0.00 (less feasible). Bangladesh had 27 meetings, resulting in a 0.20 normalized score, while Eritrea had only eight meetings, resulting in a 0.06 normalized score.[53]

- Examples for military engagement: Singapore conducted 53 relevant activities during the specified period and scored a 0.57 on the normalized scale (more feasible), while Turkmenistan conducted three activities during the same period and scored a 0.04 (less feasible). India had 30 engagements, resulting in a 0.33 normalized score, while Bangladesh had 27 engagements, resulting in a 0.29 normalized score.[54]

Sources: 2020 study in *International Studies Quarterly*; and National Defense University, *Chinese Military Diplomacy, 2003–2016: Trends and Implications*, 2017, with an updated data set through 2019.[55]

F5. Arms Sales or Transfers

This indicator provides a normalized value for the total trend indicator value (TIV) of major conventional arms transfers from China to a given country between 2000–2020 in millions of U.S. dollars.[56] Zero scores can indicate that the value of deliveries is less than $0.5 million.

How countries are scored: Countries scored higher (more feasible) if they purchased a higher value of arms from China. For example, with 8,777 TIV (an assessed value of roughly $8.8 billion dollars) in arms transfers, Pakistan scored a 1.00 on the normalized scale (more feasible), while Ghana had 130 TIV and scored a 0.01 on the normalized scale (less feasible).[57] Bangladesh had a TIV of 2,605, or a 0.33 a normalized score, while Myanmar had a TIV of 1,439, or a 0.19 normalized score.

Source: SIPRI arms transfers database.[58]

F6. Tensions in Relations

This indicator provides a composite value that includes a binary value of whether a country has a contiguous border with a major power (Russia or the United States) and a binary value of whether the country has engaged in conflict opposite China between 1949 and 2007.

How countries are scored: Countries scored better (more feasible) if they were not contiguous with Russia or the United States. Countries also scored better (more feasible) if they had not fought a war with China between 1949 and 2007. For example, Kazakhstan scored a 0.5 because of its contiguous border with Russia (less feasible), while Iraq had no contiguous border or past conflict and scored a zero (more feasible). A higher

---

[53] The maximum value in our subset of 108 countries was 136 political engagements (Japan), and the minimum value was 0 engagements (multiple countries).

[54] The maximum value in our subset of 108 countries was 92 military engagements (Pakistan), and the minimum value was 0 engagements (multiple countries).

[55] Hackenesch and Bader, 2020; Allen, Saunders, and Chen, 2017. National Defense University provided us with an interim update of the Allen, Saunders, and Chen data set that included information through calendar year 2019. A newer version with 2020 and 2021 data is forthcoming. See Center for the Study of Chinese Military Affairs, Chinese Military Diplomacy Database, version 4.00, National Defense University, forthcoming.

[56] SIPRI uses the TIV to estimate prices of like equipment across countries, because sometimes the deal amount is not known or the equipment may be provided at below-market rates. It provides these TIV amounts in millions of U.S. dollars. In other words, SIPRI is assessing the equipment value provided across countries rather than the stated or unstated dollar amounts of military aid and/or sales programs.

[57] The maximum value in our subset of 108 countries was 8,777 TIV (Pakistan), and the minimum value was 0 TIV (multiple countries). Zero scores can indicate that the value of deliveries is less than $0.5 million.

[58] SIPRI, undated. Data retrieved on March 15, 2021.

composite value indicates greater historical and/or current frictions with countries or powerful neighbors and has a negative impact on feasibility.

Source: Authors' analysis of geographic borders using ArcGIS and Correlates of War's interstate war data.[59]

F7. Official Recognition of the PRC over the ROC

This indicator provides a binary value indicating whether a country has full diplomatic relations with the PRC over the ROC (Taiwan).

How countries are scored: This is a binary indicator for all countries scored except Bhutan.[60] A higher indicator value signifies there are formal obstacles to building relations with the PRC and its military given the lack of diplomatic relations. Countries scored lower (more feasible) if they recognize mainland China instead of Taiwan. Countries scored higher (less feasible) if they maintain full diplomatic relations with Taiwan.

Source: Ministry of Foreign Affairs of the ROC website.[61]

---

[59] ArcGIS, undated; Sarkees and Wayman, 2010.

[60] Bhutan does not have official diplomatic relations with either China or Taiwan, and Bhutan is required under Article 2 of the 2007 India-Bhutan Friendship Treaty to "cooperate closely with [India] on issues relating to [both countries'] national interests," including matters of foreign policy (Ministry of External Affairs of the Government of India, India-Bhutan Friendship Treaty, March 2, 2007, p. 1). However, India and China have official diplomatic relations, and Bhutan and China have carried out 24 rounds of ministerial-level talks to resolve their mutual border dispute. For the purposes of this analysis, we have scored Bhutan as a 0.5. However, even if we scored it a 0.00 (full PRC relations and no Taiwan relations) or a 1.00 (no PRC relations and full Taiwan relations), Bhutan would still score in Tier 4 for feasibility (i.e., the bottom 25 percent of countries scored) and would therefore be excluded from our top-ranked potential host nations.

[61] Ministry of Foreign Affairs of the ROC, undated.

Country Scores

This appendix contains the scores for the 108 countries that we scored across our 17 framework indicators, focusing on two dimensions: desirability and feasibility. For more information on our framework, see Chapter 3 and Appendix A. Table B.1 provides each country's region (based on its location within a U.S. combatant command AOR), each country's total score for each dimension, and the tier (quartile) in which each country ranked. Tier 1 consists of the top 25 percent of countries (i.e., countries 1–27 of 108). Each tier contains 27 countries.

Table B.2 provides each country's scores for each of the ten desirability indicators. Table B.3 provides each country's scores for each of the seven feasibility indicators.

TABLE B.1

Country-Level Composite Scores and Tiers, by Dimension

Country	U.S. Combatant Command	Desirability		Feasibility	
		Total Score	Tier (Quartile)	Total Score	Tier (Quartile)
Afghanistan	CENTCOM	2.157	4	0.656	1
Algeria	AFRICOM	2.915	3	0.524	2
Angola	AFRICOM	3.808	2	0.556	2
Australia	INDOPACOM	4.690	1	−1.609	4
Bahrain	CENTCOM	4.142	1	0.408	2
Bangladesh	INDOPACOM	4.641	1	0.950	1
Benin	AFRICOM	1.479	4	−0.153	3
Bhutan	INDOPACOM	2.357	3	−0.950	4
Botswana	AFRICOM	2.167	3	−0.457	4
Brunei	INDOPACOM	5.759	1	0.116	3
Burkina Faso	AFRICOM	0.137	4	0.011	3
Burundi	AFRICOM	1.298	4	0.800	1
Cambodia	INDOPACOM	5.875	1	1.146	1
Cameroon	AFRICOM	2.537	3	0.451	2
Cape Verde	AFRICOM	3.318	2	−0.599	4
Central African Republic	AFRICOM	−0.105	4	0.512	2
Chad	AFRICOM	1.130	4	0.650	1
Comoros	AFRICOM	1.876	4	0.371	2
Congo (DRC)	AFRICOM	1.271	4	0.621	1
Congo, Republic of	AFRICOM	2.819	3	0.715	1
Cote d'Ivoire	AFRICOM	2.335	3	0.061	3
Djibouti	AFRICOM	3.383	2	0.701	1
Egypt	CENTCOM	2.775	3	0.659	1
Equatorial Guinea	AFRICOM	2.968	2	0.876	1

Table B.1—Continued

Country	U.S. Combatant Command	Desirability		Feasibility	
		Total Score	Tier (Quartile)	Total Score	Tier (Quartile)
Eritrea	AFRICOM	1.326	4	0.851	1
Eswatini (Swaziland)	AFRICOM	0.830	4	−0.561	4
Ethiopia	AFRICOM	1.249	4	0.024	3
Fiji	INDOPACOM	3.437	2	−0.026	3
Gabon	AFRICOM	3.173	2	0.499	2
Gambia	AFRICOM	2.322	3	0.142	3
Ghana	AFRICOM	2.682	3	−0.309	4
Guinea	AFRICOM	2.335	3	0.383	2
Guinea-Bissau	AFRICOM	1.183	4	0.378	2
India	INDOPACOM	3.923	2	−0.310	4
Indonesia	INDOPACOM	6.280	1	0.393	2
Iran	CENTCOM	3.975	2	0.839	1
Iraq	CENTCOM	2.563	3	0.575	2
Japan	INDOPACOM	4.929	1	−0.646	4
Jordan	CENTCOM	2.989	2	0.102	3
Kazakhstan	CENTCOM	3.531	2	0.077	3
Kenya	AFRICOM	3.455	2	0.304	2
Kiribati	INDOPACOM	3.127	2	−0.620	4
Kuwait	CENTCOM	4.298	1	0.177	3
Kyrgyzstan	CENTCOM	3.059	2	0.592	2
Laos	INDOPACOM	3.142	2	1.135	1
Lebanon	CENTCOM	3.792	2	0.398	2
Lesotho	AFRICOM	1.826	4	−0.058	3
Liberia	AFRICOM	2.508	3	−0.052	3
Libya	AFRICOM	2.542	3	0.757	1
Madagascar	AFRICOM	2.754	3	0.113	3
Malawi	AFRICOM	0.615	4	−0.047	3
Malaysia	INDOPACOM	5.595	1	0.174	3
Maldives	INDOPACOM	5.026	1	0.143	3
Mali	AFRICOM	1.055	4	0.393	2
Marshall Islands	INDOPACOM	2.883	3	−2.159	4
Mauritania	AFRICOM	2.413	3	0.377	2
Mauritius	AFRICOM	2.591	3	−0.459	4
Micronesia (Federated States of)	INDOPACOM	4.209	1	−1.259	4
Mongolia	INDOPACOM	3.458	2	−0.471	4
Morocco	AFRICOM	2.935	2	0.318	2
Mozambique	AFRICOM	2.416	3	0.476	2
Myanmar	INDOPACOM	5.652	1	0.929	1
Namibia	AFRICOM	4.047	1	−0.190	4
Nauru	INDOPACOM	2.355	3	−1.945	4
Nepal	INDOPACOM	2.805	3	0.321	2
New Zealand	INDOPACOM	4.006	2	−1.194	4
Niger	AFRICOM	0.249	4	0.225	3
Nigeria	AFRICOM	2.255	3	0.395	2

Table B.1—Continued

Country	U.S. Combatant Command	Desirability		Feasibility	
		Total Score	Tier (Quartile)	Total Score	Tier (Quartile)
North Korea	INDOPACOM	1.848	4	0.602	1
Oman	CENTCOM	4.377	1	0.328	2
Pakistan	CENTCOM	4.415	1	1.995	1
Palau	INDOPACOM	4.574	1	−2.074	4
Papua New Guinea	INDOPACOM	3.766	2	−0.007	3
Philippines	INDOPACOM	4.974	1	−0.275	4
Qatar	CENTCOM	4.516	1	0.027	3
Rwanda	AFRICOM	1.933	4	0.035	3
Samoa	INDOPACOM	3.409	2	−0.346	4
Sao Tome and Principe	AFRICOM	2.096	4	−0.362	4
Saudi Arabia	CENTCOM	4.256	1	0.413	2
Senegal	AFRICOM	2.450	3	−0.179	3
Seychelles	AFRICOM	4.511	1	−0.563	4
Sierra Leone	AFRICOM	2.442	3	0.027	3
Singapore	INDOPACOM	7.303	1	−0.180	3
Solomon Islands	INDOPACOM	4.011	2	−0.375	4
Somalia	AFRICOM	1.608	4	0.880	1
South Africa	AFRICOM	3.141	2	0.025	3
South Korea	INDOPACOM	5.788	1	−1.232	4
South Sudan	AFRICOM	−0.271	4	0.653	1
Sri Lanka	INDOPACOM	5.246	1	0.335	2
Sudan	AFRICOM	2.171	3	0.958	1
Syria	CENTCOM	2.207	3	1.021	1
Tajikistan	CENTCOM	3.936	2	0.876	1
Tanzania	AFRICOM	3.739	2	0.498	2
Thailand	INDOPACOM	5.908	1	0.276	2
Timor Leste	INDOPACOM	4.026	1	−0.156	3
Togo	AFRICOM	2.334	3	0.180	3
Tonga	INDOPACOM	3.435	2	−0.363	4
Tunisia	AFRICOM	2.883	3	−0.195	4
Turkmenistan	CENTCOM	2.070	4	0.963	1
Tuvalu	INDOPACOM	1.866	4	−1.799	4
Uganda	AFRICOM	1.668	4	0.447	2
UAE	CENTCOM	5.574	1	0.043	3
Uzbekistan	CENTCOM	3.031	2	0.778	1
Vanuatu	INDOPACOM	4.165	1	−0.435	4
Vietnam	INDOPACOM	2.036	4	0.638	1
Yemen	CENTCOM	2.937	2	0.843	1
Zambia	AFRICOM	1.848	4	0.233	2
Zimbabwe	AFRICOM	1.618	4	0.693	1

TABLE B.2
Country-Level Scores, by Desirability Indicator

Country	Military Utility						Economic Utility		Political and Other Risks		Total Desirability Score
	D1. Known Chinese Interest in Basing and Access	D2. Within Rapid Steaming Distance of China	D3. Within Military Airlift Range of China	D4. Coastal Country	D5. Close Proximity Penalty	D6. Level of Human Development	D7. Level of Chinese Investment	D8. BRI Member or Participant	D9. Political Stability and Absence of Violence	D10. Risk of Climate Change	
Afghanistan	0	0	1	0	0	0.21	0.03	1	0.03	0.12	2.157
Algeria	0	0	0	1	0	0.64	0.00	1	0.42	0.15	2.915
Angola	1	0	0	1	0	0.34	0.04	1	0.57	0.14	3.808
Australia	0	1	0	1	0	1.00	1.00	0	0.87	0.18	4.690
Bahrain	0	0	1	1	0	0.83	0.00	1	0.45	0.14	4.142
Bangladesh	0	1	1	1	0	0.43	0.06	1	0.39	0.25	4.641
Benin	0	0	0	1	0	0.27	0.00	0	0.63	0.42	1.479
Bhutan	0	0	1	0	0	0.47	0.00	0	0.90	0.01	2.357
Botswana	0	0	0	0	0	0.62	0.00	1	0.88	0.33	2.167
Brunei	0	1	1	1	0	0.81	0.03	1	0.92	0.00	5.759
Burkina Faso	0	0	0	0	0	0.11	0.00	0	0.44	0.40	0.137
Burundi	0	0	0	0	0	0.07	0.00	1	0.23	0.00	1.298
Cambodia	1	1	1	1	0	0.36	0.09	1	0.67	0.25	5.875
Cameroon	0	1	0	1	0	0.31	0.02	1	0.37	0.16	2.537
Cape Verde	0	0	0	1	0	0.49	0.00	1	0.84	0.02	3.318
Central African Republic	0	0	0	0	0	0.01	0.00	0	0.19	0.30	−0.105
Chad	0	0	0	0	0	0.01	0.01	1	0.36	0.25	1.130
Comoros	0	0	0	1	0	0.29	0.00	0	0.62	0.03	1.876
Congo (DRC)	0	0	0	1	0	0.16	0.12	0	0.16	0.17	1.271
Congo (Republic of)	0	0	0	1	0	0.33	0.02	1	0.52	0.05	2.819
Cote d'Ivoire	0	0	0	1	0	0.26	0.00	1	0.43	0.36	2.335
Djibouti	1	0	0	1	0	0.24	0.00	1	0.54	0.40	3.383
Egypt	0	0	0	1	0	0.57	0.06	1	0.35	0.20	2.775
Equatorial Guinea	0	0	0	1	0	0.36	0.00	1	0.61	0.00	2.968
Eritrea	0	0	0	1	0	0.12	0.00	0	0.48	0.28	1.326
Eswatini	0	0	0	0	0	0.39	0.00	0	0.56	0.12	0.830

Table B.2—Continued

Country	Military Utility						Economic Utility		Political and Other Risks		Total Desirability Score
	D1. Known Chinese Interest in Basing and Access	D2. Within Rapid Steaming Distance of China	D3. Within Military Airlift Range of China	D4. Coastal Country	D5. Close Proximity Penalty	D6. Level of Human Development	D7. Level of Chinese Investment	D8. BRI Member or Participant	D9. Political Stability and Absence of Violence	D10. Risk of Climate Change	
Ethiopia	0	0	0	0	0	0.17	0.01	1	0.31	0.24	1.249
Fiji	0	0	0	1	0	0.63	0.00	1	0.83	0.02	3.437
Gabon	0	0	0	1	0	0.56	0.00	1	0.62	0.01	3.173
Gambia	0	0	0	1	0	0.19	0.00	1	0.63	0.49	2.322
Ghana	0	0	0	1	0	0.39	0.02	1	0.65	0.38	2.682
Guinea	0	0	0	1	0	0.15	0.06	1	0.50	0.38	2.335
Guinea-Bissau	0	0	0	1	0	0.16	0.00	0	0.53	0.50	1.183
India	0	1	1	1	0	0.46	0.16	0	0.45	0.15	3.923
Indonesia	1	1	1	1	0	0.59	0.24	1	0.53	0.09	6.280
Iran	0	1	1	1	0	0.71	0.05	1	0.39	0.17	3.975
Iraq	0	0	0	1	0	0.51	0.12	1	0.10	0.16	2.563
Japan	0	1	1	1	0	0.95	0.11	0	0.89	0.02	4.929
Jordan	0	0	1	1	0	0.61	0.02	0	0.54	0.18	2.989
Kazakhstan	0	0	1	0	0	0.78	0.19	1	0.64	0.09	3.531
Kenya	1	0	0	1	0	0.38	0.01	1	0.37	0.30	3.455
Kiribati	0	0	0	1	0	0.43	0.00	1	0.87	0.17	3.127
Kuwait	0	0	1	1	0	0.75	0.01	1	0.65	0.11	4.298
Kyrgyzstan	0	0	1	0	0	0.55	0.01	1	0.51	0.01	3.059
Laos	0	0	1	0	0	0.40	0.12	1	0.76	0.13	3.142
Lebanon	0	0	1	1	0	0.64	0.00	1	0.27	0.12	3.792
Lesotho	0	0	0	0	0	0.24	0.00	1	0.59	0.01	1.826
Liberia	0	0	0	1	0	0.16	0.01	1	0.55	0.21	2.508
Libya	0	0	0	1	0	0.60	0.00	1	0.11	0.16	2.542
Madagascar	0	0	0	1	0	0.24	0.00	1	0.56	0.06	2.754
Malawi	0	0	0	0	0	0.16	0.00	0	0.60	0.15	0.615
Malaysia	0	1	1	1	0	0.76	0.19	1	0.69	0.04	5.595
Maldives	0	1	1	1	0	0.63	0.00	1	0.70	0.31	5.026
Mali	0	0	0	0	0	0.07	0.00	1	0.22	0.23	1.055

Table B.2—Continued

Country	Military Utility						Economic Utility			Political and Other Risks		Total Desirability Score
	D1. Known Chinese Interest in Basing and Access	D2. Within Rapid Steaming Distance of China	D3. Within Military Airlift Range of China	D4. Coastal Country	D5. Close Proximity Penalty	D6. Level of Human Development	D7. Level of Chinese Investment	D8. BRI Member or Participant		D9. Political Stability and Absence of Violence	D10. Risk of Climate Change	
Marshall Islands	0	1	0	1	0	0.56	0.00	0		0.82	0.50	2.883
Mauritania	0	0	0	1	0	0.28	0.00	1		0.50	0.37	2.413
Mauritius	0	0	0	1	0	0.75	0.01	0		0.86	0.03	2.591
Micronesia	0	1	1	1	0	0.41	0.00	0		0.91	0.11	4.209
Mongolia	0	0	1	0	0	0.62	0.05	1		0.82	0.03	3.458
Morocco	0	0	0	1	0	0.53	0.00	1		0.57	0.17	2.935
Mozambique	0	0	0	1	0	0.11	0.05	1		0.46	0.21	2.416
Myanmar	1	1	1	1	0	0.34	0.07	1		0.39	0.15	5.652
Namibia	1	0	0	1	0	0.46	0.03	1		0.80	0.24	4.047
Nauru	0	0	0	1	0	0.67	0.00	0		0.80	0.11	2.355
Nepal	0	0	1	0	0	0.38	0.01	1		0.48	0.06	2.805
New Zealand	0	0	0	1	0	0.98	0.04	1		1.00	0.01	4.006
Niger	0	0	0	0	0	0.00	0.05	0		0.37	0.17	0.249
Nigeria	0	0	0	1	0	0.26	0.13	1		0.20	0.33	2.255
North Korea	0	1	1	1	3	0.33	0.02	1		0.51	0.02	1.848
Oman	0	0	0	1	0	0.76	0.01	1		0.81	0.21	4.377
Pakistan	1	0	1	1	0	0.30	0.15	1		0.11	0.13	4.415
Palau	0	1	1	1	0	0.79	0.00	0		0.85	0.06	4.574
Papua New Guinea	0	1	0	1	0	0.29	0.02	1		0.50	0.05	3.766
Philippines	0	1	1	1	0	0.59	0.04	1		0.40	0.05	4.974
Qatar	0	0	1	1	0	0.83	0.00	1		0.83	0.14	4.516
Rwanda	0	0	0	0	0	0.27	0.00	1		0.66	0.00	1.933
Samoa	0	0	0	1	0	0.58	0.00	1		0.92	0.09	3.409
Sao Tome and Principe	0	0	0	1	0	0.42	0.00	0		0.72	0.05	2.096
Saudi Arabia	0	0	1	1	0	0.84	0.06	1		0.53	0.17	4.256
Senegal	0	0	0	1	0	0.21	0.00	1		0.63	0.39	2.450

Table B.2—Continued

Country	Military Utility						Economic Utility		Political and Other Risks		Total Desirability Score
	D1. Known Chinese Interest in Basing and Access	D2. Within Rapid Steaming Distance of China	D3. Within Military Airlift Range of China	D4. Coastal Country	D5. Close Proximity Penalty	D6. Level of Human Development	D7. Level of Chinese Investment	D8. BRI Member or Participant	D9. Political Stability and Absence of Violence	D10. Risk of Climate Change	
Seychelles	1	0	0	1	0	0.73	0.00	1	0.81	0.03	4.511
Sierra Leone	0	0	0	1	0	0.11	0.04	1	0.63	0.33	2.442
Singapore	1	1	1	1	0	0.99	0.36	1	0.99	0.03	7.303
Solomon Islands	1	0	0	1	0	0.31	0.00	1	0.75	0.05	4.011
Somalia	0	0	0	1	0	0.00	0.00	1	0.12	0.51	1.608
South Africa	0	0	0	1	0	0.57	0.12	1	0.60	0.15	3.141
South Korea	0	1	1	1	0	0.95	0.12	1	0.73	0.01	5.788
South Sudan	0	0	0	0	0	0.07	0.00	0	0.09	0.43	-0.271
Sri Lanka	1	1	1	1	0	0.71	0.05	1	0.63	0.14	5.246
Sudan	0	0	0	1	0	0.21	0.00	1	0.19	0.23	2.171
Syria	0	0	1	1	0	0.31	0.04	0	0.01	0.15	2.207
Tajikistan	1	0	1	0	0	0.50	0.00	1	0.48	0.05	3.936
Tanzania	1	0	0	1	0	0.25	0.04	1	0.54	0.09	3.739
Thailand	1	1	1	1	0	0.70	0.05	1	0.46	0.30	5.908
Timor Leste	0	1	0	1	0	0.39	0.00	1	0.66	0.02	4.026
Togo	0	0	0	1	0	0.22	0.00	1	0.51	0.40	2.334
Tonga	0	0	0	1	0	0.60	0.00	1	0.86	0.03	3.435
Tunisia	0	0	0	1	0	0.63	0.00	1	0.43	0.17	2.883
Turkmenistan	0	0	1	0	0	0.58	0.01	0	0.63	0.15	2.070
Tuvalu	0	0	0	1	0	0.33	0.00	0	0.95	0.42	1.866
Uganda	0	0	0	0	0	0.27	0.05	1	0.49	0.14	1.668
UAE	1	0	1	1	0	0.90	0.08	1	0.80	0.21	5.574
Uzbekistan	0	0	1	0	0	0.59	0.01	1	0.58	0.16	3.031
Vanuatu	1	0	0	1	0	0.39	0.00	1	0.81	0.04	4.165
Vietnam	0	1	1	1	3	0.56	0.07	1	0.69	0.28	2.036
Yemen	0	0	1	1	0	0.14	0.00	1	0.00	0.21	2.937
Zambia	0	0	0	0	0	0.35	0.03	1	0.67	0.20	1.848
Zimbabwe	0	0	0	0	0	0.32	0.02	1	0.48	0.21	1.618

Table B.3. Country-Level Scores, by Feasibility Indicator

Country	Regime Alignment with the PRC			China's Influence in the Country		Potential Obstacles in Relationship			Total Feasibility Score
	F1. Authoritarian Regime	F2. Aligned Voting with China	F3. Perceptions of Corruption	F4. Partner Engagement	F5. Arms Sales or Transfers	F6. Tensions in Relations	F7. Official Recognition of the PRC over the ROC		
Afghanistan	0.27	0.95	0.09	0.06	0.00	0.0	0.0		0.656
Algeria	0.32	0.96	0.32	0.08	0.12	0.0	0.0		0.524
Angola	0.31	0.95	0.20	0.10	0.01	0.0	0.0		0.556
Australia	0.98	0.26	0.86	0.47	0.00	0.5	0.0		-1.609
Bahrain	0.11	0.90	0.39	0.01	0.00	0.0	0.0		0.408
Bangladesh	0.39	0.95	0.18	0.25	0.33	0.0	0.0		0.950
Benin	0.65	0.88	0.38	0.01	0.00	0.0	0.0		-0.153
Bhutan	0.61	0.90	0.74	0.00	0.00	0.0	0.5		-0.950
Botswana	0.72	0.88	0.63	0.02	0.00	0.0	0.0		-0.457
Brunei	0.28	0.96	0.63	0.07	0.00	0.0	0.0		0.116
Burkina Faso	0.54	0.92	0.37	0.00	0.00	0.0	0.0		0.011
Burundi	0.13	0.97	0.09	0.05	0.00	0.0	0.0		0.800
Cambodia	0.23	1.00	0.12	0.49	0.01	0.0	0.0		1.146
Cameroon	0.15	0.72	0.17	0.03	0.02	0.0	0.0		0.451
Cape Verde	0.93	0.89	0.61	0.05	0.00	0.0	0.0		-0.599
Central African Republic	0.08	0.77	0.18	0.01	0.00	0.0	0.0		0.512
Chad	0.16	0.91	0.12	0.01	0.01	0.0	0.0		0.650
Comoros	0.42	0.91	0.12	0.00	0.00	0.0	0.0		0.371
Congo (DRC)	0.19	0.84	0.08	0.05	0.00	0.0	0.0		0.621
Congo (Republic of)	0.19	0.94	0.09	0.06	0.00	0.0	0.0		0.715
Cote d'Ivoire	0.44	0.80	0.32	0.01	0.00	0.0	0.0		0.061
Djibouti	0.23	0.90	0.20	0.23	0.00	0.0	0.0		0.701
Egypt	0.17	0.92	0.28	0.13	0.05	0.0	0.0		0.659
Equatorial Guinea	0.04	0.92	0.05	0.04	0.00	0.0	0.0		0.876
Eritrea	0.01	0.95	0.12	0.03	0.00	0.0	0.0		0.851
Eswatini	0.18	0.90	0.28	0.00	0.00	0.0	1.0		-0.561
Ethiopia	0.21	0.93	0.34	0.15	0.01	0.5	0.0		0.024

Table B.3—Continued

Country	Regime Alignment with the PRC			China's Influence in the Country		Potential Obstacles in Relationship		Total Feasibility Score
	F1. Authoritarian Regime	F2. Aligned Voting with China	F3. Perceptions of Corruption	F4. Partner Engagement	F5. Arms Sales or Transfers	F6. Tensions in Relations	F7. Official Recognition of the PRC over the ROC	
Fiji	0.60	0.85	0.33	0.05	0.00	0.0	0.0	-0.026
Gabon	0.21	0.87	0.24	0.07	0.00	0.0	0.0	0.499
Gambia	0.46	0.93	0.33	0.00	0.00	0.0	0.0	0.142
Ghana	0.83	0.86	0.41	0.05	0.01	0.0	0.0	-0.309
Guinea	0.38	0.95	0.21	0.02	0.00	0.0	0.0	0.383
Guinea-Bissau	0.44	0.89	0.09	0.01	0.00	0.0	0.0	0.378
India	0.67	0.87	0.37	0.36	0.00	0.5	0.0	-0.310
Indonesia	0.59	0.92	0.33	0.35	0.04	0.0	0.0	0.393
Iran	0.15	0.96	0.17	0.11	0.09	0.0	0.0	0.839
Iraq	0.29	0.94	0.12	0.03	0.01	0.0	0.0	0.575
Japan	0.97	0.55	0.82	0.59	0.00	0.0	0.0	-0.646
Jordan	0.34	0.89	0.49	0.03	0.00	0.0	0.0	0.102
Kazakhstan	0.22	0.93	0.34	0.21	0.00	0.5	0.0	0.077
Kenya	0.48	0.95	0.25	0.08	0.01	0.0	0.0	0.304
Kiribati	0.94	0.65	0.33	0.00	0.00	0.0	0.0	-0.620
Kuwait	0.37	0.91	0.39	0.02	0.01	0.0	0.0	0.177
Kyrgyzstan	0.28	0.97	0.25	0.15	0.00	0.0	0.0	0.592
Laos	0.12	0.97	0.22	0.50	0.01	0.0	0.0	1.135
Lebanon	0.43	0.94	0.17	0.06	0.00	0.0	0.0	0.398
Lesotho	0.63	0.93	0.38	0.03	0.00	0.0	0.0	-0.058
Liberia	0.60	0.74	0.21	0.02	0.00	0.0	0.0	-0.052
Libya	0.08	0.90	0.07	0.00	0.00	0.0	0.0	0.757
Madagascar	0.60	0.87	0.17	0.02	0.00	0.0	0.0	0.113
Malawi	0.66	0.82	0.24	0.03	0.00	0.0	0.0	-0.047
Malaysia	0.51	0.92	0.51	0.28	0.00	0.0	0.0	0.174
Maldives	0.40	0.89	0.41	0.06	0.00	0.0	0.0	0.143
Mali	0.33	0.94	0.24	0.02	0.00	0.0	0.0	0.393

Table B.3—Continued

Country	Regime Alignment with the PRC			China's Influence in the Country			Potential Obstacles in Relationship			Total Feasibility Score
	F1. Authoritarian Regime	F2. Aligned Voting with China	F3. Perceptions of Corruption	F4. Partner Engagement	F5. Arms Sales or Transfers		F6. Tensions in Relations	F7. Official Recognition of the PRC over the ROC		
Marshall Islands	0.94	0.11	0.33	0.00	0.00		0.0	1.0		-2.159
Mauritania	0.35	0.91	0.22	0.02	0.01		0.0	0.0		0.377
Mauritius	0.88	0.90	0.54	0.05	0.00		0.0	0.0		-0.459
Micronesia (Federated States of)	0.93	0.00	0.33	0.00	0.00		0.0	0.0		-1.259
Mongolia	0.85	0.90	0.30	0.28	0.00		0.5	0.0		-0.471
Morocco	0.37	0.92	0.37	0.10	0.03		0.0	0.0		0.318
Mozambique	0.43	0.94	0.17	0.14	0.00		0.0	0.0		0.476
Myanmar	0.28	0.93	0.21	0.30	0.19		0.0	0.0		0.929
Namibia	0.78	0.93	0.51	0.14	0.03		0.0	0.0		-0.190
Nauru	0.78	0.16	0.33	0.00	0.00		0.0	1.0		-1.945
Nepal	0.56	0.93	0.28	0.23	0.00		0.0	0.0		0.321
New Zealand	1.00	0.50	1.00	0.30	0.00		0.0	0.0		-1.194
Niger	0.48	0.93	0.26	0.04	0.00		0.0	0.0		0.225
Nigeria	0.45	0.92	0.17	0.05	0.04		0.0	0.0		0.395
North Korea	0.02	0.94	0.08	0.26	0.00		0.5	0.0		0.602
Oman	0.22	0.94	0.55	0.16	0.00		0.0	0.0		0.328
Pakistan	0.37	0.97	0.25	0.64	1.00		0.0	0.0		1.995
Palau	0.93	0.18	0.33	0.00	0.00		0.0	1.0		-2.074
Papua New Guinea	0.62	0.74	0.20	0.07	0.00		0.0	0.0		-0.007
Philippines	0.56	0.92	0.29	0.16	0.00		0.5	0.0		-0.275
Qatar	0.24	0.90	0.67	0.03	0.01		0.0	0.0		0.027
Rwanda	0.20	0.74	0.55	0.05	0.00		0.0	0.0		0.035
Samoa	0.82	0.79	0.33	0.01	0.00		0.0	0.0		-0.346
Sao Tome and Principe	0.85	0.94	0.46	0.00	0.00		0.0	0.0		-0.362
Saudi Arabia	0.06	0.88	0.54	0.10	0.03		0.0	0.0		0.413
Senegal	0.71	0.92	0.43	0.05	0.00		0.0	0.0		-0.179

Table B.3—Continued

Country	Regime Alignment with the PRC			China's Influence in the Country		Potential Obstacles in Relationship		Total Feasibility Score
	F1. Authoritarian Regime	F2. Aligned Voting with China	F3. Perceptions of Corruption	F4. Partner Engagement	F5. Arms Sales or Transfers	F6. Tensions in Relations	F7. Official Recognition of the PRC over the ROC	
Seychelles	0.78	0.87	0.71	0.05	0.00	0.0	0.0	-0.563
Sierra Leone	0.65	0.92	0.28	0.04	0.00	0.0	0.0	0.027
Singapore	0.48	0.94	0.96	0.32	0.00	0.0	0.0	-0.180
Solomon Islands	0.80	0.82	0.39	0.00	0.00	0.0	0.0	-0.375
Somalia	0.06	0.94	0.00	0.01	0.00	0.0	0.0	0.880
South Africa	0.80	0.92	0.42	0.32	0.00	0.0	0.0	0.025
South Korea	0.84	0.51	0.64	0.24	0.00	0.5	0.0	-1.232
South Sudan	0.01	0.63	0.00	0.03	0.00	0.0	0.0	0.653
Sri Lanka	0.56	0.93	0.34	0.27	0.04	0.0	0.0	0.335
Sudan	0.16	0.94	0.05	0.18	0.06	0.0	0.0	0.958
Syria	0.00	0.97	0.03	0.07	0.01	0.0	0.0	1.021
Tajikistan	0.07	0.97	0.17	0.14	0.00	0.0	0.0	0.876
Tanzania	0.34	0.94	0.34	0.19	0.05	0.0	0.0	0.498
Thailand	0.30	0.90	0.32	0.44	0.05	0.5	0.0	0.276
Timor Leste	0.72	0.88	0.37	0.05	0.00	0.0	0.0	-0.156
Togo	0.43	0.80	0.22	0.03	0.00	0.0	0.0	0.180
Tonga	0.80	0.74	0.33	0.03	0.00	0.0	0.0	-0.363
Tunisia	0.71	0.89	0.42	0.05	0.00	0.0	0.0	-0.195
Turkmenistan	0.01	1.00	0.09	0.04	0.03	0.0	0.0	0.963
Tuvalu	0.94	0.80	0.66	0.00	0.00	0.0	1.0	-1.799
Uganda	0.34	0.93	0.20	0.05	0.00	0.0	0.0	0.447
UAE	0.16	0.90	0.78	0.06	0.02	0.0	0.0	0.043
Uzbekistan	0.10	0.98	0.18	0.07	0.01	0.0	0.0	0.778
Vanuatu	0.83	0.69	0.41	0.11	0.00	0.0	0.0	-0.435
Vietnam	0.18	0.96	0.32	0.68	0.00	0.5	0.0	0.638
Yemen	0.10	0.90	0.04	0.08	0.00	0.0	0.0	0.843
Zambia	0.52	0.92	0.28	0.09	0.02	0.0	0.0	0.233
Zimbabwe	0.28	0.98	0.16	0.14	0.01	0.0	0.0	0.693

Abbreviations

AEI	American Enterprise Institute
AFRICOM	U.S. Africa Command
AI	artificial intelligence
AOR	area of responsibility
BRI	Belt and Road Initiative
CCP	Chinese Communist Party
CENTCOM	U.S. Central Command
CIA	U.S. Central Intelligence Agency
COVID-19	coronavirus disease 2019
CPI	Corruption Perceptions Index
CPIA	Country Policy and Institutional Assessment
DoD	U.S. Department of Defense
DRC	Democratic Republic of the Congo
GDP	gross domestic product
GNI	gross national income
HA/DR	humanitarian assistance/disaster relief
HDI	Human Development Index
I&W	indications and warning
INDOPACOM	U.S. Indo-Pacific Command
ISR	intelligence, surveillance, and reconnaissance
MCF	military-civil fusion
MOOTW	military operations other than war
MOU	memorandum of understanding
MSG	military strategic guideline
NEO	noncombatant evacuation operation
NUDT	National University of Defense Technology
OECD	Organisation for Economic Co-operation and Development
OSD	Office of the Secretary of Defense
PIC	Pacific Island Country
PKO	peacekeeping operations
PLA	People's Liberation Army
PLAA	People's Liberation Army Army
PLAAF	People's Liberation Army Air Force
PLAN	People's Liberation Army Navy
PPP	purchasing power parity
PRC	People's Republic of China
ROC	Republic of China (Taiwan)
SIPRI	Stockholm International Peace Research Institute

SLOC	sea line of communication
SOE	state-owned enterprise
SOF	special operations forces
SMS	*Science of Military Strategy*
SSF	Strategic Support Force
TIV	trend indicator value
TT&C	tracking, telemetry, and command
TTP	tactics, techniques, and procedures
UAE	United Arab Emirates
UAV	unmanned aerial vehicle
UN	United Nations
UNDP	United Nations Development Programme
WDI	world development indicators (World Bank)
WGI	worldwide governance indicators (World Bank)

Bibliography

Unless otherwise indicated, the authors of this report provided the translations of bibliographic details for the non-English sources included in this report. To support conventions for alphabetizing, sources in Chinese are introduced with and organized according to their English translations. The original rendering in Chinese appears in brackets after the English translation.

Academy of Military Science, *People's Liberation Army Military Terminology* [中国人民解放军军语], 2nd ed., Beijing: Academy of Military Science Press, December 2011.

AEI—*See* American Enterprise Institute.

AidData, "AidData's Global Chinese Official Finance Dataset, 2000–2014, Version 1.0," webpage, October 11, 2017. As of September 1, 2021:
http://aiddata.org/data/chinese-global-official-finance-dataset

Allen, Kenneth W., and Cristina L. Garafola, *70 Years of the PLA Air Force*, Montgomery, Ala.: China Aerospace Studies Institute, 2021.

Allen, Kenneth, Phillip C. Saunders, and John Chen, *Chinese Military Diplomacy, 2003–2016: Trends and Implications*, Washington, D.C.: National Defense University Press, China Strategic Perspectives 11, July 2017.

American Enterprise Institute, "China Global Investment Tracker," webpage, undated. As of February 19, 2021:
https://www.aei.org/china-global-investment-tracker/

ArcGIS, "Global Shipping Routes," webmap, undated. As of February 19, 2021:
https://www.arcgis.com/home/webmap/viewer.html?layers=12c0789207e64714b9545ad30fca1633

Bacani, Emmanuel Louis, "S&P: China's GDP Growth to Average 4.6% Through 2030 in 'Inescapable' Slowdown," S&P Global Market Intelligence, August 29, 2019.

Barron, Jeff, "China's Crude Oil Imports Surpassed 10 Million Barrels per Day in 2019," U.S. Energy Information Administration, March 23, 2020.

Beauchamp-Mustafaga, Nathan, "Where to Next?: PLA Considerations for Overseas Base Site Selection," Jamestown Foundation, *China Brief*, Vol. 20, No. 18, October 19, 2020.

———, "Dare to Face the 'Strong Enemy 强敌': How Xi Jinping Has Made the PLA Talk About the United States," *Sinocism*, March 4, 2021.

Becker, Jeffrey, *Securing China's Lifeline Across the Indian Ocean*, Newport, R.I.: U.S. Naval War College, China Maritime Studies Institute, China Maritime Report No. 11, December 2020.

Béraud-Sudreau, Lucie, and Meia Nouwens, "Sino-European Military Cooperation in the Twenty-First Century: From Friends to 'Frenemies?'" in Roger Cliff and Roy D. Kamphausen, eds., *Enabling a More Externally Focused and Operational PLA: 2020 PLA Conference Papers*, Carlisle Barracks, Pa.: Strategic Studies Institute, U.S. Army War College Press, July 2022, pp. 1–23.

Bertelsmann Stiftung, *BTI 2020 Country Report—North Korea*, Gütersloh, 2020.

Biden, Joseph R., Jr., *Interim National Security Strategic Guidance*, Washington, D.C.: White House, March 2021.

Blasko, Dennis J., "The 2015 Chinese Defense White Paper on Strategy in Perspective: Maritime Missions Require a Change in the PLA Mindset," Jamestown Foundation, *China Brief*, Vol. 15, No. 12, June 19, 2015.

Blasko, Dennis J., and Roderick Lee, "The Chinese Navy's Marine Corps, Part 1: Expansion and Reorganization," Jamestown Foundation, *China Brief*, Vol. 19, No. 3, February 1, 2019a.

———, "The Chinese Navy's Marine Corps, Part 2: Chain-of-Command Reforms and Evolving Training," Jamestown Foundation, *China Brief*, Vol. 19, No. 4, February 15, 2019b.

Boc, Anny, "Does China's 'Alliance Treaty' with North Korea Still Matter?" *The Diplomat*, July 26, 2019.

"British Media Says the Y-20 Has Been Delivered to the Chinese Air Force in Batches; 1,000 Aircraft Needed to Fulfill Strategic Air Delivery Requirements" ["英媒称运20已批量交付中国空军 满足战略空运1000架"], Xinhua [新华网], January 14, 2018. As of June 22, 2021:
http://www.xinhuanet.com/mil/2018-01/14/c_129790335.htm

Brooks, Stephen G., and William C. Wohlforth, "The Rise and Fall of the Great Powers in the Twenty-First Century," *International Security*, Vol. 40, No. 3, Winter 2015–2016, pp. 7–53.

Burden, Lizzy, "China's Economy Set to Overtake U.S. Earlier Due to Covid Fallout," Bloomberg, December 25, 2020.

Burke, Edmund J., Kristen Gunness, Cortez A. Cooper III, and Mark Cozad, *People's Liberation Army Operational Concepts*, Santa Monica, Calif.: RAND Corporation, RR-A394-1, 2020. As of June 22, 2022:
https://www.rand.org/pubs/research_reports/RRA394-1.html

Burke, Edmund J., Timothy R. Heath, Jeffrey W. Hornung, Logan Ma, Lyle J. Morris, and Michael S. Chase, *China's Military Activities in the East China Sea: Implications for Japan's Air Self-Defense Force*, Santa Monica, Calif.: RAND Corporation, RR-2574-AF, 2018. As of June 22, 2022:
https://www.rand.org/pubs/research_reports/RR2574.html

Burns, Richard B., Kevin M. Freese, Keith A. French, William C. Hardy, Andrew M. Johnson, Nicole M. Laster, and Anthony E. Mack, *Competition in 2035: Anticipating Chinese Exploitation of Operational Environments*, Fort Leavenworth, Kan.: Operational Environment & Threat Analysis Directorate, U.S. Army Training and Doctrine Command, G-2, August 15, 2019.

"By 2020, the Chinese Air Force Will Be Equipped with 40 Y-20s That Can Deliver a Division Long Distances" ["2020年中国空军将装备40架运-20 可远程投送1个师"], Xinhua [新华网], July 13, 2018. As of May 18, 2021:
http://www.xinhuanet.com/mil/2018-07/13/c_129912721.htm

Carnegie Endowment for International Peace, "AI Global Surveillance Technology," website, undated. As of November 23, 2020:
https://carnegieendowment.org/publications/interactive/ai-surveillance

Center for the Study of Chinese Military Affairs, Chinese Military Diplomacy Database, version 4.00, National Defense University, forthcoming.

Chase, Michael S., Jeffrey Engstrom, Tai Ming Cheung, Kristen A. Gunness, Scott Warren Harold, Susan Puska, and Samuel K. Berkowitz, *China's Incomplete Military Transformation: Assessing the Weaknesses of the People's Liberation Army (PLA)*, Santa Monica, Calif.: RAND Corporation, RR-893-USCC, 2015. As of August 31, 2021:
https://www.rand.org/pubs/research_reports/RR893.html

Chase, Michael S., Cristina L. Garafola, and Nathan Beauchamp-Mustafaga, "Chinese Perceptions of and Responses to US Conventional Military Power," *Asian Security*, Vol. 14, No. 2, 2018, pp. 136–154.

Chase, Michael S., and Jennifer D. P. Moroney, *Regional Responses to U.S.-China Competition in the Indo-Pacific: Australia and New Zealand*, Santa Monica, Calif.: RAND Corporation, RR-4412/1-AF, 2020. As of May 19, 2021:
https://www.rand.org/pubs/research_reports/RR4412z1.html

Chen Yu [陈瑜], Li Jiansi [李剑肆], and Zeng Yu [曾宇], "Research on the Building of Overseas Strategic Projection Capabilities" ["境外空中战略投送能力建设研究"], *Journal of Military Transportation University* [军事交通学院学报], Vol. 21, No. 2, February 2019, pp. 5–8, 40.

Chen Zheng, "China Debates on the Non-Interference Principle," *Chinese Journal of International Politics*, Vol. 9, No. 3, Autumn 2016, pp. 349–374.

China Aerospace Studies Institute, *Science of Military Strategy (2013)*, trans., "In Their Own Words: Foreign Military Thought" series, Montgomery, Ala.: China Aerospace Studies Institute, Air University, 2021.

China Power Team, "Does China Dominate Global Investment?" China Power Project, Center for Strategic and International Studies, September 26, 2016, updated January 28, 2021.

———, "How Is China's Energy Footprint Changing?" China Power Project, Center for Strategic and International Studies, February 15, 2016, updated March 17, 2022.

"China to Deepen Military Cooperation with Caribbean Countries, Pacific Island Countries: Defense Minister," Xinhua, July 8, 2019.

"China to Help Bangladesh Build Submarine Base, Senior Official Says," Radio Free Asia, September 12, 2019.

"Chinese Economy to Overtake U.S. 'by 2028' Due to Covid," BBC, December 26, 2020.

"Chinese Ships Drill in Mediterranean en Route to Joint Exercises with Russia," Radio Free Europe/Radio Liberty, July 12, 2017.

CIA—*See* U.S. Central Intelligence Agency.

Clemens, Morgan, "The Maritime Silk Road and the PLA: A Paper for China as a 'Maritime Power' Conference," Arlington, Va.: CNA, July 28–29, 2015.

"Commentary: Chinese Military Contributes to World Peace," Xinhua, September 18, 2020.

Connable, Ben, Abby Doll, Alyssa Demus, Dara Massicot, Clint Reach, Anthony Atler, William Mackenzie, Matthew Povlock, and Lauren Skrabala, *Russia's Limit of Advance: Analysis of Russian Ground Force Deployment Capabilities and Limitations*, Santa Monica, Calif.: RAND Corporation, RR-2563-A, 2020. As of May 18, 2021: https://www.rand.org/pubs/research_reports/RR2563.html

Cooper, Cortez A., *The PLA Navy's "New Historic Missions": Expanding Capabilities for a Re-emergent Maritime Power*, Santa Monica, Calif.: RAND Corporation, CT-332, 2009. As of August 16, 2021: https://www.rand.org/pubs/testimonies/CT332.html

Costello, John, and Joe McReynolds, *China's Strategic Support Force: A Force for a New Era*, Washington, D.C.: National Defense University Press, China Strategic Perspectives 13, October 2018.

Cuenca, Oliver, "Ethiopia-Djibouti Line Reports Reduced Revenue Due to Vandalism," *International Railway Journal*, December 16, 2020.

Dauvergne, Peter, "A Dark History of the World's Smallest Island Nation," *MIT Press Reader*, July 22, 2019.

Defense Intelligence Agency, *China Military Power: Modernizing a Force to Fight and Win*, Bethesda, Md., January 2019.

"Djibouti and China Sign a Security and Defense Agreement," AllAfrica, February 27, 2014.

Dobbins, James, Howard J. Shatz, and Ali Wyne, "A Warming Trend in China–Russia Relations," *The Diplomat*, April 18, 2019.

———, *Russia Is a Rogue, Not a Peer; China Is a Peer, Not a Rogue: Different Challenges, Different Responses*, Santa Monica, Calif.: RAND Corporation, PE-310-A, October 2018. As of August 17, 2021: https://www.rand.org/pubs/perspectives/PE310.html

Dossani, Rafiq, Jennifer Bouey, and Keren Zhu, *Demystifying the Belt and Road Initiative: A Clarification of Its Key Features, Objectives and Impacts*, Santa Monica, Calif.: RAND Corporation, WR-1338, 2020. As of March 3, 2021: https://www.rand.org/pubs/working_papers/WR1338.html

Downs, Erica, *China-Pakistan Economic Corridor Power Projects: Insights into Environmental and Debt Sustainability*, New York: Columbia University, October 2019.

Downs, Erica, Jeffrey Becker, and Patrick deGategno, *China's Military Support Facility in Djibouti: The Economic and Security Dimensions of China's First Overseas Base*, Arlington, Va.: CNA, July 2017.

Duchâtel, Mathieu, Oliver Bräuner, and Zhou Hang, "Protecting China's Overseas Interests: The Slow Shift Away from Non-Interference," Stockholm International Peace Research Institute, SIPRI Policy Paper No. 41, June 2014.

Dunst, Charles, "In Cambodia, 'Rule of Law' Means Hun Sen Rules," *Foreign Policy*, December 12, 2019.

Duri, Jorum, and Kaunain Rahman, "Pacific Island Countries: Overview of Corruption and Anti-Corruption," Bergen, Norway: CMI U4 Anti-Corruption Resource Centre and Transparency International, August 2020.

Dutton, Peter A., Isaac B. Kardon, and Conor M. Kennedy, *Djibouti: China's First Overseas Strategic Strongpoint*, Newport, R.I.: U.S. Naval War College, China Maritime Studies Institute, China Maritime Report No. 6, April 2020.

Dutton, Peter A., and Ryan D. Martinson, eds., *Beyond the Red Wall: Chinese Far Seas Operations*, Newport, R.I.: U.S. Navy War College, China Maritime Study No. 13, May 2015.

Easton, Ian M., and L. C. Russell Hsiao, *The Chinese People's Liberation Army's Unmanned Aerial Vehicle Project: Organizational Capacities and Operational Capabilities*, Arlington, Va.: Project 2049 Institute, March 11, 2013.

Education Policy and Data Center, "Somalia: National Education Profile, 2018 Update," Washington, D.C., 2018.

Ekman, Alice, *China's Smart Cities: The New Geopolitical Battleground*, Paris: French Institute of International Relations (IFRI), December 2019.

Erickson, Andrew S., "U.S. Wary of Its New Neighbor in Djibouti: A Chinese Naval Base," *Andrew S. Erickson Blog*, February 25, 2017. As of July 6, 2021:
https://www.andrewerickson.com/2017/02/u-s-wary-of-its-new-neighbor-in-djibouti-a-chinese-naval-base/

Erickson, Andrew S., and Joel Wuthnow, "Barriers, Springboards and Benchmarks: China Conceptualizes the Pacific 'Island Chains,'" *China Quarterly*, Vol. 225, March 2016, pp. 1–22.

Ethirajan, Anbarasan, "China Debt Dogs Maldives' 'Bridge to Prosperity,'" BBC, September 17, 2020.

Fravel, M. Taylor, *Active Defense: China's Military Strategy Since 1949*, Princeton, N.J.: Princeton University Press, 2019.

Freedom House, "Countries and Territories," webpage, undated. As of June 22, 2021:
https://freedomhouse.org/countries/freedom-world/scores

———, "Fiji: Freedom in the World 2020," webpage, 2020a. As of June 22, 2021:
https://freedomhouse.org/country/fiji/freedom-world/2020

———, "Kiribati: Freedom in the World 2020," webpage, 2020b. As of June 22, 2021:
https://freedomhouse.org/country/kiribati/freedom-world/2020

———, "Marshall Islands: Freedom in the World 2020," webpage, 2020c. As of June 22, 2021:
https://freedomhouse.org/country/marshall-islands/freedom-world/2020

———, "Micronesia: Freedom in the World 2020," webpage, 2020d. As of June 22, 2021:
https://freedomhouse.org/country/micronesia/freedom-world/2020

———, "Palau: Freedom in the World 2020," webpage, 2020e. As of June 22, 2021:
https://freedomhouse.org/country/palau/freedom-world/2020

———, "Samoa: Freedom in the World 2020," webpage, 2020f. As of June 22, 2021:
https://freedomhouse.org/country/samoa/freedom-world/2020

———, "Tonga: Freedom in the World 2020," webpage, 2020g. As of June 22, 2021:
https://freedomhouse.org/country/tonga/freedom-world/2020

———, "Tuvalu: Freedom in the World 2020," webpage, 2020h. As of June 22, 2021:
https://freedomhouse.org/country/tuvalu/freedom-world/2020

———, "All Data, FIW 2013–2021," data file, 2021. As of September 1, 2021:
https://freedomhouse.org/report/freedom-world

Garafola, Cristina L., "Will the PLA Reforms Succeed?" *China Analysis*, European Council on Foreign Relations, March 2016.

Garafola, Cristina L., and Timothy R. Heath, *The Chinese Air Force's First Steps Toward Becoming an Expeditionary Air Force*, Santa Monica, Calif.: RAND Corporation, RR-2056-AF, 2017. As of August 30, 2021:
https://www.rand.org/pubs/research_reports/RR2056.html

Garcia Herrero, Alicia, and Jianwei Xu, "How Big Is China's Digital Economy?" Brussels: Bruegel, Working Paper No. 4, May 17, 2018.

Gelpern, Anna, Sebastian Horn, Scott Morris, Brad Parks, and Christoph Trebesch, *How China Lends: A Rare Look into 100 Debt Contracts with Foreign Governments*, Peterson Institute for International Economics, Kiel Institute for the World Economy, Center for Global Development, and AidData at William & Mary, 2021.

Gentile, Gian, Yvonne K. Crane, Dan Madden, Timothy M. Bonds, Bruce W. Bennett, Michael J. Mazarr, and Andrew Scobell, *Four Problems on the Korean Peninsula: North Korea's Expanding Nuclear Capabilities Drive a Complex Set of Problems*, Santa Monica, Calif.: RAND Corporation, TL-271-A, 2019. As of August 30, 2021:
https://www.rand.org/pubs/tools/TL271.html

Gettinger, Dan, "Drone Databook Update: March 2020," Annandale-on-Hudson, N.Y.: Center for the Study of the Drone at Bard College, March 2020.

Goodkind, Daniel, *The Chinese Diaspora: Historical Legacies and Contemporary Trends,* Washington D.C.: U.S. Census Bureau, August 2019.

Gordon, Ilana, "Welcome to Nauru, the Most Corrupt Country You've Never Heard Of," *Dose*, Medium, April 18, 2017.

Green Belt and Road Initiative Center, "Countries of the Belt and Road Initiative (BRI)," webpage, March 2020. As of June 22, 2021:
https://green-bri.org/countries-of-the-belt-and-road-initiative-bri/

Green, Will, and Taylore Roth, *China-Iran Relations: A Limited but Enduring Strategic Partnership*, Washington, D.C.: U.S.-China Economic and Security Review Commission, June 28, 2021.

Greitens, Sheena Chestnut, "Dealing with Demand for China's Global Surveillance Exports," Washington, D.C.: Brookings Institution, April 2020.

Grieger, Gisela, "Briefing: China's Growing Role as a Security Actor in Africa," Brussels: European Parliamentary Research Service, October 2019.

Grossman, Derek, Nathan Beauchamp-Mustafaga, Logan Ma, and Michael S. Chase, *China's Long-Range Bomber Flights: Drivers and Implications*, Santa Monica, Calif.: RAND Corporation, RR-2567-AF, 2018. As of August 30, 2021:
https://www.rand.org/pubs/research_reports/RR2567.html

Grossman, Derek, Michael S. Chase, Gerard Finin, Wallace Gregson, Jeffrey W. Hornung, Logan Ma, Jordan R. Reimer, and Alice Shih, *America's Pacific Island Allies: The Freely Associated States and Chinese Influence*, Santa Monica, Calif.: RAND Corporation, RR-2973-OSD, 2019. As of August 30, 2021:
https://www.rand.org/pubs/research_reports/RR2973.html

Gunness, Kristen, "The Dawn of an Expeditionary PLA?" in Nadège Rolland, ed., *Securing the Belt and Road Initiative: China's Evolving Military Engagement Along the Silk Road*, Washington: D.C.: The National Bureau of Asian Research, September 2019.

Hackenesch, Christine, and Julia Bader, "The Struggle for Minds and Influence: The Chinese Communist Party's Global Outreach," *International Studies Quarterly*, Vol. 64, No. 3, September 2020, pp. 723–733.

Harkavy, Robert E., *Strategic Basing and the Great Powers, 1200–2000*, New York: Routledge, 2007.

Hartnett, Daniel M., "The 'New Historic Missions': Reflections on Hu Jintao's Military Legacy," in Roy Kamphausen, David Lai, and Travis Tanner, eds., *Assessing the People's Liberation Army in the Hu Jintao Era*, Carlisle, Pa.: Strategic Studies Institute, U.S. Army War College Press, April 2014, pp. 31–80.

Heath, Timothy R., "The 'Holistic Security Concept': The Securitization of Policy and Increasing Risk of Militarized Crisis," Jamestown Foundation, *China Brief*, Vol. 15, No. 12, June 19, 2015. As of September 1, 2021:
https://jamestown.org/program/the-holistic-security-concept-the-securitization-of-policy-and-increasing-risk-of-militarized-crisis/

———, "China's Evolving Approach to Economic Diplomacy," *Asia Policy*, No. 22, July 2016, pp. 157–192.

———, *China's Pursuit of Overseas Security*, Santa Monica, Calif.: RAND Corporation, RR-2271-OSD, 2018. As of August 17, 2021:
https://www.rand.org/pubs/research_reports/RR2271.html

———, "The Ramifications of China's Reported Naval Base in Cambodia," *World Politics Review*, August 5, 2019.

Heginbotham, Eric, Michael Nixon, Forrest E. Morgan, Jacob L. Heim, Jeff Hagen, Sheng Tao Li, Jeffrey Engstrom, Martin C. Libicki, Paul DeLuca, David A. Shlapak, David R. Frelinger, Burgess Laird, Kyle Brady, and Lyle J. Morris, *The U.S.-China Military Scorecard: Forces, Geography, and the Evolving Balance of Power, 1996–2017*, Santa Monica, Calif.: RAND Corporation, RR-392-AF, 2015. As of August 30, 2021:
https://www.rand.org/pubs/research_reports/RR392.html

Heijmans, Philip, "Hun Sen—and China—Win Cambodia Elections," *Newsweek*, July 29, 2018.

Heritage Foundation, "Explore the Data: All Index Data," 2021 Index of Economic Freedom data set, 2021. As of June 22, 2021:
https://www.heritage.org/index/explore

Hillman, Jennifer, and David Sacks, *China's Belt and Road: Implications for the United States*, New York: Council on Foreign Relations, Independent Task Force Report No. 79, 2021.

Government of the People's Republic of China, "One Belt, One Road Portal" ["中国一带一路网"], webpage, undated. As of October 17, 2022:
https://eng.yidaiyilu.gov.cn/

Hillman, Jonathan E., and Maesea McCalpin, "Watching China's 'Safe Cities,'" Washington, D.C.: Center for Strategic and International Studies, November 2019.

Horn, Sebastian, Carmen Reinhart, and Christoph Trebesch, "China's Overseas Lending," Kiel, Germany: Kiel Institute for the World Economy, Kiel Working Paper No. 2132, June 2019.

Hu Xin [胡欣], "The Expansion of National Interests and the Construction of Overseas Strategic Strong Points" ["国家利益拓展与海外战略支撑点建设"], *Forum of World Economics & Politics* [世界经济与政治论坛], No. 1, 2019, pp. 21–35.

Huang Zijuan [黄子娟], "How Many Y-20s Does Our Military Require? Experts Teach You How to Calculate" ["我军需要多少运-20？专家教你计算"], *China Military Online* [中国军网], June 8, 2016.

Huawei, "Huawei Smart City Brochure," July 27, 2017.

———, "Huawei Smart City Overview Presentation," June 10, 2018.

Hsu, Kimberly, Craig Murray, Jeremy Cook, and Amalia Feld, *China's Military Unmanned Aerial Vehicle Industry*, Washington, D.C.: U.S.-China Economic and Security Review Commission, June 13, 2013.

International Institute for Strategic Studies, "The 2019 Military Balance Chart: China's Armed Forces," wall chart in *The Military Balance 2019*, Washington, D.C., February 2019.

International Monetary Fund, "Report for Selected Countries and Subjects," data set, World Economic Outlook Database, October 2020. As of January 12, 2021:
https://www.imf.org/en/Publications/WEO/weo-database/2020/October/weo-report

———, "Kiribati: Staff Concluding Statement of the 2021 Article IV Mission," March 2, 2021.

Jane's, "United States Defense Budget Overview," *Sentinel Security Assessment–North America*, February 20, 2019.

———, "China Defense Budget Overview," *Sentinel Security Assessment–China and Northeast Asia*, June 8, 2020.

Jiang Deliang [姜德良], Zhang Ren [张韧], and Ge Shanshan [葛珊珊], "Natural Risk Scenario Simulation Assessment of Overseas Support Bases Based on Uncertain Knowledge" ["知识不确定条件下的海外保障基地自然风险情景模拟评估"], *Marine Science Bulletin* [海洋通报], Vol. 36, No. 5, October 2017, pp. 504–511, 537.

Jiang Shan [江山] and Zhang Junsheng [张峻生], "'Jiaolong' Attacks: Overcoming the Enemy to Achieve Victory Is Inseparable from Hard Work" ["'蛟龙'出击：克敌制胜，离不开千锤百炼"], *China Military Online*, August 20, 2020.

Joint Chiefs of Staff, *DOD Dictionary of Military and Associated Terms*, Washington, D.C., November 2021.

Jones, Charlie Lyons, and Raphael Veit, *Leaping Across the Ocean: The Port Operators Behind China's Naval Expansion*, Barton ACT: Australian Strategic Policy Institute, February 2021.

Kamphausen, Roy, and David Lai, eds., *The Chinese People's Liberation Army in 2025*, Carlisle, Pa.: Strategic Studies Institute, U.S. Army War College Press, July 2015.

Kamphausen, Roy, David Lai, and Tiffany Ma, eds., *Securing the China Dream: The PLA's Role in a Time of Reform and Change*, Seattle, Wash.: The National Bureau of Asian Research, 2020.

Kania, Elsa, *The PLA's Unmanned Aerial Systems: New Capabilities for a 'New Era' of Chinese Military Power*, Montgomery, Ala.: China Aerospace Studies Institute, August 2018.

Kania, Elsa B., and John Costello, "Seizing the Commanding Heights: The PLA Strategic Support Force in Chinese Military Power," *Journal of Strategic Studies*, Vol. 44, No. 2, 2021 pp. 218–264.

Kao, Ernest, "China Considered Using Drone in Myanmar to Kill Wanted Drug Lord," *South China Morning Post*, February 20, 2013.

Kardon, Isaac B., "China's Overseas Base, Places, and Far Seas Logistics," in Joel Wuthnow, Arthur S. Ding, Phillip C. Saunders, Andrew Scobell, and Andrew N.D. Yang, eds., *The PLA Beyond Borders: Chinese Military Operations in Regional and Global Context*, Washington, D.C.: National Defense University Press, 2021, pp. 73–105.

Kardon, Isaac B., Conor M. Kennedy, and Peter A. Dutton, *Gwadar: China's Potential Strategic Strongpoint in Pakistan*, Newport, R.I.: U.S. Naval War College, China Maritime Studies Institute, China Maritime Report No. 7, August 2020.

Kennedy, Conor, "Strategic Strong Points and Chinese Naval Strategy," Jamestown Foundation, *China Brief*, Vol. 19, No. 6, March 22, 2019.

Kostecka, Daniel J., "Places and Bases: The Chinese Navy's Emerging Support Network in the Indian Ocean," *Naval War College Review*, Vol. 64, No. 1, Winter 2011, pp. 59–78.

Kulp, Scott A., and Benjamin H. Strauss, "New Elevation Data Triple Estimates of Global Vulnerability to Sea-Level Rise and Coastal Flooding," *Nature Communications*, Vol. 10, October 2019.

Legarda, Helena, and Meia Nouwens, "Guardians of the Belt and Road: The Internationalization of China's Private Security Companies," Mercator Institute for China Studies, August 16, 2018.

Lelyveld, Michael, "China's Carbon Targets Spark Rift with Russia," Radio Free Asia, November 6, 2020.

Li, Jason, "Conflict Mediation with Chinese Characteristics: How China Justifies Its Non-Interference Policy," Stimson Center, August 27, 2019.

Li Jian [李剑], Chen Wenwen [陈文文], and Jin Jing [金晶], "The Structure of Indian Ocean Maritime Rights and the Indian Ocean Expansion of China's Maritime Rights" ["印度洋海权格局与中国海权的印度洋拓展"], *Pacific Journal* [太平洋学报], May 2014, Vol. 22, pp. 68–76.

Li Kexin [李克欣], Qiu Haohan [李克欣], and Zhai Siyu [翟思宇], "A Glimpse of the Strong Military with He Long, Special Warfare Company Commander in a Navy Marine Corps Brigade" ["海军陆战队某旅特战连连长何龙强军精武掠影"], *China Military Online*, August 11, 2020.

Li Qingsi [李庆四] and Chen Chunyu [陈春雨], "Analysis of China's Overseas Port Chain Basing Strategy" ["试析中国的海外港链基地战略"], *Regional and Global Development* [区域与全球 发展], No. 2, 2019.

Li Shougeng [李守耕], Chen Tieqi [陈铁祺], and Wang Feng [王丰], "Research on Pre-Positioned Reserves Methods for Combat Readiness Materiel" ["战备物资预置储备模式研究"], *Journal of Military Transportation University* [军事交通学院学报], July 2019, pp. 57–60, 70.

Liff, Adam P., and Andrew S. Erickson, "Demystifying China's Defense Spending: Less Mysterious in the Aggregate," *China Quarterly*, Vol. 216, December 2013, pp. 805–830.

Lin, Bonny, Michael S. Chase, Jonah Blank, Cortez A. Cooper III, Derek Grossman, Scott W. Harold, Jennifer D. P. Moroney, Lyle J. Morris, Logan Ma, Paul Orner, Alice Shih, and Soo Kim, *Regional Responses to U.S.-China Competition in the Indo-Pacific: Study Overview and Conclusions*, Santa Monica, Calif.: RAND Corporation, RR-4412-AF, 2020a. As of May 19, 2021:
https://www.rand.org/pubs/research_reports/RR4412.html

———, *U.S. Versus Chinese Powers of Persuasion: Does the United States or China Have More Influence in the Indo-Pacific Region?* Santa Monica, Calif.: RAND Corporation, RB-10137-AF, 2020b. As of August 16, 2021:
https://www.rand.org/pubs/research_briefs/RB10137.html

Lin, Bonny, and Cristina L. Garafola, *Training the People's Liberation Army Air Force Surface-to-Air Missile (SAM) Forces*, Santa Monica, Calif.: RAND Corporation, RR-1414-AF, 2016. As of August 25, 2021:
https://www.rand.org/pubs/research_reports/RR1414.html

Lin, Bonny, Cristina L. Garafola, Bruce McClintock, Jonah Blank, Jeffrey W. Hornung, Karen Schwindt, Jennifer D. P. Moroney, Paul Orner, Dennis Borrman, Sarah W. Denton, and Jason D. Chambers, *Competition in the Gray Zone: Countering China's Coercion Against U.S. Allies and Partners in the Indo-Pacific*, Santa Monica, Calif.: RAND Corporation, RR-A594-1, 2022. As of August 12, 2022:
https://www.rand.org/pubs/research_reports/RRA594-1.html

Long, Drake, "Cambodia, China and the Dara Sakor Problem," *The Diplomat*, October 21, 2020.

Lostumbo, Michael J., Michael J. McNerney, Eric Peltz, Derek Eaton, David R. Frelinger, Victoria A. Greenfield, John Halliday, Patrick Mills, Bruce R. Nardulli, Stacie L. Pettyjohn, Jerry M. Sollinger, and Stephen M. Worman, *Overseas Basing of U.S. Military Forces: An Assessment of Relative Costs and Strategic Benefits*, Santa Monica, Calif.: RAND Corporation, RR-201-OSD, 2013. As of August 30, 2021:
https://www.rand.org/pubs/research_reports/RR201.html

Lu, Hui, Charlene Rohr, Marco Hafner, and Anna Knack, *China Belt and Road Initiative: Measuring the Impact of Improving Transportation Connectivity on Trade in the Region—A Proof-of-Concept Study*, Santa Monica, Calif.: RAND Corporation, RR-2625-RC, 2018. As of March 3, 2021:
https://www.rand.org/pubs/research_reports/RR2625.html

Luce, LeighAnn, and Erin Richter, "Handling Logistics in a Reformed PLA: The Long March Toward Joint Logistics," in Phillip C. Saunders, Arthur S. Ding, Andrew Scobell, Andrew N.D. Yang, and Joel Wuthnow, eds., *Chairman Xi Remakes the PLA*, Washington D.C.: National Defense University Press, 2019, pp. 257–292.

Luo Zhaohui [罗朝晖], Wan Jie [万捷], and Li Hongyang [李弘扬], "Research on Factors in Site Selection of Overseas Military Base of Chinese Navy" ["我国海军海外基地选址因素研究"], *Logistics Technology* [物流技术], June 2019, pp. 141–144.

Luxner, Larry, "What China's March to Net-Zero Emissions Means for the World," Atlantic Council, January 20, 2021.

Ma Liang [马良], Zhang Lin [张林], and Liu Xinke [刘新科], "Overseas Security Method of Assessing Point Location Based on Rough and Evidence Reasoning Bases" ["基于粗集和证据推理的海外基地保障点选址评估"], *Command Control & Simulation* [指挥控制与仿真] Vol. 36, No. 1, February 2014, pp. 88–93.

Macan-Markar, Marwaan, "China Debt Trap Fear Haunts Maldives Government," *Nikkei Asia*, September 15, 2020.

Matthews, Miriam, Katya Migacheva, and Ryan Andrew Brown, *Superspreaders of Malign and Subversive Information on COVID-19: Russian and Chinese Efforts Targeting the United States*, Santa Monica, Calif.: RAND Corporation, RR-A112-11, 2021. As of August 30, 2021:
https://www.rand.org/pubs/research_reports/RRA112-11.html

Mazarr, Michael J., Gian Gentile, Dan Madden, Stacie L. Pettyjohn, and Yvonne K. Crane, *The Korean Peninsula: Three Dangerous Scenarios*, Santa Monica, Calif.: RAND Corporation, PE-262-A, 2018. As of August 30, 2021:
https://www.rand.org/pubs/perspectives/PE262.html

McCaslin, Ian Burns, *Red Drones over Disputed Seas: A Field Guide to Chinese UAVs/UCAVs Operating in the Disputed East and South China Seas*, Arlington, Va.: Project 2049 Institute, August 2017.

McLeary, Paul, "New Pentagon No. 2 Hits China in First Speech as Tensions Rise," *Breaking Defense*, March 19, 2021.

McReynolds, Joe, ed., *China's Evolving Military Strategy*, Washington, D.C.: Jamestown Foundation, 2016.

Mercator Institute for China Studies, "MERICS BRI Tracker: Database and Project Design," database, September 18, 2019. As of September 1, 2021:
https://merics.org/en/merics-bri-tracker-database-and-project-design

"Military Report: Special Report on the 70th Anniversary of the Founding of the People's Navy, Guaranteed to Win, Logistical Forces Extend to the Far Seas" ["军事报道: 人民海军成立70周 年特别报道保障打赢后勤力量向远海大洋延伸"], video, China Central Television, April 19, 2019. As of January 23, 2022:
https://www.youtube.com/watch?v=Z4DyQGgTIjk

Miller, Terry, Anthony B. Kim, and James M. Roberts, *2021 Index of Economic Freedom*, Washington, D.C.: Heritage Foundation, 2021.

Ministry of External Affairs of the Government of India, India-Bhutan Friendship Treaty, March 2, 2007.

Ministry of Foreign Affairs of the People's Republic of China, "Foreign Ministry Spokesperson Geng Shuang's Regular Press Conference on February 19, 2019," 2019.

———, "Foreign Ministry Spokesperson Geng Shuang's Regular Press Conference on July 22, 2019," July 23, 2019.

———, "Foreign Ministry Spokesperson Wang Wenbin's Regular Press Conference on July 16, 2020," July 17, 2020.

———, "State Councilor and Foreign Minister Wang Yi Gives Interview to Xinhua News Agency and China Media Group on International Situation and China's Diplomacy in 2020," December 30, 2021.

———, "Interview on Current China-US Relations Given by State Councilor and Foreign Minister Wang Yi to Xinhua News Agency," August 6, 2020.

Ministry of Foreign Affairs of the Republic of China, "Diplomatic Allies," webpage, undated. As of June 21, 2021: https://en.mofa.gov.tw/AlliesIndex.aspx?n=1294&sms=1007

Ministry of National Defense of the People's Republic of China, "Defense Ministry's Regular Press Conference on Nov. 26," November 26, 2015a.

———, "Defense Ministry's Regular Press Conference on Dec. 31," December 31, 2015b.

Morgan, Forrest E., Benjamin Boudreaux, Andrew J. Lohn, Mark Ashby, Christian Curriden, Kelly Klima, and Derek Grossman, *Military Applications of Artificial Intelligence: Ethical Concerns in an Uncertain World*, Santa Monica, Calif.: RAND Corporation, RR-3139-1-AF, 2020. As of August 31, 2021: https://www.rand.org/pubs/research_reports/RR3139-1.html

Mullen, Andrew, "China's Service Sector: What Is It and Why Is It Important to the Economy?" *South China Morning Post*, March 3, 2021.

Mulvenon, James, "Chairman Hu and the PLA's 'New Historic Missions,'" *China Leadership Monitor*, No. 27, January 2009.

Narin, Sun, "Defense Minister Says Ream Being Made into a Geopolitical Issue by 'Them,'" Voice of America Khmer, June 9, 2021.

Nouwens, Meia, "The Evolving Nature of China's Military Diplomacy: From Visits to Vaccines," London: International Institute for Strategic Studies, May 2021.

Observatory of Economic Complexity, "China," webpage, 2020. As of December 31, 2020: https://oec.world/en/profile/country/chn

OECD—*See* Organisation for Economic Co-operation and Development.

Office of the Director of National Intelligence, *Annual Threat Assessment of the U.S. Intelligence Community*, Washington, D.C, April 9, 2021.

Office of the Secretary of Defense, *Annual Report to Congress: Military and Security Developments Involving the People's Republic of China 2018*, Washington, D.C.: U.S. Department of Defense, May 2018.

———, *Annual Report to Congress: Military and Security Developments Involving the People's Republic of China 2019*, Washington, D.C.: U.S. Department of Defense, May 2019.

———, *Military and Security Developments Involving the People's Republic of China 2020: Annual Report to Congress*, Washington, D.C.: U.S. Department of Defense, August 2020.

———, *Military and Security Developments Involving the People's Republic of China 2021: Annual Report to Congress*, Washington, D.C.: U.S. Department of Defense, November 2021.

"On January 21, 2019, Xi Jinping Attended the Opening Ceremony of the Seminar on Key Provincial and Ministerial-Level Leading Cadres, Insisting on Bottom Line Thinking, and Focusing on Preventing and Resolving Major Risks, and Delivered an Important Speech" ["习近平2019年1月21日出席省部级主要领导干部坚持底线思维着力防范化解重大风险专题研讨班开班式并发表重要讲话"], Xinhua, January 21, 2019.

Organisation for Economic Co-operation and Development, "The Belt and Road Initiative in the Global Trade, Investment and Finance Landscape," in *OECD Business and Finance Outlook 2018*, Paris: OECD Publishing, 2018.

———, "FDI Stocks (indicator)," webpage, undated. As of December 31, 2020: https://www.oecd-ilibrary.org/finance-and-investment/fdi-stocks/indicator/english_80eca1f9-en

O'Rourke, Ronald, *China Naval Modernization: Implications for U.S. Navy Capabilities—Background and Issues for Congress*, Washington, D.C.: Congressional Research Service, March 8, 2022.

OSD—*See* Office of the Secretary of Defense.

Page, Jeremy, Gordon Lubold, and Rob Taylor, "Deal for Naval Outpost in Cambodia Furthers China's Quest for Military Network," *Wall Street Journal*, July 22, 2019.

Pal, Alasdair, and Devjyot Ghoshal, "Report on Alleged Chinese Corruption in Maldives Due by June: Minister," Reuters, January 16, 2020.

Panda, Ankit, "Cambodia's Hun Sen Denies Chinese Naval Base Again—but What's Really Happening?" *The Diplomat*, June 2, 2020.

Parameswaran, Prashanth, "Why Did China's Navy Gain Use of a Malaysia Port Near the South China Sea?" *The Diplomat*, November 24, 2015.

Pearson, Elaine, "China's Bully Tactics Haven't Silenced Australia," Human Rights Watch, December 3, 2020.

Peltier, Chad, Tate Nurkin, and Sean O'Connor, *China's Logistics Capabilities for Expeditionary Operations*, Jane's, 2020.

Peng Guangqian [彭光谦] and Yao Youzhi [姚有志], eds., *Science of Military Strategy* [战略学], Beijing: Academy of Military Science Press, 2001.

———, *Science of Military Strategy*, trans., Beijing: Academy of Military Science Press, 2005.

Peter, Zsombor, "Laos Braces for Promise, Peril of China's High-Speed Railway," Voice of America, March 4, 2021.

Pettis, Michael, "Debt, Not Demographics, Will Determine the Future of China's Economy," *Fortune*, June 17, 2021.

———, "The Problems with China's 'Dual Circulation' Economic Model," *Financial Times,* August 25, 2020.

Pettyjohn, Stacie L., and Jennifer Kavanagh, *Access Granted: Political Challenges to the U.S. Overseas Military Presence, 1945–2014*, Santa Monica, Calif.: RAND Corporation, RR-1339-AF, 2016. As of August 30, 2016: https://www.rand.org/pubs/research_reports/RR1339.html

"PLA Donates Anti-Epidemic Supplies to Vietnamese Military," *China Military Online*, April 29, 2020.

PricewaterhouseCoopers, *The Long View: How Will the Global Economic Order Change by 2050?*, The World in 2050 report, London, February 2017.

Rasheed, Aishath Hanaan Hussain, "Work of Asset Recovery Commission Ongoing: Gov't Spokesperson," *Raajje*, February 11, 2021. As of September 1, 2021: https://raajje.mv/95210

Ratner, Ely, "Advance Policy Questions for Mr. Ely Ratner, Nominee to Be Assistant Secretary of Defense for Indo-Pacific Security Affairs," responses, Washington, D.C.: Senate Armed Services Committee, undated.

Ray, Rebecca, Kevin P. Gallagher, William Kring, Joshua Pitts, and B. Alexander Simmons, "Chinese Overseas Development Finance: Geospatial Data for Analysis of Biodiversity and Indigenous Lands," database, Boston University Global Development Policy Center, 2019. As of January 5, 2021: https://www.bu.edu/gdp/chinas-overseas-development-finance/

Reconnecting Asia Project, "Reconnecting Asia Project Database," Center for Strategic and International Studies, December 2020. As of September 1, 2021: https://reconasia.csis.org/reconnecting-asia-map/

Rolland, Nadège, ed., *Securing the Belt and Road Initiative: China's Evolving Military Engagement Along the Silk Road*, Seattle, Wash.: National Bureau of Asian Research, NBR Special Report 80, September 2019. As of September 30, 2020: https://www.nbr.org/publication/securing-the-belt-and-road-initiative-chinas-evolving-military-engagement-along-the-silk-roads/

———, *China's Vision for a New World Order*, Seattle Wash.: National Bureau of Asian Research, NBR Special Report 83, January 2020.

Roser, Max, "Human Development Index (HDI)," *Our World in Data*, 2014.

"Russian Media: Y-20 About to Enter Service with the Chinese Air Force; Will Be More Important Than the J-20" ["俄媒: 运-20即将列装中国空军　比歼-20更重要"], Xinhua [新华网], June 10, 2016.

Ruta, Michele, Matias Herrera Dappe, Somik Lall, Chunlin Zhang, Erik Churchill, Cristina Constantinescu, Mathilde Lebrand, and Alen Mulabdic, *Belt and Road Economics: Opportunities and Risks of Transport Corridors*, Washington, D.C.: International Bank for Reconstruction and Development, World Bank, 2019.

Sarkees, Meredith Reid, and Frank Wayman, *Resort to War: 1816–2007*, data set, version 4.0, Washington, D.C.: CQ Press, 2010. As of June 22, 2021: https://correlatesofwar.org/data-sets/COW-war

Saunders, Phillip C., "Hearing on a 'World-Class' Military: Assessing China's Global Military Ambitions," testimony before the U.S.-China Economic and Security Review Commission, Washington, D.C., June 20, 2019.

Saunders, Phillip C., Arthur S. Ding, Andrew Scobell, Andrew N.D. Yang, and Joel Wuthnow, eds., *Chairman Xi Remakes the PLA: Assessing Chinese Military Reforms,* Washington D.C.: National Defense University Press, 2019.

Saunders, Philip C., and Joel Wuthnow, "China's Goldwater-Nichols? Assessing PLA Organizational Reforms," *Joint Force Quarterly,* 3rd Quarter 2016, pp. 68–75.

Scobell, Andrew, and Nathan Beauchamp-Mustafaga, "The Flag Lags but Follows: The PLA and China's Great Leap Outward," in Phillip C. Saunders, Arthur S. Ding, Andrew Scobell, Andrew N.D. Yang, and Joel Wuthnow, eds., *Chairman Xi Remakes the PLA: Assessing Chinese Military Reforms,* Washington D.C.: National Defense University Press, 2019, pp. 171–199.

"Sea Distances/Port Distances," Sea-Distances.org, online tool, undated. As of June 22, 2021: https://sea-distances.org/

Shih, Gerry, "In Central Asia's Forbidding Highlands, a Quiet Newcomer: Chinese Troops," *Washington Post,* February 18, 2019.

Shou Xiaosong [寿晓松], ed., *Science of Military Strategy* [战略学], Beijing: Academy of Military Science Press [军事科学院], 2013.

Singleton, Craig, "Beijing Eyes New Military Bases Across the Indo-Pacific," *Foreign Policy,* July 7, 2021.

Small, Andrew, *The China-Pakistan Axis: Asia's New Geopolitics,* London: C. Hurst & Co. (Publishers) Ltd., 2015.

Song Zhongping [宋忠平], "The Dream and Reality of China's Overseas Bases" ["中国海外基地的梦想与现实"], Xinhua, July 8, 2015.

Southerland, Matthew, "As Chinese Pressure on Taiwan Grows, Beijing Turns Away from Cross-Strait 'Diplomatic Truce,'" Washington, D.C.: U.S.-China Economic and Security Review Commission, February 9, 2017.

State Council Information Office of the People's Republic of China, *China: Arms Control and Disarmament* [中国的军备控制与裁军], Beijing, November 1995a.

———, *China: Arms Control and Disarmament,* trans., Beijing, November 1995b.

———, *China's National Defense* [中国的国防], Beijing, July 1998a.

———, *China's National Defense,* trans., Beijing, July 1998b.

———, *China's National Defense in 2000* [2000年中国的国防], Beijing, October 2000a.

———, *China's National Defense in 2000,* trans., Beijing, October 2000b.

———, *China's National Defense in 2002* [2002年中国的国防], Beijing, December 2002a.

———, *China's National Defense in 2002,* trans., Beijing, December 2002b.

———, *China's National Defense in 2004* [2004年中国的国防], Beijing, December 2004a.

———, *China's National Defense in 2004,* trans., Beijing, December 2004b.

———, *China's National Defense in 2006* [2006年中国的国防], Beijing, December 2006a.

———, *China's National Defense in 2006,* trans., Beijing, December 2006b.

———, *China's National Defense in 2008* [2008年中国的国防], Beijing, January 2009a.

———, *China's National Defense in 2008,* trans., Beijing, January 2009b.

———, *China's National Defense in 2010,* [2010年中国的国防], Beijing, March 2011a.

———, *China's National Defense in 2010,* trans., Beijing, March 2011b.

———, *The Diversified Employment of China's Armed Forces* [中国武装量的多样化运用], Beijing, April 2013a.

———, *The Diversified Employment of China's Armed Forces,* trans., Beijing, April 2013b.

———, *China's Military Strategy* [中国的军事战略], Beijing, May 2015a.

———, *China's Military Strategy*, Beijing, trans., May 2015b.

———, *China's Policies on Asia-Pacific Security Cooperation*, Beijing, January 2017a.

———, "China Ready to Promote Reform of Global Governance System," Xinhua, September 14, 2017b.

———, *China's Arctic Policy*, Beijing, January 2018.

———, *China's National Defense in the New Era* [新时代的中国国防], Beijing, July 2019a.

———, *China's National Defense in the New Era*, trans., Beijing, July 2019b.

———, *China and the World in the New Era*, Beijing, September 27, 2019c.

———, *China's Armed Forces: 30 Years of UN Peacekeeping Operations*, Beijing, September 2020.

Stockholm International Peace Research Institute, "SIPRI Arms Transfers Database," webpage, undated. As of March 15, 2021:
https://www.sipri.org/databases/armstransfers

Strobel, Warren P., and Nancy A. Youssef, "F-35 Sale to U.A.E. Imperiled over U.S. Concerns About Ties to China," *Wall Street Journal*, May 25, 2021.

Sutter, Karen M., "'Made in China 2025' Industrial Policies: Issues for Congress," Washington, D.C.: Congressional Research Service, IF10964, August 11, 2020.

Thorne, Devin, and Ben Spevack, *Harbored Ambitions: How China's Port Investments Are Strategically Reshaping the Indo-Pacific*, Washington, D.C.: C4ADS, 2017.

Tiezzi, Shannon, "Chinese Nationals Evacuate Yemen on PLA Navy Frigate," *The Diplomat*, March 30, 2015.

Transparency International, "Corruption Perceptions Index," webpage, 2020. As of June 22, 2021:
https://www.transparency.org/en/cpi/2020/index/

Turner Lee, Nicol, *Navigating the U.S.-China 5G Competition*, Washington, D.C.: Brookings Institution, April 2020.

Underwood, Kimberly, "China Advances Signals Intelligence," *Signal*, August 13, 2018.

United Nations, "UN Comtrade Database," webpage, 2021. As of February 19, 2021:
https://comtrade.un.org/data/

United Nations Development Programme, "PRK–Human Development Indicators," undated. As of June 22, 2021:
http://hdr.undp.org/en/countries/profiles/PRK

———, *Human Development Report 1998*, New York: Oxford University Press, 1998.

United Nations Office on Drugs and Crime, "Tackling Corruption, a Key to Recover with Integrity," December 9, 2020.

United Nations Pacific, "Tuvalu," webpage, undated. As of June 22, 2021:
https://pacific.un.org/en/about/tuvalu

———, "Nauru," webpage, 2021. As of June 22, 2021:
https://pacific.un.org/en/about/nauru

United States Institute of Peace Senior Study Group, *China's Impact on Conflict Dynamics in the Red Sea Arena*, Washington, D.C.: United States Institute of Peace, April 2020.

U.S. Agency for International Development, "Somalia: Education," webpage, March 19, 2021. As of August 16, 2021:
https://www.usaid.gov/somalia/education

U.S. Central Intelligence Agency, "Field Listing–Coastline," *The World Factbook*, undated.

———, "The World Factbook," webpage, August 18, 2022. As of August 16, 2021:
https://www.cia.gov/the-world-factbook/

U.S.-China Economic and Security Review Commission, *2020 Report to Congress of the U.S.-China Economic and Security Review Commission*, Washington, D.C.: U.S. Government Publishing Office, December 2020.

———, "Hearing on 'China in Latin America and the Caribbean,'" transcript, Washington, D.C., May 20, 2021.

U.S. Department of Defense, "Chad Sbragia, Deputy Assistant Secretary of Defense for China Press Briefing on the 2020 China Military Power Report," transcript, August 31, 2020.

U.S. Department of State, "2020 Country Reports on Human Rights Practices: Tonga," undated-a.

———, "2020 Country Reports on Human Rights Practices: Tuvalu," undated-b.

———, "2020 Country Reports on Human Rights Practices: Fiji," March 30, 2021a.

———, "2020 Country Reports on Human Rights Practices: Kiribati," March 30, 2021b.

———, "2020 Country Reports on Human Rights Practices: Marshall Islands," March 30, 2021c.

———, "2020 Country Reports on Human Rights Practices: Micronesia," March 30, 2021d.

———, "2020 Country Reports on Human Rights Practices: Nauru," March 30, 2021e.

———, "2020 Country Reports on Human Rights Practices: Palau," March 30, 2021f.

———, "2020 Country Reports on Human Rights Practices: Samoa," March 30, 2021g.

U.S. Energy Information Administration, "China," webpage, September 30, 2020. As of December 30, 2020:
https://www.eia.gov/international/analysis/country/CHN

Voeten, Erik, Anton Strezhnev, and Michael Bailey, "United Nations General Assembly Voting Data," data set, Harvard Dataverse, 2021. As of June 22, 2021:
https://dataverse.harvard.edu/dataset.xhtml?persistentId=hdl:1902.1/12379

Vrolyk, John, "Insurgency, Not War, Is China's Most Likely Course of Action," *War on the Rocks*, December 19, 2019.

Wang Tianze [王天泽], Qi Wenzhe [齐文哲], and Hai Jun [海军], "An Exploration of Transportation and Projection Support for Overseas Military Bases" ["海外军事基地运输投送保障探讨"], *Traffic Engineering and Technology for National Defence* [国防交通工程与技术], Vol. 16, No. 1, 2018, pp. 31–35.

Wang Yi, "Working Together to Address the New Threat of Terrorism," statement by the Minister of Foreign Affairs of the People's Republic of China at the UN Security Council Summit on Terrorism, New York, September 24, 2014, Ministry of Foreign Affairs of the People's Republic of China, September 25, 2014.

———, "Work Together to Create a Community of Shared Future for Mankind," Ministry of Foreign Affairs of the People's Republic of China, May 31, 2016.

——— [王毅], "Use Xi Jinping's Thought in the New Era for Socialism with Chinese Characteristics to Break New Ground in China's Diplomacy" ["以习近平新时代中国特色社会主义思想引领中国外交开新境界"], *People's Daily* [人民日报], December 19, 2017.

Watts, Stephen, Scott Boston, Pauline Moore, and Cristina L. Garafola, *Implications of a Global People's Liberation Army: Historical Lessons for Responding to China's Long-Term Global Basing Ambitions*, Santa Monica, Calif.: RAND Corporation, RR-A1496-3, 2022. As of December 2022:
https://www.rand.org/pubs/research_reports/RRA1496-3.html

Watts, Stephen, Bryan Frederick, Nathan Chandler, Mark Toukan, Christian Curriden, Erik E. Mueller, Edward Geist, Ariane M. Tabatabai, Sara Plana, Brandon Corbin, and Jeffrey Martini, *Proxy Warfare as a Tool of Strategic Competition: State Motivations and Future Trends*, Santa Monica, Calif.: RAND Corporation, RR-A307-2, forthcoming.

White House, *National Security Strategy of the United States of America*, Washington, D.C., December 2017.

Woetzel, Jonathan, Jeongmin Seong, Kevin Wei Wang, James Manyika, Michael Chui, and Wendy Wong, "China's Digital Economy: A Leading Global Force," New York: McKinsey Global Institute, August 2017.

Wood, Peter, Alex Stone, and Taylor A. Lee, *China's Ground Segment: Building the Pillars of a Great Space Power*, Montgomery, Ala.: China Aerospace Studies Institute, March 2021.

World Bank, "Country Policy and Institutional Assessment," webpage, undated-a. As of August 16, 2021:
https://databank.worldbank.org/source/country-policy-and-institutional-assessment

———, "World Development Indicators," webpage, undated-b. As of August 16, 2021:
https://datatopics.worldbank.org/world-development-indicators/

———, "Worldwide Governance Indicators," interactive data access tool, undated-c. As of August 16, 2021: https://info.worldbank.org/governance/wgi/Home/Reports

———, "Trade (% GDP): China," webpage, December 2020. As of January 5, 2021: https://data.worldbank.org/indicator/NE.TRD.GNFS.ZS?locations=CN

———, "Worldwide Governance Indicators," webpage, 2021a. As of June 22, 2021: https://info.worldbank.org/governance/wgi/Home/Documents

———, "Somalia Education for Human Capital Development Project (P172434): Project Information Document (PID)," Washington, D.C., PIDA28885, March 10, 2021b.

World Bank Group, "Climate Change Knowledge Portal," database, undated. As of June 22, 2021: https://climateknowledgeportal.worldbank.org/download-data

Wuthnow, Joel, "A New Era for Chinese Military Logistics," *Asian Security*, February 2021.

Wuthnow, Joel, Arthur S. Ding, Phillip C. Saunders, Andrew Scobell, and Andrew N.D. Yang, eds., *The PLA Beyond Borders: Chinese Military Operations in Regional and Global Context*, Washington, D.C.: National Defense University Press, 2021.

Wuthnow, Joel, Phillip C. Saunders, and Ian Burns McCaslin, "PLA Overseas Operations in 2035: Inching Toward a Global Combat Capability," *Strategic Forum*, No. 309, Washington, D.C.: National Defense University Press, May 2021.

"Xi Expounds Best Approach to Reunification," Xinhua, January 2, 2019.

"Xi Eyes More Enabling International Environment for China's Peaceful Development," Xinhua, November 30, 2014.

"Xi Jinping Gives Important Remarks at Central Work Forum on Diplomacy to the Periphery" ["习近平在周边外交工作谈会上发表重要讲话"], Xinhua, October 25, 2013.

Xi Jinping, "Secure a Decisive Victory in Building a Moderately Prosperous Society in All Respects and Strive for the Great Success of Socialism with Chinese Characteristics for a New Era," remarks delivered at the 19th National Congress of the Communist Party of China, Xinhua, October 18, 2017.

———, "Working Together for an Asia-Pacific Community with a Shared Future," Ministry of Foreign Affairs of the People's Republic of China, November 20, 2020.

"Xi Stresses Need to Improve Global Governance," Xinhua, April 8, 2018.

"Xi Thought Leads to China Dream," *China Daily*, January 2, 2018.

Xiao Tianliang [肖天亮], ed., *Science of Military Strategy* [战略学], Beijing: National Defense University Press [国防大学出版社], 2015.

———, ed., *Science of Military Strategy* [战略学], Beijing, National Defense University Press [国防大学出版社], 2017.

———, ed., *Science of Military Strategy* [战略学], Beijing: National Defense University Press [国防大学出版社], 2020.

Xing Zhigang, "Keeping Overseas Chinese Workers Safe," *China Daily*, July 14, 2004.

Yan Wenhu [闫文虎], "Correctly Understand the Military's Missions in the New Era" ["正确理解新时代军队使命任务"], *China Military Online* [中国军网], July 26, 2019.

Yao, Kevin, "China Pursues Economic Self-Reliance as External Risks Grow: Advisers," Reuters, August 4, 2020.

Yung, Christopher D., Ross Rustici, Scott Devary, and Jenny Lin, *"Not an Idea We Have to Shun": Chinese Overseas Basing Requirements in the 21st Century*, Washington, D.C.: Center for the Study of Chinese Military Affairs, Institute for National Strategic Studies, National Defense University Press, China Strategic Perspectives No. 7, October 2014.

Zenglein, Max J., "China's Overrated Service Sector," Mercator Institute for China Studies, October 13, 2016.

Zheng Bijian, "Xi Jinping's Dream for China and the World," *China Daily*, April 13, 2018.

Zhou Huaqi [周华奇], Li Shaoming [李少鸣], Zhang Hengyang [张恒洋], and Wang Xufei [王旭飞], "Thinking on Our Army Building Oil Support Bases Overseas" ["我军在境外建立油料保障基地的思考"], *Logistics Sci-Tech* [物流科技], No. 2, 2013.